A Plume of Dust

Brigadier John and Peggy Prendergast.

Photo by Jenny Potter

A Plume of Dust

John Prendergast

The Pentland Press Limited
Edinburgh · Cambridge · Durham

By the same author:
The Road to India
Prender's Progress

© J. Prendergast 1993

First published in 1993 by
The Pentland Press Ltd.
1 Hutton Close
South Church
Bishop Auckland
Durham

ISBN 1 85821 038 0

Typeset by Elite Typesetting Techniques, Southampton.
Printed and bound by Antony Rowe Ltd., Chippenham.

To Peggy
to whom I owe everything

Contents

Quotations from Persian poetry are from:
Persian Poems – An Anthology of Verse Translations,
edited A.J. Arberry (J.M. Dent & Sons Ltd, 1954).

Illustrations

Foreword

Introduction to a Plume of Dust by John Prendergast. Introduction written by Mark Tully.

History cannot be understood in the context of the present. Good historians write with a sympathetic understanding of the period they are describing and analysing, realising that beliefs, codes of conduct, economic circumstances, the development of knowledge were very different then. Perhaps nowhere is this sympathetic understanding more needed than in writing a history of the British Raj. I do not mean the sort of sympathy which led to a wave of Raj nostalgia some thirty years after Independence. That nostalgia distorted the past, bathed the British in a golden light, and presented Indians as knaves or sycophants who needed a good dose of muscular Christianity to redeem them. At the other extreme there is a view of the Raj which presents the British who ruled India as polo-playing, chota-peg – drinking Colonel Blimps.

Historians who want to chart a course between those two poles must understand that Victorian values which are now seen as almost childishly idealistic, were deeply meaningful to many of the British in India right up to the end of the Raj. They must also be able to sympathise with the deep love of India that so many British officers, officials, and businessmen felt for that magnificent country. It's a love which, judged with the advantage of hindsight does often seem patronising, condescending, and based on an innate sense of racial superiority. Judged with an understanding of Victorian ethics, the concept of the imperial mission, and the public school spirit that love will be seen to arise from the belief that life should be lived for some great purpose.

I was born in the British Raj, and my mother's family had roots in India going back four generations. More than twenty years in Independent India have lead me to believe that for all the undoubted goodwill of so many of the men who ruled India colonialism had disasterous consequences. I now think India with its ancient civilization could have found its own way through the Industrial Revolution and all the changes that came with it, and should have been allowed to do so. That does not mean I have any less respect for my parents, and

xi

the earlier generations of my family who lived in India. I know that they lived their lives by the light of their times, and I know that my children and grand-children will find many of my beliefs of India dated, they may even find my love of the country patronising.

Brigadier John Prendergast served in the Indian army until Independence. He and his wife Peggy both came from families who had earlier links with India. In the first pages of a Plume of Dust John Prendergast describes how he felt sailing out of Karachi at the end of his career, leaving the subcontinent, as he then feared, for ever. 'My chest was aching as I unconsciously pressed on the stern rail, straining towards that sunlit past, now lost for ever. Gone was the daylong change of light on Waziristan's shale hills. Gone was the Muezzin's call to prayer from a minaret limned against a lemon evening sky . . . Back to India! It could not be for me, I mourned.' But the Brigadier soon realised that he couldn't just leave the sub continent, and goes on to tell of the ways he found to keep up those links.

My family and I spent many hours with the Prendergasts in their beloved Corbett Park, a beautiful wild life reserve in northern India. I remember the sadness we all felt that first year when John and Peggy did not make it to Corbett. The Brigadier was not always an easy person to be associated with in Corbett Park. He had little patience with visitors who came just to picnic, and could be quite rude to those who played transistor radios too loudly. But what made all of us love the Prendergasts, although they were of a different genera-tion, was their courage, their devotion to India and of course their stories of the past. They were quite simply people we just did not meet among our genera-tion.

My parents came from the British Business Community in India and had, as far as I can remember, no close friends in the Army. It was John Prendergast who gave me a real insight into that unique relationship between a British Officer and his Indian soldiers. Readers of A Plume of Dust will come close to the Brigadier too. I hope therefore that this book will stand for many genera-tions to help them understand what motivated the officers who served in the Indian Army. Without that understanding they will never know how so few British managed to govern so many Indians for such a long time.

by Mark Tully
The BBC's Veteran Reporter and Authority on India

Chapter 1

Light at the End of the Tunnel

Early in January 1948 I leant over the ship's stern watching Karachi slip from view – the port of my entry seventeen years before upon a stage that became sharp with vivid memories and changing scenes that I could not possibly have foreseen – and now the port of my exit. Over Karachi there was still light for my straining eyes, a deep orange light thrown from a great, hot sun which seemed to sink too swiftly behind me, telling me abruptly that I had seen enough, seen my last.

My chest was aching as I unconsciously pressed on the stern rail, straining towards that sunlit past, now lost for ever. Gone was the day-long change of light on Waziristan's shale hills. Gone was the Muezzin's summons to prayer from a minaret limned against a lemon, evening sky. I could hear the green barbet's sunset call ever more faintly, full throated and peremptory as it dismissed the stately sal forest's ranks to the night, as animals stealthily took over from man. I could smell the brushwood cooking fires and hot clarified butter. I was conscious of brown-skinned peasants and the flickering light picking out their lean, smiling features. So many of them and why did they smile? Was it because the hot, hard day was rewarded by the cool night and its simple pleasures – songs round the fire to the rhythm of the tom-tom which seemed to go on endlessly? My racing thoughts took me to the other camp fires. I could see mustachioed Rajput and bearded Sikh soldiers, all by then worn far too thin after Burma's long, thrashing war and the annihilating victory over the Japanese, a victory won for the most part by those most redoubtable of soldiers the Indian sepoys and riflemen.

Like most Indians, the Rajputs could add to, and improvise, tuneful songs handed down across the wood fires. One song ended repeatedly in a cadence: *Wapas Hindustan-ko*, Back to India – for they longed to be home to play with their sons. The begetting and love of children is the one joy of the Indian poor. Back to India! It could not be for me, I mourned. I had served half my active life there, but now I had to adapt and serve out the other half in another world. As I turned away the sea was already cold steel but there was blood on its edge. Sadly, I started down into the fug of the ship's bar, where duty-free drink flowed freely and everyone was singing. Of course they sang, for they were

1

going home. My steps down the companionway echoed my thoughts. For me all the bright scene was gone for ever: gone – gone – g o n e!

Abruptly I left the bar and sat in the dimly lit saloon to think things out. For a long time I had known this day would come, but events had moved so fast that there had been little time to take stock. I was no longer in my first youth and had a little family to care for and bring up. England just had to be my new home, a home really new to me, since I had grown up and been educated in Jersey. As was the rule, I would be losing all acting rank and, as a major, would out of necessity join the British army which would, I feared, regard me as an interloper. The future looked dark with clouds and rain now that I was somewhat part worn, with only the prospect of modest pay and rank.

I think I felt the parting more heavily than many of my brother officers. Though Britain was my motherland, India was, and still is, the centre of my being. It was my childhood's playground, whether in Lahore where I was born or in Jabalpur and Mhow where my father had formed and commanded the first Independent Brigade, and where he was later Divisional Commander of the Central Provinces. All through the years of school in Jersey, after my father retired there, my return to India to command troops as my forefathers had done was my unquestioned goal. In India I was at home and in instinctive and happy sympathy with the people of the country, and we talked to each other on the same wave-length. I remember an Indian friend saying to me many years later that the country where one is born is always 'Home' for the rest of one's life; this was certainly true for me.

My own little family's exit from India was almost furtive, though the departing British were not generally the objects of violence. Rather did the bulk of the people look on apprehensively, like children who have suddenly lost their parents. For two months we had been crammed into a couple of rooms in a hutted transit camp, and I had only obtained the second room when I bitterly protested that one was hardly enough for ourselves, two children and a baby born in Karachi, as well as our Anglo-Indian nanny. Nanny had looked after the two older children as babies and wanted to go to England, after she had seen the Sikh workers cut down by Muslims outside her house in the railway colony in Quetta. Fortunately for her, we had also been in Quetta at the time, as I was on the last long Staff College course – a course that was abruptly ended in August 1947 when India was divided. Our delay, waiting for the arrival of our third child, meant that I was allotted accommodation on one of the last ships to leave India – the *Windrush*. This horrid scow was a reparation ship formerly used for *Kraft durch Freude* trips. It had neither power nor joy by then and was too enclosed for warm seas. Swift cockroaches darted everywhere. There was polio on board and some died, but our children only caught whooping-cough. The *Windrush* blew up and sank in the Mediterranean on a succeeding voyage and I wonder if the cockroaches made the shore. Must ships sink themselves in order to get rid of this pest? The ship seemed to make our withdrawal from India still more ignominious. If one had no pride of service, what was left?

* * *

At the end of the next July, 1948, I was straining my eyes through the gathering light and could already see Karachi rising above the skyline. Having said good-bye to India, there it was again, even if those shores were now Pakistan. My feelings were all joy and expectation, for it seemed as if I were being steered by the hand of fate in my entering, departing and re-entering by this port. I was looking over the bows of the BISN *Musaffari*, one of those open-decked steamers which at that time still plied between Bombay and Karachi. I could scarcely believe the sudden and happy turn of fortune. Whilst on leave before joining my new British regiment, a brief letter had arrived from the Defence Ministry. It read: 'Would you like the appointment of MA, Kabul?' Little did I know it, but it was a fatal step in my career. As usual, half of the War Office did not know what the other half was doing, and the Military Secretary's depart-ment, responsible for allotting appointments, never forgave me for leaping at this offer from another branch.

The words had danced before my eyes. I had had to think, and it began to dawn on me that MA was the abbreviation for Military Attaché. Now, surely a Military Attaché had to be tall, lean and elegant, with private means? I certainly had none of these qualifications, although descended from old and illustrious families on both sides. I was stout and broad, but I had served for years along the border of Afghanistan and I spoke Pushtu, the language of the tougher elements in that country. I was to see my beloved sub-continent again and the mysterious land beyond the Khyber. What a sudden turnabout! I learned that I would be back to temporary lieutenant-colonel and, as well as this, would be a local full colonel with an expense allowance. Future good schooling for the family now seemed feasible, though at the time all I could think was that I was going back – *back*!

Nanny had not liked the idea of Kabul, so we had found her another job, to the unconcealed delight of the two older children. Poor Nanny was rather hurt but, excellent as she was with babies, she could not cope with their growing inde-pendence. When we had docked at Bombay there was the foreshortened figure of our much loved ayah (children's nurse) who had travelled half across India to join us – quite a feat for a hill woman from the Nilgiris. It was an extraordinarily brave thing for her to do. The year before we had sent her back from Quetta on the official Staff College refugee train, the only way we could get her home, though with no assurance that she would ever get there through the storms of Partition. She had a terrible journey and was dumped on the Indian frontier losing all her possessions. It was only by chance that another ayah with whom she was travelling was recognised by a passing British officer who took the two women to Delhi with him. Yet here she was, ready to brave Pakistan and disruption again. We were delighted to see her very dark face and white-toothed smile again, and she swooped on our youngest whom she had not seen before and took over all three children and the washing of their clothes and the baby's nappies. Her adaptability was quite remarkable. She had never been on a ship before, but took it in her stride. Peggy had expected to have to look after her through the rough monsoon weather, but Ayah was equal to it and merely remarked, rather crushingly, 'Madam not washing Baby's napkins very well.'

We had signalled our old cook, Moosa, to join us at Karachi if he could and to recruit a good bearer to meet us in Peshawar *en route* for Kabul. There he was, sure enough, on Karachi docks and I looked down with affection on the old man. He had been part of our life since we had recruited him on our honeymoon in Kashmir before the war. He had then been working as an ordinary trek cook, having been left unprovided for by his former employers away on leave. I saw his worth when our little fishing safari was caught in a drenching thunderstorm which came up suddenly, as they always do in the mountains. Undeterred, he had set to and produced a hot and comforting three-course dinner in the cavern of a hollow tree. After that he had accompanied us all over India, his noble and distinctive looks adding splendour to our establishment, quite apart from his wonderful cooking and staunch character. He had looked after Peggy and the children, who loved him dearly, all the time I was away at the wars. Now he was thin and shabby. Such pension as we had been able to afford him could not have gone far. His skull cap had no turban round it and he looked abjectly poor, though we had got him another job before we left. It had however not turned out well, as his new employer kept very late hours and would not give him any travel allowance for much journeying. I knew, too, that Moosa was putting on an act: he was not above indulging in a bit of self-pity; aren't we all? He told me he had taken on a very smart-looking bearer friend of his, Ghulam Qadir, whom we had known in Quetta. He was a Kashmiri like Moosa and, like him, unable to return home from Pakistan to his own country under Indian domination.

Everything was falling into place. We had the important part of our staff assembled. As members of the 'Establishment' it was essential to have a carefully selected team of servants. It was the way of life for both British and Indians, and it was unthinkable that one should do one's own housework or bazaar shopping. Caste, the strongest trades union in the world, dictated what should be done and by whom. There was, too, a lot of entertaining in an official position, and we had to have someone to take responsibility for the children and the house when we were out. Our relationships were warm; we thought of our servants as friends rather than employees, and they seemed to like us too.

The Ministry had loaded my official car, a post-war Humber Hawk, on another ship. The car proved to be no hawk. The Afghan hills and roads tested it beyond its limits – a Land Rover would have been better, but they were then hardly on the market.

I was to relieve a Military Attaché of great note who had done fourteen years in

Kabul, including the long, tricky period of the war. Our masters had wisely kept him there as the only man who knew his subject. Such was his remarkable influence with the Afghans, so difficult to approach, that he had had certain important German firms closed down as they were bases for making trouble in India, and this at a time when we seemed to be losing the war in a series of disasters. He was Colonel Stalker Lancaster, a Gurkha officer who, owing to his high-bridged nose, was nicknamed 'The Duke'! He had warned me that a driver for the car was essential, as to run over an Afghan would bring dire consequences, even to the death penalty, so I recruited a driver with good references. He was to accompany the car by rail to Peshawar, since there were then no roads suitable for the long hot drive from Karachi – they are not much more suitable now! I thought it was all rather unnecessary, but felt bound to follow the advice of one so august.

We waited a while in Karachi for the car to arrive. I had always pressed on in the past, only to be told that I had not been expected so soon, so for once I took my time, determined to ensure that the vehicle did not go astray. I arranged for a wagon to convey it and the driver by rail, and saw them off before we left for Peshawar ourselves by train.

The journey went smoothly and it was sheer joy to see the wide plains of the Punjab again, but as we were approaching the Attock Bridge at Campbellpur, shortly before the Indus, which is the dividing line between the Punjab and the North West Frontier Province, the train was invaded by armed Ma'suds from South Waziristan, the most intractable of all the tribesmen on the Afghan border. They were left over from the war between India and Pakistan in Kashmir, into which they had been injudiciously thrown by the Pakistan government with its British advisers. Their propensity for loot and murder had turned them aside and they had failed to seize the vital landing strip at Srinagar, the key post of the war, which was then occupied first by troops from India. Mindful of the senseless murder by these tribesmen of friends of ours, the Dykes, who had been staying in the little convent at Baramullah at the entrance to the Vale of Kashmir for the birth of their third child at the beginning of the invasion, I was most apprehensive for my little family.[1] They hung on the footplates and some leant through the window. Our very dark-skinned Ayah attracted them most. For an insane second I contemplated pushing the most importunate Ma'sud to his death in the Indus far below as we crossed the bridge. Fortunately, my use of Pushtu intrigued them and they were prepared to chat. I was as disarming as I could be, but I was ready if we were attacked. However, much to my relief they got off at the other end of the bridge – a swarm of locusts drifting away in the wind.

At last I could really feel elation – I had crossed into the North West Frontier Province, the home of my early service, and the sleepers repeated, 'Home again, home again!' as I looked lovingly at the bare, soil-eroded ravines and hillocks.

---

[1] I have described my own unhappy experience with these unruly people in a previous book, *Prender's Progress*.

Entrance to Afghanistan 1948 – drawing by author.

Chapter 2

Mountain Farces

When all was assembled in Peshawar we set off in my official car, and sent the baggage and servants on by lorry. Soon we topped the familiar Khyber Pass, so full of memories for me, and there before us was the wide sweep of Afghanistan, the secret and forbidding country I had never entered before. In those days, one had to drive down a dry tributary of the Kabul River for some thirteen miles after crossing the border at Tor Kham, avoiding boulders as best one could. Once past Jelalabad, Afghanistan's third town, we dipped in and out of side streams and dry ravines beside the Kabul River itself. Over to the right, I could see the date palms popularly believed to be the descendants of stones spat out by Alexander's army as it passed through. It may be true. Dates do not occur naturally in that part of the world, but have always been the iron rations of soldiers and travellers in the Middle East. We stuck, of course, in a sandy ravine, much to my elder son's despair. He sat on a bank and wept; he was only six. How many times, in my long-distance journeys later on, have I felt the same despair when we have broken down in a lonely place. Using branches and foliage from the tamarisk trees which lined the road to make the wheels grip, and with a little digging, we extricated ourselves.

As advised by the 'Duke', we stopped at the Sarobi rest house for the night. It was a grim place, smelling of sour cooking fat, and it took us hours to get a meal of some sort. Next morning, glad to get away, we set off very early. At that time, on leaving Sarobi, one had to cross the Lattaband Pass. It was a climb up to some 7,500 feet in a steep ascent of tight horseshoe bends, and was so named owing to the custom of camel *quafilas* and other travellers tying shreds (*latta*) of their clothing on the bushes at the summit to propitiate the spirits whom they felt might threaten them on this grim passage. There used to be other threats, dealt with by the one capable ruler in Afghanistan in the recent past, Mir Abdur Rahman, who put highwaymen in cages on the pass to be eaten by the crows. The roads have never been safer.

We arrived in Kabul, to be met by the 'Duke'. As I might have known, he had not expected me so soon. He objected to my wearing uniform since, he remarked, 'The Afghans don't like it.' I had my first 'Red Hat', however, and I was determined to wear it at least once. In spite of the 'Duke's' surprise at our

early arrival, we found he had already generously vacated our official house –
the best of the staff houses, allotted to the 'Duke' on account of his prestige.
For the same reason he was regarded as Number Two in the Embassy. I was
soon told that I would be Number Three, the normal place for a Military
Attaché in a small post.

Having come all in one piece, we were able to deploy in a well-ordered
operation, and were really in a position to give a dinner party the same day,
should we have so wished, much to everyone's surprise. A party came over
from the ambassador's house 'to help', which was very kind of them. We sat
them down, put drinks in their hands, and got on with the job we'd done so
often before. My instinct to move *en bloc* had been right and I felt insufferably
smug. How irritating we must have been, but our expertise had been learned the
hard way. Military moves to far distant places used to come suddenly, often
giving us only twenty-four hours to pack up. All too often, it would be to a non-
family posting, and my wife would officially be left to fend for herself in a
country where there was little accommodation apart from that attached to a job.
A fortnight before our first child was due to arrive I was moved from the
Tactical School in Poona to the NWFP, to raise and command the 1st Western
Tribal Legion. Peggy was in bed with high blood pressure at the time and
had only twenty-four hours in which to pack and to find somewhere to live;
needless to say there was no accommodation attached to my new promotion.
There was a wonderful comradeship in the Indian army, and a bevy of wives
descended on her to pack up our possessions; our next door neighbours put
her up until she could get a train to Peshawar, where we stayed with friends
while I raised my Legion, and Peggy had our son in the civil hospital. It was
in such circumstances that it was advisable to get your family up to the cool
hills where they could stay all the year round away from the intolerable heat
of the plains. Military postings, in addition to being sudden, were always
couched in the imperative: 'You will report, etc. on etc. . . . .' A later ambassador, seeing my posting order at the end of my tour, asked me if I was in bad
odour with my masters. I reassured him that the imperative was the usual
military tense.

New members from the Foreign Office arriving in Kabul used to wait for
months to set up house. As they spent only two years in the posting, and took a
lot of leave in England, their efforts seemed to me to be rather wasted. Their
possessions arrived at a leisurely pace in dribs and drabs after them, so that they
lived from hand to borrow in discomfort.

I have no idea how we ever learned anything about so secretive a country as
Afghanistan. In later years I doubt if the embassy really knew a single thing
about what was going on beyond its lovely gardens surrounded by high walls,
and they always seemed to be caught out by the march of events. The Afghans
played things very close to their chests, but in my time, with my small forces'
mission to look after, I would have known through them if major trouble were

brewing, though I do not know what use could have been made of this information, except to evacuate the embassy.

However, the British embassy, recently upgraded from a legation, was admirably placed to be the social centre of Kabul, particularly for foreigners. It was the only purpose-built mission, based on a fine ambassadorial residence, with a good ballroom and cinema projection room, as well as an excellent library where I found many old books about Afghanistan, some of then written by the small band of eccentric men, mostly English, who had explored the country on their own in the nineteenth century. It stood in grounds of some twenty-five acres, with discreet gendarmerie posts set in the walls outside, and the gardens contained the pleasant homes of the embassy staff and the offices. The area was elegantly laid out and there were extensive grape pergolas, the only grass tennis courts in Kabul, and a swimming pool. Especially heavy tennis balls had to be used, for these were necessary at 6,000 feet of rarified atmosphere. In the spring, a sea of daffodils vied with the vivid blue of muscaris, and in the summer there was a formal flag display of apricot coloured cannas, backed by a fountain of tall shrub roses. We had our own electricity, carpenters and builders, a medical service, water, garages, and supply trucks, which needed constant repair and maintenance on those terrible roads. In short, it was a little nineteenth century island, although we often felt like Cinderella, since the electricity used to be turned off at midnight and we would be left groping in the dark at the end of a party unless we had arranged for an extension.

Other missions, and more and more were being opened, had to content themselves with hiring the finer houses in Kabul, of which there were none of particular merit or style, while their staff had to be accommodated where they could find any house at all – a most insecure arrangement. It was so much so that in our time there, some of the women members of the US embassy got themselves mixed up in a murder carried out by their servants, who unwisely popped the corpse of a local money changer, who had been dealing with the girls, after robbing him, down the garden well. It is not surprising that the British embassy was highly regarded and, in Kabul, to be invited there was to have 'arrived'.

The splendid establishment was in some way a sop to my pride, battered by our shuffling exit from India. I feel to this day that a nation's mission must be elegant and looked up to, if it is to cut any figure in the modern political/commercial world: a shabby shop-window attracts no customers. Nevertheless, in the very cosiness and comfort behind those stout walls, it was all too easy to remain isolated from a tough, jagged country and a potentially unstable people, remnants from many an epic invasion of India. It struck me as a fair pleasance rather than a thorough-going mission.

Ours seemed a strange, artificial sort of life, as each country's mission sought to maintain friendly relations with its host and the other missions, and to keep a close touch with Afghan affairs. All our activities were directed towards the social round. Officially, we employed entirely overt means of collecting infor-

M A's house, Embassy Compound, Kabul.

mation, and it was imagined that in the endless succession of parties, an adroitly posed question might extract a breath of insight. At the same time it was felt desirable to appear important and to be popular, to further one's country's interests and standing. I do not think I ever collected in this way anything of note, and I felt all the time that I was in the cast of a comic opera.

I do not recall that there was very much effort to open up trade, nor was Afghanistan an inviting market, and the British embassy, no longer representing the Indian sub-continent as well as England, was chiefly exercised in advising and helping the new Pakistan and Indian missions. The Pakistanis were having a difficult time, since following the British withdrawal, the Afghans were promoting the idea of Pushtunistan. This doctrine laid claim to all Pathan territories beyond their border as far as the Indus, either within Pakistan itself or in its buffer belt of tribal territory – territory that I knew full well from my service with the trans-border police, or Scouts, in years gone by. The Indians were busy encouraging the idea of Pushtunistan to keep Pakistan looking northwards, away from their mutual border and Kashmir.

When I first arrived, the staff was of reasonable ability and the First Secretary remained a steady influence, but later on the personnel deteriorated steeply. Many were disgruntled at being posted to what they regarded as a backwoods mission, being completely oblivious to the riches before them. Afghanistan, once the cockpit of Asia and a vital outpost of India, was, in their eyes, of little importance, so little as to be hardly worth bothering about. One, a Welsh singing man, missed the Gilbert and Sullivan he had had in Shanghai and scowled at everything around. His childless wife, once very pretty, had nothing to interest her except to make minor trouble. She adroitly lifted our newly allotted fridge (a great innovation run on kerosene) on the grounds that the Foreign Office should come first. I couldn't be bothered to contest it, as in a small post friction can get out of hand. Indeed, people often acted very strangely, but I am certain that much of the excessive emotion was due to the dry altitude, always believed to be the reason for the strange goings-on in Kenya in the 1920s and '30s. Happily, I can say that on subsequent visits to the embassy years later the current staff had improved greatly, but I still think the FO should guard its standards more.

To return to the time of our arrival: I found the 'Duke' a fussy little bachelor, held in much awe by the officers of the embassy. He had certainly achieved much. He spoke and read fluent Persian, the court and official language, but he had no Pushtu, the language of the Pathans. He had, however, gained the confidence of the Afghan leaders who were intensely suspicious – an almost impossible feat. He did it by playing endless bridge with them, and through the years had pieced together little tit-bits of information. I felt inadequate, for I have never been keen on that smoke-clouded, sedentary game. Besides this, he was great friends with the Turkish Military Mission, bridge players all, who were training the army, and was able through them to work out the detailed structure of the armed forces. The Afghans would never let anyone near their conscript army, possibly because they were ashamed that it was so backward and manifestly underpaid.

After years in this atmosphere, Lancaster had become as secretive as the Afghans, and suspected every member of the staff of indiscretion: indiscretion about what? I was to ask myself later. It must have been a terrible wrench for him to leave Kabul with its fine climate, a post in which, by perseverance, he had done so much, and where he was so well known and respected, although by then he had obviously been there far too long.

On taking over a post, it was customary to buy furnishings from the outgoing incumbent. Much of the 'Duke's' was badly worn beyond the threadbare and he asked a steep price. I would not respond and we had enough of our old Indian fittings with us to get the house running, but I did take all I reasonably could, though in the ill-paid army one was often driven to unseemly haggling. This led to a little stuffiness. Yes, I thought him a stuffy little man, though I listened to all he had to impart and tried to extract lucidity out of the fog he created with the aid of vast libations of his favourite tipple – sticky gin and It; as he talked his eyes would dart conspiratorially at the four walls.

At this time Sir Giles Squire, a keen gardener, presided over us. He did very little directly, but did it very well and we all liked and respected him, as did the

Afghans. He was the last Head of Mission appointed by the former government of India from the Political Service – a service that had the knack of commanding respect. Sir Giles had at one time been Consul-General in Meshed, and before the war the Indian government had been able to control most of Iran from that post. Paradoxically I was the first Military Attaché to be appointed by the War Office in England, although I had come from the Indian army and had been recommended for the position by a distinguished Indian army general. Perhaps for this reason, since much of the Indian Political Service had been recruited from the Indian army, Sir Giles made me feel very much at home, although the Foreign Office tended to regard the military as uncomfortable bedfellows.

Lady Squire had great influence in Kabul as she set a high moral tone which was to the Muslims' liking. She kept in close touch with the few English women who had married Afghans and who, in so doing, had cut themselves off from the world behind the *purdah*. She was not everybody's cup of tea, being an ardent member of Moral Rearmament, but she never overpressed her beliefs, though I understand that various members of the embassy used to be prayed for at her morning meetings. She was one of the few people in Kabul, besides the Czechs and White Russians, to take a disapproving posture *vis à vis* the Russians, and would not attend their functions, a noticeable gesture in a small capital.

In due course, after Sir Giles's departure and in the full uniform allowed for the occasion, I, together with the other officers of the embassy and heads of other missions, went to meet our new ambassador at Charassia, some ten miles out of Kabul and the official entry point where all heads of missions were welcomed by the Chef de Protocol. I imagine this reception so far out of the capital stemmed from former times when an ambassador had to be looked over and his credentials examined before being allowed in. This must have been deemed particularly necessary in the case of British legates sent up to offer terms during the troubled times of the nineteenth century in which war and peace followed each other in rapid succession.

The road out was deeply potholed and I remember the French ambassador's car – a vast American limousine with soft, marshmallow springs – setting up such a rhythmic undulation that the chauffeur had to stop, get out and lean on the bonnet to quell the heaving. His Excellency had meanwhile turned the colour of *crême de menthe frappé*.

Our new ambassador came from the former Consular Service, recently amalgamated into the Diplomatic Corps, and we were anxious to see if he would be congenial in our small, intimate mission. He arrived and greeted the Chef de Protocol with a torrent of very good Persian, spoken in the orotund manner accompanied by much bowing and scraping, which is the Iranian way of observing good manners by making a show of abject humility in an elaborate routine: such expressions as, 'Your humble slave petitions . . .' It was a remarkable effort, but it fell like a lead balloon. The Chef de Protocol, accustomed to the bluffer Afghans' greeting in clipped Persian, looked slightly horrified and taken aback. This undistinguished little man was to be our head. I cannot recall anything particular about the two years of his ambassadorship, except that he was unpopular with his staff and always tetchy. My masters were the War Office and I did not have much to do with him. He was so undistinguished that it was difficult not to overshadow him at parties and he had the unfortunate habit of getting slightly tipsy and showing it, though in the Foreign Office he should have had plenty of practice.

Many of the parties given by Afghans were 'stag', for Afghan women were strictly in *purdah* as a sharp reaction to ex-King Amanullah's attempt to westernise the country. No alcohol was served and the general décor of the houses and palaces was depressing. They went in a great deal for dark green, relieved by still darker maroon. I used to wait endlessly while my ambassador played bridge, for I could not leave before him. Everybody seemed to gravitate towards the huge, grim-looking stoves known as *bokharies*, black, ugly and iron-flued: no charming Nuremburg tiles!

I revisited Kabul in 1967 and was then introduced to Afghan ladies of the court. They were very much out of *purdah* and I confirmed the views of Britons in the early nineteenth century that they were very beautiful, many of them with remarkable green eyes. *Purdah* did not seem to be strictly observed in the time of Alexander Burnes, and British officers such as Warburton married Afghan ladies whom they met in Kabul, and even taught them ballroom dancing. Some of these modern women had good degree qualifications and their burst out from behind the curtain to assume responsible roles was dramatic.

The fine gardens of the embassy had a great appeal for the Afghan court. They were pleased to call themselves *Duranis* (*Dur-i-Durani*, the Pearl of Pearls), being descended from Persian invaders led by the Emperor Nadir Shah in the eighteenth century, and Persians have gardening in their bones. Long before Nadir Shah's time that remarkable Mughal ruler, Babur, made Kabul his capital and laid out gardens such as he said he found woefully lacking in India. There was a day when the rulers came and visited our gardens, and were greatly taken with several specimens of white specie roses which foamed over their supports like fountains. I was interested to see that the party – rulers all and very tough – could take time off to fondle and smell their delicate petals.

At that time the country was governed by an oligarchy of the puppet King Zahir Shah's uncles, brothers of his murdered father, General and King Nadir Shah. In the party were two well-known nephews of the royal family. One of them, Prince Naim, was tall and elegant and had been educated in pre-war France. He was always charming and delighted to talk French. The second interested me more. Prince Daud, cropheaded, tough and sinister, had been educated in Nazi Germany and was always convinced that he, as the son of the eldest of the royal brothers, the late Hashim Khan, was the rightful ruler of

Afghanistan. On being introduced to this rather brutal looking man, I had a question immediately shot at me in very clipped Persian. My wretched ears, damaged by loud battle noises, are not very good, and of course I missed the point of his remark so that I was rather at a loss. He didn't wait to bandy words with such a moron as I and passed on. I felt that there was a strong man if ever I saw one.

He was a strong man but a headstrong one, and his greed for power when he seized the kingdom in 1973 in the absence of his cousin, King Zahir Shah, was Afghanistan's next step on the slippery slope. He called himself 'President' to be more acceptable, 'King' by then being unfashionable, and put his arm round the Bear's neck for support. It was fatal. Within five years his family and friends were slaughtered before his eyes in a slow and deliberate way, the ultimate in cruelty, and then he himself was shot, all in the Bear's good time. The corpses were dragged through the streets as a warning against any attempt at independence – an attempt that Daud, at last realising his situation, had been trying to make by approaching the Arabs and offering oil-drilling rights to the French. Daud's ambition had opened the door to the disasters that were to follow.

Chapter 3

The Last Frame of the Great Game

The tiny forces' mission which I mentioned earlier consisted of a squadron-leader flying instructor, a technical and mechanical instructor of the same rank, and two sergeants on the mechanical side, all from the Royal Air Force, plus an army signals instructor. They were accompanied by their families. The Afghans had a small force of British bi-plane fighters and in time we did sell them a number of Avro Ansons, with a good back-up of spares – quite a package – but this was the work of Squadron-Leader Charles Woolley whose enthusiasm brought it off. I merely had to give the project my blessing and encouragement and liaise with the Afghans, but at least we on our side of the house managed to do some trade. We chose Avro Ansons because they were so robust that they could survive when forgetfully landed with their wheels up.

I was soon to realise that the whole concept of the mission was very wrong, for the team were paid by the Afghans, who also had to bear the cost of their housing. Such conditions were totally foreign to the country, as for many years the Afghans had been accustomed to receiving gifts of arms and finance from European countries, resulting in an unworkable mixture of weapons and differing ammunition. The fact that the Royal Air Force personnel were Afghan employees weakened their position profoundly. I found that they were all discontented, mainly because their accommodation, though suitable for the poorer Afghans, was not really adequate for Europeans. They were in arrears of pay too. The country was in severe economic difficulties, as the secret of producing the fine curled skins of the Karakuli sheep's unborn lambs had been discovered, and the trade had been taken over by SW Africa (now Namibia). The export trade in grapes, many of them too delicate to travel, dried fruit and *krout* (dried curd) was not sufficient for the government's needs. I found the British officers deeply upset and their leader had been hauled before the ambassador by my predecessor. Colonel Lancaster had been so long in Afghanistan that he could only see the Afghan point of view.

I realised that my little army would have to be better looked after, or the mission would cease to be a credible body. Almost weekly, therefore, I donned my best uniform and aiguillettes ('chicken guts') and called upon the Afghan Chief of Staff, literally to dicker for better terms. The Chief gave ground but

15

little, though there were minor improvements. I pointed out that the instructors had to have their authority backed. Recently they had criticised an Afghan officer for failing to signal the red light on an impending wheels-up landing. He had turned on the instructors, screaming at them, '*Sag, sag!*' ('Dog, dog', an extreme insult).

This Royal Air Force mission were very fine men. On a brief official visit to London, the briefer the better for me who loves the wide, open spaces, I called in at the RAF Secretariat. I told them of the problems and what little I had done to improve things. They seemed very pleased and said it was unheard of for anyone from the military to make the effort to visit them.

The Afghan Chief of Staff was a very likeable man and our meetings were friendly, accompanied by that reviving drink, green tea imbued with white cardamom and cinnamon. It was uphill going, as he really had very little financial power: the King's uncles kept everything under their own very tight control. I felt I was in the invidious position of an unusually extortionate tax collector. It was particularly difficult since for years the country had been accustomed, as I have said, to receiving arms and financial help as a free gift, not as a hard driven bargain with HM Treasury.

I did try to fix up courses for his officers with British service training establishments in England and this was a moderate success. But one Afghan officer, misinterpreting the behaviour of an English waitress who was coquettish and, by Afghan standards, fair game, being unveiled and short skirted, made a pass at her and was reported. Alas, the report was sent straight to the Afghan army and not to me. The Chief expressed his regrets and said the officer would be recalled and shot. I was aghast and pleaded for him, but it seemed to be of no avail. Life is held cheaply in this hard country and ideas of honour are strict.

Gradually affairs moved more smoothly, but I put so much effort into my visits that I felt jaded, for I had to discuss everything in my limping Persian, which I was currently trying to improve. In supporting the little mission, perhaps I was slow to realize that British influence was receding from the area faster than I could grasp. Faster indeed than the Russians could immediately understand, though subsequent events have shown that they at last saw that a gaping vacuum had opened up.

I still had my pride in the Empire, a glow that was only chilling slowly, and I was fired by the great feats of arms achieved in Afghanistan by British and Indian troops in efforts to secure a friendly ruler in a friendly Afghan buffer state. Unfortunately, we had an unerring instinct for choosing the wrong ruler. The Treasury got cold feet after each outstanding military success and, as so often happens, the army had then been starved of support, which resulted in the crushing local defeats of the Kabul Gorge and Maiwand. The Indian government had from time to time been attracted by the Hindu Kush as a natural forward boundary, and as the army was alternately nourished and starved, there was a series of forward pushes and withdrawals. None of this advance and retreat detracted from our gallantry and astounding feats of arms, but every time we withdrew a little, the Afghans came hounding after us, sure of the 'invaders'' weakness, which was in fact that of the Treasury.

This period in which we and the Russians manoeuvred for the control of Afghanistan was known as the 'Great Game', and I saw its dying flicker in my efforts for the little mission, but I'm a romantic. If an intended buffer state is weak, it is impossible for statesmen to decide firmly where its borders should be set. The Great Game was a see-saw, with the Bear at the other end of the plank. As we fell, so the Russians rose, but even Gortchakov cried in exasperation as long ago as 1864 that the greatest difficulty for a statesman is in knowing where to stop in trying to secure a stable frontier. This is as apposite today as it was a hundred years ago.

I saw my role in this situation as both mollifying the Afghan army and making life more pleasant for the mission. I invited the Chief to a dinner party – no easy thing to do as all invitations had to go through the Afghan Foreign Ministry and were often not passed on. We pulled out all the stops for him and I really think the Chief enjoyed himself. The army had previously held aloof and no officer had ever dined at the embassy. I invited his chief aide several times. In a small embassy where nothing happened, it was quite a coup. I used to invite the members of the mission to my house and introduce them to other diplomats, telling them to guard their tongues. All in all, their lot was greatly improved, but I could not meet their desire to travel about and shoot. The Afghans were too suspicious of foreigners, and I myself desperately needed to tour the country as part of my job and to explore it in all its hostile, jagged beauty, and dared not compromise the slow progress I was making to get more freedom to travel: a freedom seldom granted to members of the Corps Diplomatique.

Above all I wanted to see this exciting land of weird-shaped mountains which seemed just to have poked their sharp heads through the upland desert flatness, across which dust devils raced and spun, and mirages formed their mysterious, watery images. Peggy and I did not want to go on leave to England, as to do so would have been to miss a great experience.

Other members of the embassy did not appear to feel the urge to use shotgun or fishing rod, but the Afghan court were keen shots. They used to shoot duck in a strange manner. Mounted on horseback they would gallop to a lake's edge and fire off both barrels at the rising birds before they could get away. I am a keen fisherman and happily the court were ardent followers of angling. They had all the latest tackle from the House of Hardy, still an august temple for its followers. We talked and talked, and I was invited to distant rivers in the very regions I sought to visit, so I had an entrée to the court equivalent to the 'Duke's' bridge. All the southern tributaries flowing into the Oxus from the northern slopes of the Panshir range hold trout, but even when we went there by invitation and spent the night in a rest house, I used to hear our every move reported to Kabul over the telephone by the man in charge.

In my second year the *Alice in Wonderland* atmosphere was stirred by a ripple. It should have been a tidal wave. The Russian embassy, housed in a substantial private house, had been manned only by a Second Secretary, a pale, sad and wizened individual – just a caretaker. Without warning, a retired General arrived as ambassador – an impressive figure who was getting down to learning tolerable English remarkably quickly. Why English and not Persian? I can only think that Russia still felt we were the paramount power in the area. With him were no fewer than three Military Attachés. I felt that this alone might have caused some perturbation, for most European countries rated only a visiting MA, who would come from a larger mission elsewhere for a short spell. Only Britain, America, India, Pakistan and Iran had full time attachés and I, on account of the Royal Air Force mission, had most stature. A number of Russian secretaries also arrived, including one or two or their farouche women officials who can be so brash and pushing.

Kabul stirred drowsily and muttered, 'Just the jolly Bears – good allies, but rather rough.' Invitations to the Russian embassy followed, and I presume the newsletters of each mission were full of useless tattle, assigning deep motives to passing remarks. I, too, wrote our embassy newsletter for the ambassador, and I confess it was a thin, gossipy column, for by then I had lost my chief informant in the person of the embassy surgeon, a capable Pakistani who had been so helpful to my predecessor. As Pakistan fell into worse odour with the Afghans he became afraid to mingle with them and exercise his knack for collecting news. Some years later a former official in the British High Commission in New Delhi told me that I had been the only person in Kabul who knew anything about Afghanistan and had given them any useful information. If my news was acceptable, how arid the rest must have been! Of course, I reported the Russian changes, but it was the ambassador's job to interpret them, and in all I really contributed frustratingly little.

For some strange reason, the Russians made a play for me and I could never understand their marked advances. Perhaps they thought I was the British Number One Commissar since I was heavy, stout and just like a bulky Russian general. I have never been able to fathom this friendliness, for I gave away no information and indeed, like everybody in Kabul, knew nothing. Even the Russian ambassador's wife joined in when invited to attend a tennis tea party at our embassy for the second time. She declared she would only come if 'The Colonel' was playing. At the first party I had played my usual rather violent and erratic game which appeared greatly to have pleased her.

I was asked to dinner at the Russian embassy as the sole guest and I had to drink against my three military opposite numbers. I felt outnumbered, but determined to keep reasonably sober and not to make the mistake of some British diplomats in Moscow who had collapsed with their faces in the soup after many toasts on empty stomachs. I found, as I have before, that if I ate a large number of canapés, I could keep my head. These were spread liberally with caviare and, being oily, helped me to remain in one piece. The barman, a particularly tough-looking individual, might easily have poured water into his masters' glasses since vodka is colourless. I remember the conversation as heavy and dull with a tendency to invite me to denigrate the Americans. I would not be drawn. Yes, there *was* someone behind the curtain which pulsated from time to time. I had only a fork if I should wish to treat him or her as Polonius, through the arras. I took my leave early and in good order from this strange, dull and bibulous party where there were Secretaries as well as the military, but no beautiful Olga Polovsky who might perhaps have emerged had I shown discontent with my lot or dislike of the Americans.

I invited the Russian attachés to dinner with their stout, pleasant wives who were brassily hennaed in high-piled coiffures and dressed in figured chiffon velvet – *Coronation Street* barwomen. I liked the three officers, but found them lacking in both appearance and personality. The senior had an alarming smile of all gold-faced teeth. The youngest professed himself homesick and ill, and seemed under psychological strain. I plied them liberally with Scotch and this spirit, much stronger than vodka, seemed to make them reel about a bit. I dilated on the freedom of speech and action we enjoyed in the west, but I never got an inkling of their future plans. Perhaps there were as yet none formulated. As I had only overt means at my disposal to obtain information, I felt helpless. However much you top up a Russian, he's not likely to give much away. Did the leader talk too much when he got home? Perhaps so, because he was relieved by another very soon after.

Possibly the reason why the Russians so obviously thought me more important than I really was, was because the Afghans allowed me so much freedom, unlike some others. I am sure that the existence of the Royal Air Force mission and the sale of the Avro Ansons piqued them. They did follow me once, but only as far as Charassia – a narrow gap in the hills which surround Kabul, guarded by a marsh. It was once the scene of a British victory in the confused fighting round the capital, before its capture by Roberts in 1879. There, snipe lurked under the lea of the uncut reeds in the centre of the marsh, so that it was at some risk that we got in range of them as the bog quaked and gurgled under our feet. Having shot some, we extricated ourselves from the glutinous mud covering us from head to foot, and on the bank were members of the Soviet embassy all in dark city suits. They looked puzzled, for we had only three brace of snipe. Perhaps they wondered why we got our clothes so filthy for such a paltry return, clothes being so hard to come by in Russia. It must have reinforced their conviction that I was only shooting as a cover for something sinister. They asked if they might photograph us and I rashly agreed. I would like to have seen the reports to their friends at home on the decadent British or perhaps on that slippery customer, the British Military Attaché.

It was at about this time that I took over the running of the embassy gardens. The new ambassador had handled the Afghan gardeners rather roughly, and they were in revolt. In the east it is sometimes as well to let things roll on. The gardeners were not capable of sustained digging, debilitated by their poor diet. I got them going again by jollying them along, and was then approached by the newly burgeoning Soviet embassy. They asked me for flower seeds and when I enquired what kind they wanted, they said it didn't matter so long as they were red!

After the Military Attachés' visit, two Russian Secretaries descended on us. I think they were the First and Second of that rank, but all was so anonymous. Even their faces were anonymous, like their clothes. It was very unusual for a Russian Secretary to visit a Military Attaché, and I was on my guard, or rather, I said to myself, 'Be on your guard!' On guard against what? They pressed me very hard over Pakistan and said that the British were still in full power behind a façade, or words to that effect. I was no believer in the folding up of the Empire and replied rather tetchily, 'Why don't you read the Pakistan papers?' but felt they still did not realize what a great void had opened up south of the Oxus; after all, Russians themselves don't give up territory easily. Pakistan could not replace the British influence in Afghanistan, for in addition to being distracted over Pushtunistan, she was still laying claim to Kashmir, which led inevitably to exhausting wars with India.

Chapter 4

Down to Earth

In September 1950, towards the end of our time in Kabul, Peggy and I were able to do a trek on foot with pack ponies up the Panshir Valley, using vertiginous tracks with falls of thousands of feet to cross the Hindu Kush (Hindu Killers). In the past, Indian captives had died in large numbers on account of the cold, while being dragged as slaves over the passes: hence the name. So precipitous were the tracks that in one place I could only force myself along by crawling abjectly on all fours, averting my eyes from the dead camels that had slipped over the cliff. Peggy stepped blithely across – how little sensitivity women have! Walking up the valley was an amazing experience. Although wide at its entrance it narrowed progressively, walled in by high mountains. The forbidding nature of this rocky passage was relieved by scattered cypresses and mulberry trees, which vied darkly with the gold and silver of poplars and willows. The sun shone warmly on the light mud walls of towered, isolated villages. Now, alas, this fertile valley has been devastated and destroyed in the struggle against the Russians.

We were beyond the regions accurately surveyed and mapped but, aided by an altimeter and a compass, we found the remote Nawak Pass at 16,000 feet. We had heard from a party of French explorers of a wonderful fishing lake beyond the pass at the head of the Kokcha River which flows into the Oxus. A German had disappeared there some years before. We were able roughly to fix its position and to reach this legendary, limpid lake, to see beyond it in the far distance the great peak of Tirich Mir standing in solitary majesty at the pivotal point of four countries – Afghanistan, Russia, China and Chitral (Pakistan). The usual crossing of the Hindu Kush was the Kawak Pass leading direct to the Oxus, believed to have been used by Alexander and his army.

Crossing a high ridge, well before the pass, I saw an armed man edging down the narrow track towards us and leading a camel train. By his baggy white trousers, shirt with a cotton sheet slung over his shoulder and high-set skull cap with the turban tightly wound, I could see that he was an Afridi, probably from the high Tirah, the remote mountain area beyond the Vale of Peshawar, whose limits the British had never been able to dominate. Its knife-edged ridges were so narrow that military supply was considered too vulnerable. Like many

My wife – gone cowgirl. Peggy on the crossing of the Hindu Kush.

The really imposing Bactrian camel.

Englishmen, I would have liked to see this country which, in spite of its ridges, was rich in trees, where close-packed deodars provided cover for defenders, so that to me as to all frontier soldiers it was a mystery land. Wishing to be polite I once told my Afridi *Subedar* in the Scouts that I would like to visit his country. We were great friends, but he said firmly, 'I would shoot you if you did.' For a fleeting moment I wondered if this Afridi would take advantage of an unarmed Englishman, his old enemy, and shoot us, sending us to join the camels' bones lying beside the river some thousands of feet below, too far down for us to see the turning fall of the foaming torrent, so that the water looked stationary like drawn out cotton wool.

I thought it wise to greet him in Pushtu in a friendly way, and his reply was equally friendly in the Pathan's frank man-to-man manner. He said life was rather dull now, as raiding Muslim Pakistan was no great sport, the British and Hindus having all gone during Partition – it lacked the spice of Holy War. He twitched at his baggy trousers, now a natural flax colour rather than white, after endless washing, saying indignantly that cloth was now five times as expensive as in the time of the British. He did not seem entirely convinced when I said the whole world was more expensive. On parting I edged up the narrow track to pass the camel *quafila* still politely waiting for my small safari to come through.

After a short climb I stopped our little convoy for a breather as the path had been steep. I was a little worried because our feet were becoming increasingly sore as we had had to wade through numerous little rivulets, and because in

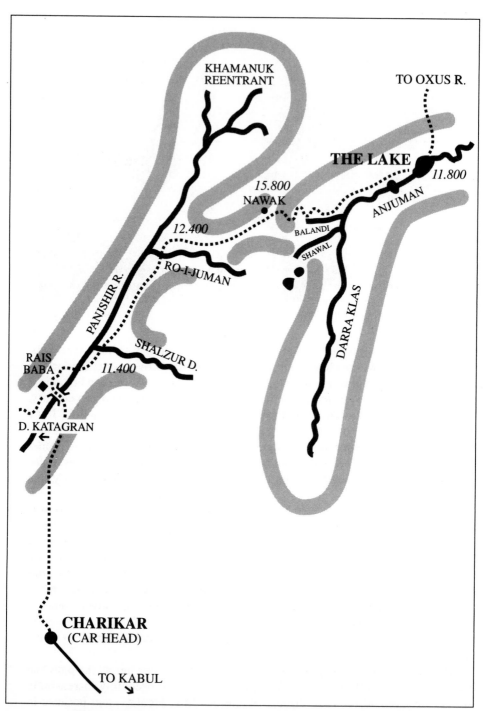

The trek over the Hindu Kush

the embassy's confines we had become unused to walking. I was always forced to do more office work than I could wish for, since my masters were always asking for reports, as if the Afghan authorities kept me provided with a steady flow of information. Nothing, of course, could have been further from the truth and I was, I fear, compelled to resort to inspired guess-work on their behalf.

In spite of sore feet, there was a feeling of well-being in the high, rarified atmosphere and with the unwonted exercise. As usual, it set my dim faculties pondering. I looked back at the friendly little convoy far below us, with its Afridi leader. From what he had said to me he was bored with life and missed the past. No longer, when things became unbearably dull after the crops had been brought in, largely by the women, could he and his friends get up a nice little raiding party to go and kidnap the Hindu girl who had flashed her eyes at them when they were shopping in Bannu. No longer was there a chance of raiding a military convoy for the ammunition and rifles which were prized above all else. Our Afridi had been carrying a rifle and a heavy bandolier crammed with .303 ammunition. This self-imposed and customary load on a long march gave him status – the rifle was almost a phallic symbol.

Since my young days when I served with Pathans I have returned many times to the Frontier and talked with fathers and sons, and they all showed this nostalgia for the past. I could believe what they said because it is not in the Pathan nature to be sycophantic. They talked of forays and raids into the settled territories as if they were discussing a test match. They referred again to successful ambushes and laughed and said, 'We had you pinned down, lying under your trucks,' or 'Do you remember so and so, Sahib? We whipped his bales off smartly.'

These forays and small campaigns are given much prominence by writers and historians, so that it must appear that, under the British, the Frontier was continually on the boil. In fact, long periods of tranquillity brought about by the payment of Danegeld were the general rule. The armed police in the buffer zone between the settled territories and Afghanistan were recruited from the Pathans in large numbers – Pakistan has now doubled this force. It gave Pathans employment, pensions, interest and sport. The government of the North West Frontier Province could not really have done better, but you cannot keep the imp mischief permanently bottled. The raider had always the option, if things got too sticky, of calling off his action and if poor old Gul Baz got his, it was a passport to Paradise. I can think of no better description than saying that we carried on a kind of cricket-with-blood relationship.

In later years, the Russians could not play this enlightened game, since their puppet rulers tried to break down the tribal structure by introducing land reforms and by lifting the *purdah*, thus striking at the very heart of tribalism, which, after all, seemed a suitable way to survive in this barren country. Individualism cannot serve a monolithic communism directly.

As we continued our journey, we made good progress at times, for we were travelling light and the pack ponies were led by the usual mare on heat, encouraging a sort of pursuit and obviating the need to goad the listless and scrawny load carriers behind. I kept my eyes on the leader of the packmen who pushed on briskly. He was easy to follow as he sported a woman's striped nylon fur coat. The next night a stallion got his mare, and we were nearly trampled on in the dark in our flimsy parachute silk tent. We had nicknamed him Umberto after a randy Italian diplomat back in Kabul.

Further on our way, we skirted Kafiristan and our men were reluctant to stop when I halted for a meal. On their advice we pressed on, as they said Kafirs raided down with bows and arrows, stealing sheep and killing shepherds. The intransigent Kafirs (heathens) are divided into two clans – the black coats and the white. They were invaded by Abdur Rahman and officially declared to be Muslims. The name of their land was changed from Kafiristan (The Land of the Unbelievers) to Nuristan (The Land of the Light [of Islam]), but the Afghan government never had much control over them – 'The Light of Islam' waned over the years. There is a suggestion that these fair-skinned people can claim descent from Alexander's army, but this has never been proved, and it appears more likely that they are of Persian origin. Originally fire worshippers, their social structure was unusual, in that they saved all their money and possessions to throw a party in order to rise a grade in society, which would be confirmed by symbols on their front doors. When they had saved enough again, they would try for another grade. They sound charming and harmless, but were, and are, extremely unpleasant to strangers. They seem to have changed little today from the people described so vividly by Colonel Robertson in the last century.

We saw few people in this remote area, but a small convoy carrying lapis lazuli and headed by an armed soldier filed past. The mines in Badakshan whence they had come are one of the few places in the world where it is found. Soon afterwards they were followed by a train of dzos, a cross between the cow and the yak and, as they threaded their way down through the rocks above us, we saw miniature mountain rabbits, pikas, popping out of their holes, and beyond them, strange little beasts in a family group – red-brown marmots. High above on the flanking mountains of the pass, my ranging eyes were checked by what seemed to be a string of pale beads, and I realised it was a flock of wild *ovis*. From my position the only things I could see were their light coloured, round bellies. A packman remarked to his assistant that I had very long sight, at which I felt gratified because in the east eyesight is more developed than amongst us.

It was an enchanting journey in the clear air. The mountains constantly changed colour from one brilliant hue to another as the unshielded sun changed its angle. It was as though nature were compensating them for their barrenness by flooding them with light and colour.

Before we reached the heights, the local Governor asked us to tea and noted that Peggy was knitting fast and diligently. Even as an honorary man, she was not expected to take part in the conversation. He remarked to his companions that he would take a stick to his old woman; she couldn't knit a stitch. Then, after the heavy silence that always falls between conversationalists who come from such distant parts and have differing interests and experiences, he volunteered, 'I see you've brought your travelling wife with you.' I imagine he himself had the four that the Muslim religion allows, one for each job. I tried to explain that I had only one wife, but he didn't seem convinced. After all, someone must have been looking after the children in Kabul.

The lake was totally deserted and we stayed there for a week, creeping into our tiny tent at night in all our clothing in the bitter cold of September. So clear was the sky, and so bright the stars, that we could see them through the skin of the tent itself. We were quite alone except for a couple of our packmen and a daily visit from afar on horseback from one of the Governor's men to see that we were not molested. Even from the high pass we had crossed we could not see a single human dwelling. Our altimeter showed 15,800 on top of the pass.

In the shadows at the edge of the lake I would choose our breakfast trout and put a dry fly over it. There were monsters further out who would take no fly, wet or dry. Using a small fly spoon I caught a four-pounder. Then against the sandy bottom a dark shadow moved. It was as if a piece of the bank had detached itself. Surely this was a really big trout. I was determined to catch it and I let my spoon go down deep to it, varying the speed of withdrawal with little sharp jerks. The shadow turned and followed the spoon up, up towards my feet, but it was only in the last two yards, when I felt I had not ensnared it, that a large head with hooked jaws emerged and seized the spoon. In nine cases out of ten this sudden apparition would have made me snatch the spoon away, but I paused for a vital second and the jaws, as big as a hound's, closed on it. I struck, and after this there was nothing spectacular. The fish went down deep and spent a long time boring and putting a great strain on my tackle, but I gradually brought it to the shore. When it was half stranded, for it was far too big for my net, Peggy slipped her thumbs up its gills and lifted it out. She said that it lay on the bank and looked at us sadly; she was always compassionate with living things. There was much gold, and clusters of red spots down its flanks, for though it was an old *ferox*, there was no sign of diminishing condition. It was as deep as a fiddle case and we photographed it with a litre bottle of Long John disappearing down its throat. It weighed just over 15 lb. and was the record for Afghanistan for at least twenty-five years. I know this, because that number of years later I met the former Court Minister in Delhi, a very pleasant individual and a skilled fisherman. He told me then that the record still stood. Does it still stand to-day?

A previous ambassador, one McConnachie, had noted that the trout in Afghanistan are migratory, so he deduced that they are not *Salmo fario*, or

The record trout in Afghanistan for many years.

Anjuman Lake: Me and hangers-on and The Fish.

ordinary brown trout, which are supposed to be strictly local in their habits. He got them recognised as a separate species by the august Bombay Natural History Society and it was declared that the fish had also an extra vertebra. It was acclaimed as *Salmo fario McConnachiensis* after its discoverer. I felt however that these were ordinary brown trout in appearance, so I sent some specimens in a jar of formalin to *The Field*, which had them identified at St. Thomas's Hospital as mere brown trout. I think their unfamiliar migratory habit, whereby the trout fall back into the warm water near the Oxus in cold weather and swim high up into the cold tributaries in the heat, is due to the tremendous contrast in temperatures in this land-locked, lofty country so far from the moderating influence of the sea.

Reluctantly, as the snow clouds closed behind us over the pass, we descended from the heights back to Kabul, confined within its ring of hills. Our tour in Afghanistan was coming to an end and there was a number of goodbye parties – a very large number. It was hard to see how we could stand the strain. I do not suggest that we were particularly popular, but in a close-knit Corps Diplomatique it had become the fashion, a sort of spontaneous combustion.

Two parties stand out in my memory. We desperately wanted a break from late nights and this Indian invitation appeared to be a routine official affair. There was nothing to indicate that it was a farewell to us, especially as the whole Corps seemed to be going. Their Military Attaché did ask me casually if we were coming, but we said to each other afterwards that no one would notice if we didn't. At the last moment, however, we thought we had better turn up, as the ambassador was going. On our arrival late it was clear that we were the principal guests, and had only just avoided committing an unforgiveable offence and hurting people who were showing us great friendship, knowing my love of India and its people. My blood runs cold even now to think of it. We were warmly greeted by the ambassador, a former Wing-Commander in the Royal Indian Air Force who had gone out of his way to invite the members of my service mission who were not usually noticed, and even served champagne in which to drink our healths in an embassy that was officially dry.

I found the ambassador a very pleasant, genial and friendly man, though his small stature and large turban did not make him an imposing figure. At one official party early in his tour of duty, he heroically decided that he must entertain his guests and demonstrate that he was a man of culture. He took out a fiddle and scratched and sketched a few notes, adopting an unprofessional stance which reminded me inescapably of Ted Ray playing the fool with the same instrument. Realising from the ill-suppressed giggles of the French contingent that his efforts were not succeeding, he changed his approach. He flung himself upon the piano stool and started playing a sort of chopsticks with his clenched fists, his large white turban bobbing from side to side. By then his decorous audience was aching with barely restrained laughter. I was writhing in embarrassment, for I was all on his side, but the ambassador seemed oblivious,

Peggy at an Indian Embassy party.

and I had a wild picture of him leading his squadron into a slab-sided mountain, for he had entered the social world of the Corps Diplomatique head on. He could have consulted Sir Giles who was still offering a great deal of good advice to him and his opposite number from Pakistan.

His wife had very fine, chiselled features and green eyes. She had clearly been a beauty and was still very handsome. However, she had the habit of stating the obvious in a portentous and instructive manner, which is the irritating way of so many middle and upper class Indian women. She was full of bromides and homespun saws and took her health, guarded by many nostrums, and her god, referred to as 'The Gard', very seriously.

The altitude of Kabul was taking its toll on everyone's sanity so the second party was not quite such a surprise as it might have been.

This was the Russian farewell. The whole Corps Diplomatique was present. The ambassador, as a soldier, greeted me warmly. In his rapidly improving English he said how nice it was for us all to be at peace, at which I flippantly replied that war was good for a soldier as it brought quick promotion. As the evening went on he sidled up to me with a leer and said, 'We know all about you and what you have been doing,' which was more than I did myself. Later, he proposed my health, which was very handsome of him and, being forewarned, I tried to read off a short speech in Russian. Typically, a young Russian female on his staff came up and told me where my pronunciation had gone wrong. Hers in English was not much better, though she was pretty fluent.

The vodka was jerked back at an alarming rate, as toast after toast followed, and I was approached by a large, uniformed figure. He represented one of those smaller Arab camel-in-oil states. Muslims who break their laws against alcohol seem to go much too far. He was a strange-looking individual, not unlike de Gaulle in his latter years, tapered at the top with a narrow head and long neck, no chest and a large keep-bag sort of stomach: not the pear shape of the old rugger blue, just a rotten pear from the start.

He asked, 'Colonel, hao many wodka you haf' drink?'

I replied breezily, exaggerating a little, 'Oh, about ten.'

He put one forefinger along his nose and winked knowingly. 'I vill beat,' he promised. Later he came up again and asked the same question in the same manner. Raising the stake, I replied that I had drunk about twenty. He rolled off, promising to beat this feat too. Still later on in this turgid evening, I saw him slowly sliding down the wall whilst two small aides kept desperately pushing him up, their feet squeaking on the linoleum floor.

The Russians then decided to heighten the tempo of the party and, although no food had yet appeared, produced pink champagne. This devilish drink cut a swathe through the decorous Corps. The party became a shambles. Impressed clearly on my memory is my fussy little ambassador on all fours behind a sofa. The Iranian ambassador, normally a very suave, attractive character, was also on all fours. My ambassador emerged from behind his sofa and barked at his Iranian counterpart, who hastily withdrew, to advance in his turn and bark, at which my ambassador withdrew and so on and so on!

I remember, too, being warmly kissed goodbye by the Iranian. I don't like being kissed by males, but it was well meant. I left the battlefield for my car, stepping high as if over large balloons but with enormous dignity. Peggy, accustomed to much, for once looked disapproving. How strangely people acted in Kabul!

You may think this is a tale just of the fleshpots but after four and a half years in Norway and Burma when I slept on the bare earth, grateful for the shelter of a tree, and charged lodging allowance by the ever-vigilant Field Cashier, I felt no shame. In any case, I was soon cut down to size by an embassy wife who said that these farewell parties had just been a fashion and had little to do with my worth. I did not think she was sniping at me. She was just naturally tactless.

Chapter 5

The Earth Proves Flat

And so we left, in October 1950. We wound down the Lattaband Pass for the last time in the well-loaded little Hawk. It was possible to reach Peshawar in a day by then, and there was no need to make two stages of it as the 'Duke' had once advised. I had long ago rejected his advice concerning the need for a driver for reasons of economy and safety. My driver was appalling; the 'Duke's' had been worse.

Soon we were pressing the Hawk up the black soil bluff above Tor Kham to surmount the Khyber once more: a small pass compared with those in Turkey, Iran and Afghanistan, but a giant in history, whose every stone has been soaked with the blood of Afghans, Afridis, British and Indians. Crossing over the top, we wended our way down the long, gentle gradients to the Peshawar Vale. I consciously and with concentration tried to imprint this journey on my mind: all the old places – Landi Kotal up on the left, Asad Khel pumping station, historical Ali Masjid and modern Shagai Fort where I had heard World War II declared over the wireless. I could see no earthly means by which I could ever return, so this was to be absolutely final. The pass seemed peopled with ghosts. Never to see Peshawar again was a thought hard to bear. I said goodbye to the military badges on the rock faces, a record of the bravery of simple soldiers who fought for an Empire in which there was then justifiable pride. They had played their little part, a little part in the Great Game.

What had my part been? I had felt my inadequacy in making any real mark in Afghanistan, but consoled myself with the knowledge that England had switched off interest there, where she no longer had a strong political stake. On the credit side, we had had a fascinating three years in a country in which I had travelled more than most other Europeans, though I had not mixed with the Afghan people as I would have liked, as this would immediately have aroused suspicions of spying which would have meant the end of my freedom to travel on those 'fishing trips'.

I had liked the proud Afghans and felt for them. Their fairyland, poor little Afghanistan, had been the sandwich between Britain and Russia for the last two centuries. Looking at the old histories, I could see that the Russians had not changed: they were still the greatest imperialists in the modern world, pushing

33

ever eastwards over great distances. Where was Samarkand of the golden gates
or Ferghana, the birthplace of Babur? The bright domes of inspiration had been
doused by the drab tides of communism. In former times, any sign of weakness
by Britain would have brought the Bear right into Afghanistan, and then into
India; the house of cards held together by prestige and self-confidence would
have come tumbling down. What was to stop Russia now? The preparations for
the next move were already being made before I left Kabul.

My time in Afghanistan left me philosophically ready to return to regimental
soldiering, though the prospect loomed dark and sunless. The years passed and
I commanded the 1st battalion of the York and Lancaster Regiment, who to my
surprise made me very welcome in Germany, the Sudan and Egypt; and finally
147 Midland Brigade in England. Finding no savour in 'home' service and
unwilling to be abroad when the children were reaching the critical stages of
their education, I somewhat rashly applied for retirement although I was still
only fifty. I did not really want a superior to whom I had to be answerable any
more, but unless I could create an absorbing interest, I knew retirement could
be a slow death.

    Having a liking for the sea, and having till then no firm base, we bought a
nineteenth century house that had seen better days, on the East Suffolk coast.
We bought it because, set against a black backdrop of ilex, it had a strange
beauty. Together with a large stretch of foreshore and many trees, we purchased
it out of my army gratuity for less than £4,000. Even at that time I was not sure
that it was a good buy, but we were captivated by its charm. I thought that as it
lay some seven hundred yards back from the cliff edge we should be safe
enough. The tides licked lovingly at my low cliffs and after every storm I
counted my losses in feet, sometimes in yards.

    When I bought it, feeling slightly vainglorious, I told the house agent that I
would eventually sell it for a bomb. 1960 was just the start of the property
boom and coastal houses in the south were already selling at huge prices. I
guessed that the Suffolk coast would soon be favoured.

    Superficially the house was in a shabby condition though basically sound, so
I set to, to redecorate the lofty rooms. We lived there in Greyfriars for four
years, doing it up round us and landscaping the garden. I found, though, that the
purchasing power of my pension dwindled rapidly against inflation, and it did
mean that I had to impose upon myself what I call the Big Silence. I always
missed the carefree life of India where friends dropped in at any time. We did
find friends, but they too were doing the jobs of gardener, boot black and do-it-
yourself builder and decorator, and had no energy to get together, save for a
Babel-like sherry party at which everyone stood face to face and channered like
hyenas.

    It was all so uneventful. One day, stifling vertigo on a high ladder, I heard
the cooing of a collared dove, that little success story that has come to our

shores from the east in comparatively recent years. The soft cooing was infinitely sad:

> Then from a wood was heard unseen to coo
> The Ringdove: *Yusuf, Yusuf, Yu* . . .
> (For thus her sorrow broke her note in twain
> And just where broken took it up again.)
> . . . *suf, Yusuf, Yusuf, Yusuf* – But one note
> Which still repeating, she made hoarse her throat,
> Till checkt: 'Oh, you with your idle sighs
> Block up the road to better enterprise,
> Sham sorrow all, or as bad as sham if true
> When once the better thing is come to do.
>
> *Parliament of the Birds – Attar (1119-1230?)*
> *trans. E. Fitzgerald*

I dropped my paint brush, so sharp was the pang of nostalgia. The sad little voice had called me right back to Peshawar and I could hear the doves there and smell the almost erotic scent of orange blossom once more. Why work with my face to a wall throughout the summer's days? Why 'Block up the road to better enterprise . . . When once the better thing is come to do'? To go to India: that was the message – a call over the distances from her – a call that had been faint, but insistent these past fifteen years, and now an imperative that I must obey.

I thought hard to see how a return could be made. I could not, on the face of it, afford such a long journey, for there were still some education fees to pay. For days and weeks I considered the problem, and then it was partly solved. A grand old cavalry uncle died and left me a modest legacy. It was good of him to remember me, but I had devoted a large part of my leave before joining the British army to illustrating a book that he had written about Pathans. He had offered to pay me for my services, but I had declined, saying it would not be seemly between relations. I could have done with even an avuncular half-crown at the time, but so is virtue sometimes rewarded.

Peggy and I decided that the only way we could go would be to travel by motor caravan and live in it. In those days almost nothing appeared to be known about driving overland to India and the AA was no help. I did know, however, that in places the going would be rough, so I bought a long wheel-base, diesel Land Rover Dormobile as the accepted tough image, go-anywhere vehicle, though I was later to modify my ideas on transport, as through the years I began to obey the steady call, beamed over the lofty Taurus and Anti-Taurus mountains, over the Elburz and the Hindu Kush beyond.

In those days, in 1963, we had under three months in term time to do this expensive journey, which would mean that we would reach India only to have to return, motoring in great haste. We decided therefore to do a shorter trial run to find out conditions for ourselves and to choose a route to the ultimate goal. It was, after all, pioneering a new form of activity. By hard driving and hard living, we did an intensive tour of Turkey and Iran, to return in time for the Christmas holidays. Even this was unsatisfying. Both these countries had so much to offer, but we could only scratch at the surface. Time was still against us, so we had to bash endlessly along atrocious roads with little opportunity to explore or to get to know the people, who in general treated us with great courtesy and kindness. Shopping for food was fun, since passers-by all joined in to help, determined to see that we were not cheated.

The Land Rover with its strange, raising-roof design and austere let-down beds was extremely uncomfortable, for we were not in our first youth. The makers obviously assumed that the human spine was the only necessary spring. When we took the trouble to visit the coach builders and suggest improvements, we were surlily greeted. Many years later the vehicle was unaltered, rapidly becoming obsolete – what price British enterprise?

We found the going desperately rough, and the art was to drive every inch of the road, scanning it closely for large potholes, so as to wend a less bumpy way round and forward, and to keep the vehicle in one piece. For example, it took us four and a half days from the Iranian border with Turkey to Teheran. In later years, with better roads, it normally took us a day, using a series of more suitable campers. The Land Rover's diesel engine became easily puffed on the hills and had a shattering roar all the livelong day. As a result the purser (Peggy), usually so competent, found she was a quaking jelly but still had to cope with border formalities, made so tedious and so complicated by countries then unused to this type of travel.

Although a little daunted by the bad roads and the wear and tear to be suffered by the vehicle, which would add to the cost, we decided that the road to India was possible. This trial run had been a valuable and interesting reconnaissance in two large countries which seemed to hold out as stiff a challenge as anything ahead, since I knew Afghanistan's lofty heights already.

Six months after our return, the agent through whom I had bought Greyfriars rang me up and said, 'Brigadier, you remember four years ago you said you would make a bomb on the sale of your house some day; well, that day has come. People are looking for houses all along our coast.'

I, feeling that I was really setting the price rather high, said, 'I should expect fourteen thousand.'

He replied, 'I should try fifteen.'

After one or two inspections by would-be buyers, a very nice couple came in a vast American station wagon. They seemed to like the house and I was at pains to point out that the rates were very low. They looked mystified. Their name suggested that they were very wealthy and petty cash was unfamiliar to them. Greyfriars was looking beautiful, for we had put still more work into it and its grounds. All the same I felt that through the surface I could see the cracked plaster and the old faults which I had rectified. Our visitors left and told the agent they liked the house. They put down a deposit and sent a surveyor to inspect it.

By then I could see a long vista of visits to India opening out if only the sale would go through. We heard nothing for two most anxious months – anxious because in 1964 such a sum as I had asked was considered a substantial one and a satisfying advance on the £5,000 I had put into the property altogether. I reasoned that I could get a bungalow as an English *pied-à-terre* and yet be able to afford to spend winters in India living in a motor caravan. Were I to relinquish England entirely, I felt that we would drift into the ranks of expatriate and roving tax-dodgers, cut off from family and loyalties. I needed roots in my country, even if only to worry over its problems. If only we could get a decision; in my little world it was big business, even if it meant little to the purchasers. At last my resolution cracked and I wrote to them, to find that they had been away in Portugal. They replied pleasantly, 'Didn't you know? Of course we want it.' And so we were through.

We changed house thrice more after that, and each time were able to add to our travel fund. In fact I had, almost by chance, created a retirement job for myself and a remunerative one. I had my independence, though I cannot pretend that the work was not absolutely back-breaking. As well as high ladders, it has included landscaping considerable areas, even to wielding a pickaxe in my seventies. I tried to make beauty round me and, again quite by accident, it attracted people prepared to pay me substantial sums for it, so that in the end I made myself quite comfortably off.

Hark, loud and clear from heaven the drum of parting calls – let none delay!
The cameleer hath risen amain, made ready all the camel-train,
And quittance now desires to gain: why sleep ye, travellers, I pray?

Rumi (1207–73): trans. R.A. Nicholson.

At last, in October 1967, when our younger son went up to Cambridge, we set out to India in the Land Rover and travelled all over the country, visiting sites of historical interest or childhood memory. This journey took us to places we had never been able to visit during my service there. We met many different people and made numerous Indian friends as we had not been able to do before, serving in the country in the days of the Raj.

The following year my two sons, one on leave from the army and the other on vacation, skilfully converted a Hawson steel commercial van to my plans. It was a happy time. Much beer was consumed and the two boys, natural mimics, were first Welsh, then Italian and lastly Indian craftsmen. I felt it was the first time we had really done something together in our peripatetic lives. The van

My sons' conversion of a diesel steel Hawson van.

had none of the discomfort of the over-rugged and cramped Land Rover. We did two very interesting trips in this vehicle, wandering about India, but its rather flat diesel engine was a gutless wonder.

This form of travel overland, spending the whole winter in India, developed into a study of caravan design and to a deeper interest in the problems of this way of life, which led eventually to my writing a book on the subject and getting it published. Later, with a better financial position and careful budgeting, I was able to have a vehicle built to my own design on a Bedford truck chassis. It was not the ultimate of my desire, as there was a limit to what I could afford, even though I sold my good shot-gun and some of my precious Persian rugs. My greatest delight came to me late in life – driving in a powerful, high-cabbed vehicle with double back wheels for a feeling of stability. I seemed to

Locally built camper for later journeys.

Interior of camper no. 3, locally made to my own specifications: strong, simple and spacious for living in over long periods.

be able to command the very roof of the world as I soared up steep inclines and drifted down winding slopes on my way to India's plains. Driving was equal to the satisfaction of arriving.

The new vehicle gave us still greater comfort for protracted living. We did four happy winters in it in India, encountering disasters, some rather frightening at the time, which lent spice to our travels and adventures. Having seen so much of the country on our earlier journeys, we eventually decided to settle down in one ideal spot for the winter, partly in order to cut down the prohibitively expensive wear and tear on the vehicle, and partly to put down roots.

Glimpses of the Indian jungle in childhood had always attracted me and so, almost by chance, while returning from Ranikhet in the Himalayan foothills, a place of happy childhood memories, we had turned in to Corbett National Wildlife Park. We were so happy there that we returned again, and eventually spent six winters altogether in the area. When the Bedford truck wore out, we flew out one year and lived in the Park accommodation. Lastly, by superhuman effort we raised enough money to buy a stock motor caravan (still a Bedford, and all we could get quickly) to pay one final visit before the route was engulfed in war and revolution.

To recapitulate, we went out to India for the first time in 1967 in the Land Rover. This journey was followed in 1968 and 1970 in the Hawson. We then did four journeys in the big Bedford in 1971–2, 1972–3, 1973–4 and 1974–5.

Before starting off from UK. The next generation also 'go' minded.

We flew out in 1976 and did our last journey in the Bedford Motorhome in 1978–9. All these winters in India amounted to a magic extension of four and a half years of our life in that country in relatively modern times, to cap my previous army service there. By so doing, for a moderate outlay, we gathered more riches than most people.

Chapter 6

Tumbleweed in the Wind

First Journey to India (1967)

In November 1967, after travelling through Europe, Turkey and Iran we at last reached Islam Qila on the Iranian border with Afghanistan, but by then we were not the only people making the journey. We were much daunted to find the passengers from two large, shabby, chartered buses completely filling up the customs office and spilling out into its noisome yard. They seemed to have come from all over Europe and America in a motley rout. I tried to look over the tall, gangling phalanx surmounted by a fuzz of frizzy hair, but it was hopeless – young men are taller than I am. I feared that many such youngsters would lack essential documents, as had happened at other places on our way. Indeed, one bearded individual, whose hair distribution made him look like some minor Hebrew prophet, was seated on the only chair before the clerk's tiny table, arguing wildly and holding everything up. Apparently, though I don't understand American very well, his girl friend had got fed up with him and the bumpy roads and had flown home, leaving him with a car registered in *her* name. The Afghan clerk reasoned that as the car was not *his*, he could not take it out of the country. Logic can be absolutely flattening. The crowd stood patiently by, pathetically docile. Young hippies had infinite patience and seemed to expect to be pushed about by bossy officials on the borders – Iranians were particularly rough with them.

My heart fell into my boots, for I always suffer an extreme psychological shock at being held up after scurrying diligently down long, empty roads. I feel like a greyhound springing out of the slips, only to find its leash still attached. Eastern borders are painstakingly slow over documentation in any case. Forms are filled in in triplicate – there is no carbon paper and large ledgers are laboriously entered up with details already shown on the forms. I knew the whole process of clearing our vehicle would take hours and hours and hours. We should be there till dark when the border would close for the night.

The prophet stamped out leaving a small gap in the crowd. I managed to catch the clerk's eye and cried, *'Stere ma'she, Babu Sa'ab!'* ('May you never

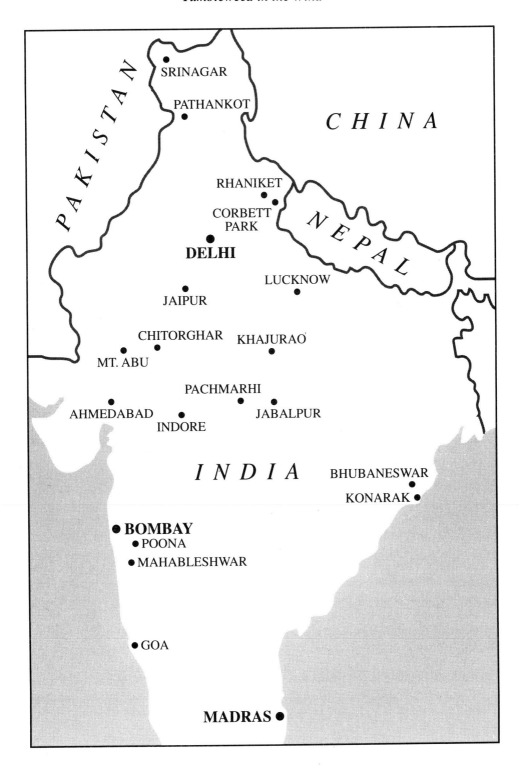

Mount Ararat: at the Turkish border.

be tired, Mr Clerk, Sir!') He looked puzzled; perhaps it was my clipped moustache and checked cap that caught his eye.

He replied, '*Kwa ma'she*' ('May you never be poor!'), got up and came
towards me, thrusting the throng aside and excusing himself, saying, 'I must go
and have a cup of tea.' We shook hands and I continued with the usual elaborate
greetings: '*Jor ye?*' ('Are you well?') '*Balbach tol de jor di?*' ('Are your children well?'), and so on and so on. He asked me where I'd learned Pushtu and I
replied mendaciously that I'd learnt it at the British embassy in lovely Kabul.
Had I been more truthful and said I'd learnt it in Waziristan, almost enemy
territory for him, I would have struck a sour note. Friendly and manly as he is,
the Afghan is both brittle and volatile.

He said to me, 'Hang on and I'll get the forms and you can fill them in in
the back office which is cool and clean. I'll take the forms out and we'll look
at your car.' This was pure balm to my ears. Any customs officer can take
one's car apart if he feels like it and have all one's food and possessions spread

out on the ground to be nosed over and leg-upped by horribly mangy pi-dogs.

He stepped lightly up into the Land Rover, looked round cursorily and nipped out again. I politely asked him, had I permission to go? I had. As we left a girl in the crowd muttered reproachfully, 'T'ain't fair!'

I replied loftily, 'I am a senior citizen,' delving deep into the welfare state, 'And have taken the trouble to learn the language.' She was ill-favoured, though youthful, and not worth a senile ogle, for she had drowned-rat hair and was dust-coloured all over, yet I felt rather sorry for her. How she roughed it; I admired her courage.

We went through the whole rigmarole again when showing our passports at the police office across the way and were equally successful. Our precious visa forms, lovingly brought from England were scrabbled up and flipped into the wastepaper basket. I, the creaking geriatric, leapt nimbly into my vehicle and we were off.

Afterwards, as I hummed bonnet down towards the haunt of dove and orange blossom, I thought about those youngsters. How did they get the money to travel? Where did they get the confidence? For they all roughed it unbearably. Marco Polo's call must have been imperative and I felt a wave of sympathy for them for I am a natural 'Darwish' myself.

> When the heart wanders, seeking endless change,
> And from its own safe solitude doth range,
> Not peace it finds, nor any virtue more:
> But though a man had merchandise in store
> And rank and wealth and lands, his heart being still,
> He may live Allah's Darweesh, if he will.
>
> *Sa'di (1184?–1292): trans. Sir Edwin Arnold*

I liked to sort things out in my bumbly mind, for the engine's song was for once sweet and kind, and I felt I must work out the dividing line between the honest traveller and the scrounger. I have met so many shaggy youngsters whom I have learned to admire, using their qualifications to work a little and travel a little. They are quite different from the scroungers who have done unbelievable damage to the image of the west, once so respected, in their search for cheap narcotics for which they will sell their very souls, while living off people poorer than themselves. If in your travels you are offered hospitality, be careful not to throw away a dry crust after you have eaten. You may not know it but dry crusts are hard to get. Unfortunately, the scroungers followed one or two narrow routes to the east and gave the impression of large numbers, though they were few in reality. They were taken for the modern youth of the west, most of whom were busy working like our own little family, or trying to get work in their own countries.

At last, in the far distance, I saw the minarets of the Empress Gauhar Shad's tomb and ecclesiastical school in Herat. They looked like slender factory chimneys. In the clear atmosphere we seemed to motor for hours over bare plains while our landmarks grew no bigger. When we did eventually reach Herat, we visited the mosques and tombs for the first time. The main mosque was remarkable for its fine tile work but, unlike the great mosques of Isfahan and Meshed, the overall design was not harmonious, as if its creators had had little vision of the whole. This mosque, a masterpiece nevertheless, has now, I believe, been damaged by a Russian official asked politely by the mullahs to remove his shoes when entering.

We then set off down the Russian-built concrete road to Kandahar. After a pause, it is always a considerable effort to pull one's thoughts together, to savour a long-hoped-for event and, in doing so, much of the savour can be squeezed out, but not so on this journey, for it is a part of my nature to thrust forward and the indomitable roar of the diesel engine assorted well with my mood. So, on a bare upland road, filled with hazards, it was as if my thoughts were whisked away to revive long forgotten memories, to whirl like the dust-devils orchestrated by the engine, for from the desert sand there was no sound. Across this hot plateau, made more uncomfortable by its dryness, lips became cracked and my face stiffened as if it were a mask. As far as I could see mirages formed and reformed as a mocking back-drop to our journey. Nothing was steady: great limpid lakes appeared and faded where there was but sand, clumps of trees wobbled as if unable to support the belt of haze above, and vanished. Real pointed mountains poked their jagged crests through the general flatness. Red dust-devils screwed up and tossed dry lumps of tumbleweed. The devils spun and chased each other across this bewitched land.

Off to the left lay a long, shale ridge, unusually dark in colour – Maiwand. Sombre it was and sombre its tale. For thither a mixed body of British and Indian soldiers had set out from Kandahar in May 1880, to face a force under Ayub Khan, son of the former Amir Sher Ali: an army of Duranis. The British force, a brigade strong under Brigadier-General Burrowes, with only light artillery, moved in the belief that there was little more than a small uprising collecting. They were over-confident after so much success against the Afghans. The march out of Kandahar was made in the heat of the day, some 110°F in the shade and searingly dry – surely a foolish step. The soldiers were in tight red tunics, that attracted the sun's rays and broiled the wearer. On closing with the reported enemy, Burrowes was horrified to find a force of 25,000 Afghans covering a copious spring, with heavy pieces of artillery to hold the British at a distance. The water was the key to the battle. Our forces, outnumbered seven times, arrived already parched with thirst and were held back from the water by guns of a longer range. In short, the British were soundly defeated by the Afghans. Have you ever been parched with thirst? I assure you the process of becoming kippered is a feeling beyond all other sufferings.

And so my thoughts wandered. Perhaps the dust devils were the souls of dead soldiers, I mused, and remembered that there had been a little white terrier called Bobby, the pet of the 66th regiment, who had joined the last stand as the thin line fought it out back-to-back to the end. Bobby snarled and snapped at the spurts of dust kicked up by ricochets. He was wounded and lost in the general scattering of the broken force, but three days later he turned up at Kandahar in sore distress. Later, he was awarded a medal by Queen Victoria, along with Lord Robert's charger, who had accompanied his master on the march from Kabul to relieve Kandahar after the disaster. I am not averse to a bit of sloppy sentimentality myself. A year afterwards Bobby was run down and killed in London by a hansom cab. He was stuffed, and remains bemedalled and glass-eyed in the Regimental Museum of the Royal Berkshires, now the Wiltshire Regiment, in Salisbury.

I smiled as I thought of my dogs in India in former times – little Banger, huffy Cholmondley the golden spaniel, and dear Mrs Brown, the water spaniel whom I had rescued, lost and exhausted, in Waziristan, dropped from a heedless motor convoy.

My mind swung back to those grim hills. I once found the story in the embassy files in Kabul of a Highlander, huge in lofty bonnet and full regalia who had crawled, wounded, into an Afghan village after the battle and there lay, calling for water. The Afghans were too frightened, and perhaps unwilling, to go to his rescue. It took him three days to die. I thought sadly of the song, 'Will ye no' come back again?', and I sorrowed for all those loyal, simple private soldiers. They did serve, I am sure, out of feelings of patriotism, feelings of identity with the county regiment or their clan under the laird, and all under Queen Victoria, their Commander-in-Chief, who suffered with them, as she shows in her letters.

Thus musing, I saw over to the right the high pink roll of Seistan's desert, with some black pencils at its foot. With a shock I realized that these, and what looked like scattered pebbles, were all tall cypresses and villages, over-topped by the advancing sand. How oppressive for those still living at its foot, the crest two or three hundred feet above them and hungry. The sandy bank is supposed to move a mile eastwards each year. It certainly looked much closer than it did so long before when I was Military Attaché.

In those days I used to bump my official car over infinitely rough roads, now so smooth since a good American highway took over at Kandahar in rivalry with the Russian one from Herat and the north. The Humber Hawk used to boil if we turned away from the head wind, and its *ersatz* buna tyres punctured readily. So bumpy was the road then that I could not feel a puncture. When it was at last discovered, we poured the inner tube out of the tyre in pieces no bigger than a jig-saw puzzle. We even sewed up one badly split tube with needle and thread before applying one of those useful vulcanising kits to the wound.

My roving thoughts were brought sharply back as I saw the two steep humps which overlook Kandahar: humps tipped out of a child's sand bucket, hills as weird as ever. We spent a night in the yard of the sleazy hotel for protection, a smelly night, loud with the clop of pony traps and always the yowl of pi-dogs, but the little shop up the road had a complete tea-set of fragile Gardener china. Peggy said we hadn't enough money to buy it and she was, alas, right. We have now learnt that if one sees something rare and desirable, one should buy it regardless, even if it hurts. It hurts more to think back on a lost opportunity.

Next day we turned eastwards and began the slow steady climb up to Ghazni. I had had a look round this area nearly twenty years before, but I wanted to refresh my memory of this famous city of which so little is left. A thousand years ago the walls used to be twenty miles in circumference. Its heyday was short, but the city was large by the standards of those days. As a younger man, I was perhaps cursory in my inspection and was disappointed with the unpretentious tombs of Mahmud, the great sultan, and his father, Sabaktaghin. On this visit, my interest mounted, though the extensive excavations of recent times had not then taken place.

There was still not much to rave about at Ghazni at first glance – just a mud fort, two simple tombs and Mahmud's two victory towers, small and insignificant by modern standards. Some say they have been taller, but I doubt it, for they have balance and their caps are well tiled. It is generally believed that crocks of gold were once discovered in the old city by a ploughman, so that more ploughmen and their oxen ploughed hopefully on and on to level the mud walls to the ground and leave little of its splendours. The thirst for crocks of gold was still there. There were vendors of coins, alas of base metal, well counterfeited and prematurely aged. You could buy them by the bucketful. They were even pierced and threaded on strings.

What manner of man was Mahmud, conceived by a ruler-adventurer out of a slave girl, an all-too-common occurrence which led to so much blood-letting at the time of accession? History suggests that he was a mean man as well as being a great conqueror and ruler, for he became the target of Firdausi's great hate poem, *The Satire on Mahmud*. He owed much to Firdausi because this fine poet, whose name means, I think, 'One from Paradise', has left us with the vivid and detailed story of Mahmud's exploits in the *Shah-Nama*: 66,000 lines of poetry! There were no war correspondents in those days. The sultan failed to reward him adequately – hence the outpouring of hate:

> Such as thou art, the vileness of thy birth
> Precludes each generous sentiment of worth.
> Nor kingly origin, nor noble race
> Warms thy low heart, the offspring of disgrace.

> *Firdausi (932–1020?), trans: J. Champion.*

You and I could have said it more starkly: 'You mean bastard!'

I read all about Mahmud in a translation of the *Shah-Nama* into Pushtu of all strange things. Sir George Roos-Keppel, then Chief Commissioner of the North West Frontier Province, had put this epic into that language and in Arabic script, for Pathans had no writing of their own. I studied it in a mud hut in a North Waziristan Armed Police camp, girt by barbed wire and roasting hot. The tribesmen were occupying our water supply in the Khaisora Valley at the time and a decision had to be made to go and drive them off, or to parley with them, for the British authorities were ready to admit that scarce water was wanted by all. Though so distracted, yet I read the marvellous tale.

The sultan later repented of his treatment of Firdausi, and sent a convoy westwards towards Meshed, bearing a rich load of silver to recompense the great war reporter, only to meet his bier coming out from his home.

Mahmud was called the Conqueror of India and Breaker of Idols. His deep forays into that huge country round about the year 1000 AD gave some validity to this title, but what manner of army moving at footpace could pin down vast India, with the constricted gut of the northern passes at its rear? Ghazni was an ideal pivot for Mahmud to raid east, north and deep south to seize treasure to finance his empire. How did those uplanders, accustomed to a bracing climate, survive the swampy heat of India? What prodigious marchers they must have been, for the pace would surely be that of the slowest, the foot slogger, the creaky bullock cart and the supercilious camel – what terrible thirst! Mahmud, lusting for power and wealth, for nothing moves men more, chose to see in himself a sword bearer for Islam, but in truth, he had to raid and rob annually to maintain his precarious ascendancy. He had to pay his soldiers to keep them to heel and he needed money for his 'Good Life', though his iconoclasm won him the title of 'Idol Breaker', putting the seal of sanctity on his activities.

In spite of the tremendous march, his army was still fresh when it arrived at the gates of sacred Somnath, at the southern tip of the Kathiawar peninsula. Somnath was a huge temple complex and the epitome of all that had been advanced in learning and artistic culture in India, which had once led the world in science. It was guarded by fifteen thousand militant priests. They fought Mahmud almost to the last man, and then all was open to the smashing and looting.

My thoughts seemed to focus on the mud wall opposite me and a bright pageant passed before my eyes. One or two remaining priests were trying to edge the Sultan and his wreckers away from the strange and mysterious centre-piece of the chief temple, for there was gold to be stripped everywhere. But Mahmud's acquisitive eyes were focused on this centre-piece: an image 'miraculously' suspended in the air. He called for his wise men, for he had very wise men with him drawn from the ranks of Arab mathematicians and scientists. Perhaps they were in advance of the Indians who were by then past their peak.

'Go and have a look behind that damned idol,' said Mahmud. 'It must be fixed to something.'

'No,' replied the Arabs. 'See, we can pass a spear round the back. There is nothing, O Smasher of Idols – live for ever.'

'Well,' snorted Mahmud, 'The damn thing can't hang in the air.'

'Yes, it does,' said the wise men. 'It is held by the pull of lodestones.'

As they prized some away, the great idol canted to one side. More poking and it crashed to the ground and out of it poured a huge mound of rose-coloured pearls as big as peas, like the seeds of the pomegranate. Here was the treasure of Somnath, beyond all dreams. Mahmud took the temple gates away with him, but they and the pearls have long gone.

The picture suddenly faded and only the brown mud wall was left as a brash local truck, hooting madly, made me jump aside, my mystic experience shattered; then back to the caravan and down to the junction with the main road where we had spent the night in the parched garden of the shanty hotel. Our arrival had been all too much for the manager, and he had flung himself down on his mat in prayer in order not to be disturbed. I did not want a meal which would, I knew, be bad. We just wanted a key to the WC. Later, having respected his prayers I had approached him again upon which he again sought his prayer mat and bowed down to the ground, his eyes anxiously following me. After a welcome night's rest, somewhat spoilt by barking dogs, and a visit to the city, we set out, and once my engine was warm, I could put the Land Rover up the steady slope which in the course of a couple of miles rose very steeply a further two thousand feet to top the pass at 9,000 ft.

We remained at about this height for some seventy miles, slowly dropping down to Kabul towards the end. Arriving in the historic capital, full of memories of the past, we looked for the big, distinguished embassy. In my mind's eye it had always stood on a slight rise. I found it with difficulty, surrounded now by a thick press of modern, flat-topped, concrete houses. When I had served there it had been four miles out of town on the edge of a wide *maidan* (plain) where I used to shoot snipe, and the road had been like Monte Casino after the bombing.

We stayed for a few days with the Timbrells, the then Military Attaché and his wife. Both were tall and good-looking, had taken the trouble to learn Persian and were clearly very keen: an ideal couple for the job. Tim Timbrell had been in the Indian army and spoke Hindustani fluently as well as Persian. He went on to be Deputy Military Adviser to the High Commissioner in New Delhi, where we met him again some years later. Alas, he had to leave the day after our arrival in Kabul for hospital investigation in England, owing to an alarming loss of weight. This splendid figure of a man, and earnest soldier, put up a tremendous fight against cancer of the spine for ten more years, during which he saw his son and two handsome daughters through school.

We took his wife Pat, who was distraught, to dinner at the Bagh-i-Bala (The Upper Garden Palace) where Abdur Rahman ruled and died. In my time it had been a semi-ruined building, whose dark portals looked down on the embassy like the empty eye sockets of an old skull. Now it was a smart restaurant. The next night Pat took us to an official diplomatic gathering at the Turkish embassy, and we were welcomed by Afghan friends of long ago. We were introduced for the first time to the Afghan ladies, by then out of their strict *purdah*. I suppose now the Bear and its friends have chopped down all those beautiful women.

In the embassy houses I noticed something was wrong. The soft-footed Pakistani servants of our time had gone – gone was Ghulam Qadir whom we had left with my successor. The Afghans had reasonably insisted that their countrymen should get the jobs. These were untrained and clonked noisily about the house in heavy British army boots, could not cook and knocked off early. However, the almond trees, the first heralds of spring which I had planted so long ago were flourishing. Those had been happy times!

Tim Timbrell was the last Military Attaché in Kabul, for the administration in its wisdom decided to abolish the post and cover the country by an annual visit from the Defence Attaché, Teheran. From then on, I felt that the embassy would sit behind its high walls and know even less of what was going on outside. The Afghans too would feel more lonely than ever.

Chapter 7

'Pass, Friend'

On the First Journey to India (1967)

Next morning we said good-bye to Pat and set off down the abrupt gut of the Kabul gorge – how different from the old Lattaband Pass which had been just a scrape road with roughly executed rain ditches winding tightly round the mountains. The new road was American made and of fine, smooth tarmac: a considerable engineering feat and in many places buttressed to the sheer cliff so that I felt that one stick of dynamite could bring it all tumbling down as shock waves smacked from one flat cliff side to another. Any small party of irregulars could have done this and the havoc would be completed by the waters of the Kabul River piling up in the gorge. Never was there such a long gut with so many potential hernias: so easy to isolate Kabul from Jelalabad and the road out of Afghanistan.

It was an emotional experience to approach the Khyber Pass again and it was my birthday – 15th November. In later years I tried to hit off this day each time. I did so on my sixtieth and went on for many years afterwards until Russia closed the gut.

As we climbed up the big black bluff above Tor Kham, keeping an eye open for Pakistani trucks, bouncing down like gorgeously ornamented goats and their drivers with their near-miss dexterity, I remembered to move over to the left (the *right* side) after I had crossed the border. We had met an American there who complained he could find none of the wonderful, tall Pathans he had come to see in the Khyber, the ultimate goal of his journey. I felt he wouldn't get much further anyway. His VW shock absorbers were terribly mashed up. I explained to him that the Pathan is tall in comparison generally with the Indian and wears a high head-dress, but he cannot compare with the vitamin-primed American. He then set off up the right hand (*wrong*) side of the road to certain death, while I tore after him hooting madly to warn him.

We could see smugglers coming up a side track to the border, in full view; the open market just off the Pass could sell their wares from the whole world cheaply, while these Pathans were at last happy to be doing something illicit, but unchecked. The black market bazaars helped to keep the turbulent tribes

52

A Pathan party at the mouth of the Khyber Pass. Author holding hat.

quiet and the new North West Frontier Government was glad to turn a blind eye. In all the time of the British Raj we never had such a good idea – perhaps we lacked oriental subtlety.

It had been a pleasant border crossing, for the Khyber Rifles, learning that I was an old Tochi Scout from a sister corps, had insisted on turning out the guard, giving me a General Salute, despite my deprecatory protests. The police and customs welcomed me as an old friend – I spoke the magic Pushtu! I enquired after their relations whom I had known and they offered scalding green tea and hard boiled eggs while a bank of beardy-weirdy travellers eyed us curiously.

Once more in our lives we passed Landi Kotal up on our left: over the black shale of the pass proper, and how soon we were over, then down and down, shrieking my loud horn to make a cluster of schoolboys scatter. Did they teach nothing but stone throwing at the school? A smashed windscreen is not uncommon and is rated a bullseye. Some horrid little beasts had started to use catapults – harder to detect; the Pathan nature must out.

Here was an intense green slick, where a quenching spring relieved all that rocky dryness. I looked up at the defended posts high above, which I had laboriously visited on foot on inspections so many years ago. I was glad to see that the well-preserved units' crests from the Afghan wars were still on the roadside rocks. We passed Ali Masjid fort, once impregnable but now many years obsolete, for the coming of the rifle with its longer range to replace the musket had made it easy for the tribesmen to pick off sentries on the walls from the surrounding hills. Once more we passed red-brick Shagai Fort, its replacement, and surely as obsolete as its predecessor in the face of new and heavier weaponry, but garrisoned now by the Khyber Rifles. Its bright red brick still clashed with the sandy dun colour of the valley. Then at last we drove through the gateway of Jamrud Fort at the foot of the pass.

We entered Peshawar's lovely cantonments under tall avenues of pepul trees and pulled into the old Gymkhana Club. I was back to my heart's home. There were the well mown grass tennis courts and the cries of the players in 1930s' English: 'Well played, Bubbles, old boy!', 'Jolly good shot, Bunty!' – yes, indeed, there were Pakistani ladies playing there – a thing unheard of in my past. The pop of the squash balls in the four courts still echoed across the gardens. In these now shabby courts Pathan markers had been trained by the British and had become world beaters. The gardens still flowered, carefully tended by the *malis* (gardeners), painstakingly planted and hand-watered as they had always been, with deep shade under the dark leaved, generous fruited citron trees. Old standards were hanging on as precariously as the faded blue back-drop screens of the tennis courts.

In 1947 the club had been generously handed over lock, stock and barrel and with a hefty credit balance to our inheritors. Now the poor turnover of funds was just beginning to make it threadbare at the seams. Instead of the crowd milling three-deep round the horseshoe bar at bi-weekly dances where the bar takings had been the club's main source of income, there were now only decorous parties for tombola, and film sessions. Pakistani officers could not afford much since alcohol was prohibitively taxed and public drinking was frowned upon. Later it was banned altogether by a fundamentalist government. Even the horseshoe bar had been torn out and a huge, dark cavern with subdued coloured lights had taken its place, though the large, badly set up, cocked head of a *sambhur* stag still presided. In the past I had thought it looked down tolerantly at the revelry below, but now its head slanted still more and, I felt, rather sadly. And I was sad too since the substantial rank of uniformed and bearded barmen was thinner than in my time. Those barmen, Khalil Mohmands, and less warlike than the Mohmands of the hills round the Peshawar Vale, were great characters and friends to us subalterns, and we practised our mispronounced Pushtu on them. Death and old age had taken so many of them away. I was sad also because the club had been the centre of a carefree life and a relief from hard service on the Frontier. I hated to see the change: it was almost a shrine for me, but the Pakistanis had done their best though, typically, the club secretary had an architect son who had inflicted his skill on this holy of holies, but who forebore to keep it in good repair.

At least he had left the tinted photographs of the Masters of the Peshawar Vale Hunt round the walls. They seemed to look out with the steely eyes of unconscious authority. They were as good as the pink coated gentlemen of England. Though their quarry was but a jackal, the going was extremely rough over hard ground and twenty foot deep, collapsed underground watercourses or *quanats*. They had often crossed into tribal territory, but hostile tribes chivalrously held their fire.

Beyond the bar there was a little lawn – oh, and how I loved every yard of the ground – where the club members and their wives used to gather on Sunday mornings for pre-lunch drinks. An Indian regimental brass band, impeccably starched, would pump out Lehar and the Strauss-Lauss lot with great accuracy but little feeling. Allsop lager beer was drunk and gin-piaz. I found this salty drink rather esoteric for it was drunk in a modern, flat champagne glass with angostura bitters, water and little pearl onions. Sunday lunch, a most delectable affair, did not usually start before three o'clock in the afternoon and, shame on it, the orange-labelled Veuve Cliquot was very much in evidence, though not exactly lashed about. We were not a loose-living lot, but we were a society within a society, isolated and far from home. All this gaiety was superimposed on a hard life of physical effort and privations beyond the understanding of our own shores. Our work took us out to the risk of ambush or a cut-in raid by a tribal *lashkar* should a single tactical mistake be made, so that our professionalism was always sharpened. Disease still infiltrated into our midst, although we lived in well laid out cantonments. To die in the heat was to be buried the same evening. Nobody had time to glance as you passed. Now the lawn was empty and silent and Sunday lunches were no more.

There are other secret places in the gardens. Where I tucked my caravan in among the shady trees to avoid the midday heat there was a little shrine, decked with sticks tied with bright rags and over all, at night, a dim electric bulb in a green, dust-obscured lantern. Somehow this little isolated tomb held my thoughts. It was visited at dawn and dusk by an old man with a long white beard and fine Pathan features, softened in his case to an expression of sweetness. There he said his prayers twice daily. Greeting him politely, I asked who was the holy man buried there who would answer his prayers. But as is so common in the east, I was gently fobbed off with an evasive answer. After all, I was but part of the intruding swirl round this little island.

Under the trees I was awakened by the muezzin's soft call to prayer at dawn. The mullahs had trained voices, tuned to carry over the flat roofs of Peshawar from the tall, slender minarets. Later in the day I was puzzled by a rhythmic metallic clank which, pursued to its source, I found to be the bell of the Church of St. John, behind the club building, where we had been married twenty-eight years before. The bell was cracked, the roof had caved in, but there were two memorials to a British regiment in Queen Victoria's reign – one for the men and one for the officers; even in death for a common cause, they were classified separately: a thing I instinctively disliked.

In the dark cavern of the bar there was a little party by the fireplace, a fireplace that in a month or two would be glowing since winter is sharp in Peshawar. I looked round as I heard Pushtu spoken in the hard dialect of the area which sounds like short bursts of machine gun fire. The voice was authoritative. Then I saw a plump man with russet-rosy cheeks: it was Mohammed Saied Khan, a friend of years before. As I greeted him warmly as a happy memory of the past, I was surprised to see he wore a black Anthony Eden hat. He looked rather like Edward G. Robinson. I knew this little man to be the Chief of Charsadda and a descendant of the rulers of Gandhara, the ruins of whose ancient pre-Kushan capital of Pushkalavati lay largely under his land. At once we were warmly embraced in the little party and more sardine toasts were ordered. I soon realized that Mohammed Saied Khan was deeply involved in politics and in this part of the world that could be a very dangerous game. You either won or lost everything. If you stayed on the fence, you straddled yourself painfully. He introduced me to a young politician just beginning to make his name. I was not struck by him as he was short and rather undistinguished looking. I inadvertently missed a chance, as so often happens to me as a would-be writer, of getting close to a man with a great political future: Zulfiquar Bhutto, who was the only statesman of international calibre Pakistan has had since Liaquat Ali Khan was murdered. We, living in comfortable security, have little conception of the pressures that led to his rise and fall in almost a Shakespearean tragedy – the tragedy that follows fatal flaws in the hero's character.

Mohammed Saied Khan insisted on asking us back to dinner that night as he did so often afterwards. Dinner turned out to be a feast of many dishes of highly spiced Pathan food. The flavours were subtle without being fiery. He had blood red original Turkoman Tekke carpets. They are badly imitated nowadays, for the Bear has killed or scattered the original weavers. It was a pleasure to run one's hand over the close pile. The very fineness of the knotting made for durability as well as beauty. They were masculine carpets as opposed to the floral tendrils of the Persian weave. He had the best collection of Gardener china of all types that I have ever seen, even to the rare green tea-set, marked with a large gold 'G'. The Gardeners were brought from Scotland in the eighteenth century by Catherine the Great to start a china factory near Moscow and the factory continued until 1917. It has continued since then, producing china of a far inferior quality. Many of its products were destined for China and Central Asia and the Pathans' sudden addiction to green brick tea has made the tea-sets greatly prized along the caravan routes. The mullahs inveighed in vain against this addiction since the tea was expensive and left nothing over for a square meal. There was a bewildering multiplicity of designs: Chinese, Russian and, most common of all, plain coloured grounds – maroon, blue or green – with medallions in white decorated with bunches of wild flowers. The figurines we can see in the Victoria and Albert Museum were not for eastern export, being forbidden representations of the human form. As was only to be expected from the Chief of Ghandara there were some splendid and much sought after Buddhist sculptures dug up on his own land.

Conversation was not absorbing because among the other guests it was all politics, politics, interrupted by sharp domestic orders from Mohammed Saied Khan to his grown-up family and a surly English daughter-in-law who was not adjusting well to her subordinate role in this patriarchal family.

We needed money for our onward journey and went to cash a cheque at Grindlays Bank down the Mall. We again met old friends among the clerks for we had had an account there when we first married. They made short cuts to speed our cheque and circumvent the elaborate convolutions of the eastern banking system: convolutions that must pre-date the Mughals. Where pay is low, petty larceny is endemic, so check and counter-check are the rule.

I saw a short, sturdy man looking at me closely. He had slightly wavy dark hair and dark eyes, but an ivory skin. His strong-nosed face had the look of authority. It was an old friend of Scout days in Waziristan, Colonel Kushwakt-ul-Mulk, the uncle of the Mehtar [1] of Chitral. In that strong face was the suggestion of his forefathers: his line claims descent from Ghenghiz Khan and Timur i' Lang. [2] We were delighted to see each other and thereafter through my many visits down the Khyber we foregathered again and again, and we met his brothers and nephews as well as his own family, including his beautiful daughter, Sultana. Much later she came to stay with us in England, together with her husband, a nephew of the late President Ayub Khan and her children.

One great feature of our visits was a lavish feast at Fuji's, the Chinese restaurant on the Mall, for there were not many places of revelry in Peshawar by then. In a way the austere stucco walls of this little café gave me some of my most tender memories: memories of cosiness enhanced by the soft light of Chinese paper lanterns. We used to hand our iced beer in at the back and it returned to us in teapots: a neat way of avoiding local sensibilities. In later years our numbers at the restaurant were increased by English people selflessly teaching in the University and at Edwardes College.[3] The British Council representative, Phil Carter, stoically kept his little library and information centre in being, although it was burnt down annually by the very students who used the reading room all day long in their quest for western knowledge.

On that first visit, a couple of days before we left for Delhi, we were walking off some of Kushi's hospitality up the four-mile long Mall, towards the grass

---

[1] The ruler – literally Prince.
[2] Timur the Lame, or Tamerlane.
[3] A school founded by the British for future Pathan leaders.

farms' depot, pestered as always by tongas[1] whose drivers could not believe that anyone who could afford to ride would rather walk. Their ponies were even more scrawny than of old for they were losing out to noisy three-wheeled motor tricycle contraptions with a box body, big enough to seat a couple of passengers. They were tinselled and as active as iridescent beetles, shiny with gilt ornaments. As a keen motorist I felt warm sympathy for the Pakistanis who love their vehicles so much. It is this underlying self-pride that gives me hope for their future.

Suddenly a voice behind us called, 'Colonel Sahib, Colonel Sahib!'

There was Ghulam Qadir, our old bearer from Kabul, now sadly aged and shabby, his white hair bravely dyed with henna. We knew already that he had had to leave Kabul with the other Pakistani servants and he was now a waiter in a shabby hotel in the bazaar. This was a come down for him, but a Kashmiri in Pathan country had little chance of getting a good job. Knowing he had gone to Peshawar, we had asked round everywhere for him, but were always told he was dead. He had given up all hope of going back to Kashmir where he, like Moosa, had some property, being very thrifty. He had attempted to return to his land and wife and family, but had been thrown back at the border and stripped of all his clothing and possessions. Philosophically he had married a new wife and started another family, resigned to his fate in Peshawar. He confirmed what we already knew – dear old Moosa had died a few years before. We had pensioned him as well as we could and he had set up in a tonga business with his sons in Rawalpindi. He did not live very long, nor did he ever see Kashmir or a beloved daughter again, since he had opted for Pakistan. There they were, just two anonymous statistics in that hasty carving-up of the sub-continent: a carving-up that took so little account of the sorrow it inflicted.

Ghulam Qadir asked us to lunch at the hotel where he worked. How long ago had he waited on us at our own table, as he did now! He produced two ice-cold Murree beers which he had managed to procure with the manager's permission. Although made in Pakistan, it was very expensive, carrying a prohibitive tax. It was an excellent meal and I made a point of praising him to the hotel proprietor.

I am always acutely embarrassed and never quite know what steps to take when poorer people offer me hospitality. I have been poor myself and know what it cost him. However, before we left we were able to give our old friend a handsome present (which we could ill afford) and did so for many years afterwards as we passed through Peshawar. Now, alas, he is dead. I feel he had no real will to live, having lost beloved Kashmir. My heart strings are always tugged when I return to the sub-continent; there is so much to remind me of happier, more carefree days. The deaths of these two old servants, our friends, made us feel that part of our lives had been finished, just as we had lost touch with Ayah some years before.

---

[1] A two-wheeled trap, largely used by the poor.

Chapter 8

A Soldier's Welcome

First Journey to India (1967)

A few days after we met Ghulam Qadir we left Peshawar for Lahore and India beyond it. After a hard day's drive over a rough and in places dusty road, fraught with hazards from the thrusting buses which completely dominated all traffic, we arrived at Lahore, my birthplace and one of the finest of eastern cities. The brilliantly painted buses, tricked out with intricate, bright metal embellishments, belonged to two companies. This meant that both of them would rush towards a single customer at full speed, braking hard at the last moment. Having wound up a high speed again with their sluggish diesel engines, they would then give way to no one.

Our visit to Lahore did not at first go very smoothly for we turned left too soon after crossing the Ravi river, short of the famous Badshai mosque – pink and white with minarets reaching to the sky. The traffic got thicker and thicker until the sub-continent's millions congealed about us. We extracted our vehicle with difficulty, though everyone tried good-naturedly to help us, and returned to the main road where we had gone wrong. After much searching we at last passed the Zamzama, which did not show its age at all in spite of Kim having climbed all over this ancient gun. We drove on down the magnificent Mall Road whose lofty trees were marred by vultures' massive nests, to park in the grounds of the Intercontinental Hotel. The manager readily gave us permission to stay there and so began the practice of many years.

It was unbelievably hot and humid in the Land Rover and we watched a glowing, copper-coloured sunset fade all too slowly. It would have been useless cleaning up and changing until it got cool. Our few and precious good clothes would have immediately become limp with sweat. The night watchman greeted us with great joy and it was difficult to fend off his offers of devoted service when he discovered that I too was originally a 15th Punjabi. His salutes were thrown with such smartness that his hand quivered and he stamped up and down, living it all over again. As usual, and as they all do, he expected me to get his son a good job in England, merely by writing a short commendatory letter – such was the faith in the Sahib. I had to explain that our island is no

59

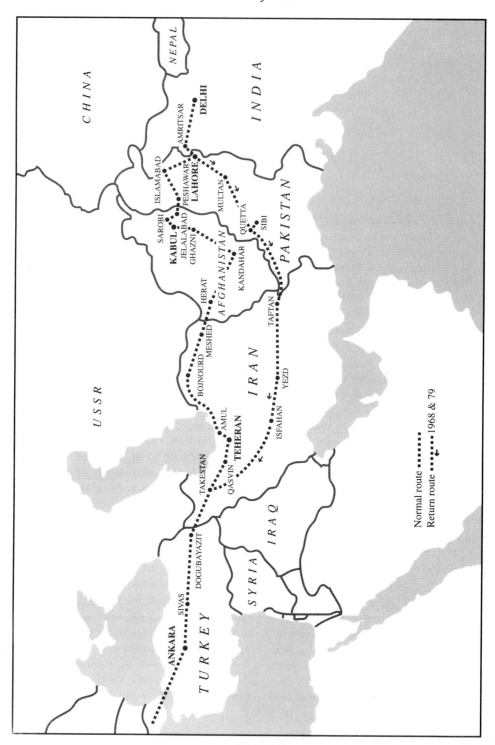

more than half the Punjab in area and, much as we liked the Pakistanis, there was already much unemployment and over-crowding in England. It is not all fun visiting old haunts, because his earnest face with its strong, curled-up military moustache showed that he expected so much of me. I felt it acutely.

From this time on our journey did not go so well. Owing to the wars and the friction between India and Pakistan it was necessary to get a pass to cross over into India, our ultimate goal. Everything was going amicably in the local office of the Home Affairs Ministry when a horrible little clerk seemed to slide out from under a mountain of dusty files to whisper to his chief that any visitors with a military rank could not have passes, 'Since,' he said, quoting a regulation, 'they might be spies!' and his dark eyes glowed at the word. Calling on my most flowery Hindustani I tried to cajole the official. This method had been extremely successful up to then, but the head clerk had turned into a clam. Only Islamabad, the capital, could give such a pass. I tried name-dropping. I tried everything. I told them, which was true, that I was the old *Ustad* (Instructor) of the then President Field Marshal, Ayub Khan, but a jack-in-office who holds the trump cards revels in his authority. Yes, they would send a telegram to Islamabad, there was nothing to worry about, but of course it was 'quite impossible' to telephone.

Daily we called in, somehow surviving the sweltering heat. For all its insulation a caravan is far hotter than a house and I wondered how I had marched so far and so hard in such heat when I was young. There was never an answer. I even sent a telegram myself to President Ayub. In Pakistan telegrams fly through the air with leaden wings and there was no immediate answer. It must eventually have got through, to no ordinary purpose judging by the recognition and helpful and friendly reception we had on our return journey. We went to the Deputy High Commission who did their best to help us. They said communication just did not work between Lahore and Islamabad and suggested we went back there, giving us the name of the office to go to and the man to see.

It was daunting to retrace our steps on a round trip of four hundred miles of hot, bumpy, dusty road and extremely galling for a thruster like me who hates being jerked back on his haunches. I got the pass on a nod and we were off down the road again: the road through Lahore to Delhi. In subsequent years I took the precaution of getting the pass at Islamabad on my way through. It was not always easy and one year there was a young post-Partition clerk who had obviously not served with the British and thoroughly enjoyed making things awkward, even to the extent of telling me to come back next day although I explained I would have nowhere to put the caravan and would have to stay in Flashman's Hotel in Rawalpindi. I pointed out that he had only to sign his name on the form I had already filled in. When this failed, I went over his head to the boss and got my pass.

I am always happy driving to Delhi down the Grand Trunk road, the main artery of the Mughals and the British. From time to time we passed Kos pillars,

pointed round stone structures some thirty feet high. I was once assured by a
senior officer with a gleam in his eye that they were of priapic significance. In
fact they marked stages for the swift Mughal postal service from the frontier to
the capital.

At first the road passed under a light green canopy of *shisham* and feathery
tamarisk trees, grown for shade and coolness. It was bright with parakeets and
the fantails of collared doves, who rose ahead reluctantly, so that one had to be
careful not to smash them on the windscreen. The road became cooler still as it
passed through lush agricultural land – the beginning of the most fertile area of
the sub-continent, watered by canals from the distant Himalayas.

The swarms of two-mile-an-hour bullock and buffalo carts I had known as a
child, with their dry wailing solid wooden wheels, had changed. The same
carts, now mounted on discarded and stripped car axles with their more silent
rubber tyres, made the bullocks' work lighter – poverty is the mother of
improvisation! The draught animals were left to travel on either side of the road
by their drivers, asleep in the back. The animals knew the road, but ignored the
highway code. In the Punjab they were being replaced by large tractors, used
for tilling and transport and towing farm carts with built up sides and half a
village crowded aboard, to follow a swifter but wobbly way to market. The
peasants had their best clothes on and seemed to be surmounted by bright
bobbles, for Sikhs and Hindus wore gay turbans in various colours and the
women's saris were brilliant with India's incomparable dyes. As Peggy said, it
was a new outing for them to be able to escape so easily from the daily round of
household chores and do some shopping. It was indeed a bumpy, dusty, hazard-
ous drive, but oh, so happy for me.

As we neared Delhi I was looking forward to visiting the Rajputana Rifles,
whose 3rd battalion I had commanded in Burma during and after the war. I
intended only to put my name in the visitors' book, to pay homage to that fine
group. I asked no more because I tend to be shy in the face of what I knew
might be regarded as an occasion for festivities. Old soldiers should fade away.
We had camped a little off the main road the previous night to tidy up before
making the call. In later years a series of delightful rest houses and restaurants,
many of which were set up by a syndicate of retired Indian officers and each
called after a bird, made their appearance along the road to Delhi, so that one
could stay the night and arrive refreshed and clean in the cool of the morning.
Our favourite was the Green Parakeet which had an excellent cook.

The Ring Road into New Delhi was a nightmare. The traffic was as thick as
the dust, and diverse, ranging from truck, bus, pony trap and bullock cart to
loose oxen, goats, camels and cripples. At times all movement ceased and it
was difficult to see which type of obstacle would have to give way first. It
called for good humour, skill and patience to edge forward to our goal in the
baking sun. The stench was horrific, for the fair city's refuse had been dumped
in mounds everywhere, closely flanking the road.

At last we turned sharply into the military cantonment in an abrupt transition from smelly shambles into spotless barracks. A passing soldier directed us and we swung into the gates of the Officers' Mess flanked by lovely flowerbeds. The Regimental Centre was so smartly laid out that I became uncomfortably aware that I was sweating through the back of my bush-shirt as the sun mounted and after the snakes and ladders effort down the Ring Road. I felt less and less like the distinguished old warrior of my romantic soul. Every pathway and road through the extensive area was bordered on either side by at least two yards of dark red ochre sand brought from some distance. Every culvert and coping stone or chain was bright with whitewash. The British army's fetish for smartness had been carried here to an extreme – a legacy that had been extended as to be almost a burden and too consuming in labour, but of course the labour force was there and dirt cheap. I found this smartness wherever I went amongst the military yet, not so far away, Connaught Place, the shopping centre of Lutyens' great lay-out of New Delhi, symbol of the pride of the British Raj, had become shabby and down at heel. The circle of broad pavements and Palladian pillars looked threadbare: whitewash had worn off and gutters were stuffed with rubbish. The pillars were spattered red with *pan* spittle as though the whole population suffered from TB. There were more beggars than ever, including to my amazement European hippies weirdly dressed, competing with real poverty. Paradox is always there in India. I could only assume that the influence of the British/Indian army had been strong enough to survive and go on, in contrast with India's natural, teeming untidiness.

As I entered the Mess I was met by a smart waiter who strode towards me as if on parade. His salute vibrated for seconds after he threw it. I put my name in the visitors' book, writing for fun, 'Quondam Commander of the 3rd Rajputana Rifles' – that would puzzle them, I thought. He offered me a drink, but I declined it with thanks because Peggy was waiting in the car. In my British days the Officers' Mess admitted no women except on special occasions.

Someone must have seen me, for word was sent to the Commandant's office and Colonel Jit Lal, the Commandant, hurried up looking agitated, and greeted me warmly. I feel some of his previous British seniors must have been very strict with him because he was patently overcome at the apparition of a florid, white-whiskered and tub-shaped old soldier. I was taking it all in: his green drill uniform in spite of the heat was smooth and ironed off at the edges to look almost like armour. He insisted that Peggy and I stay for a night or two in the guest quarters and would take no refusal. After two frosted silver goblets of iced beer I discovered without giving myself away that my own battalion, the 3rd, was shortly to hold its hundred and fiftieth anniversary celebrations at Jaipur. I had left England before the arrival of the invitation and Colonel Jit had thought I was the forerunner of a number of officers who would be gathering there.

We were soon joined on the lawn by a stocky, widely mustachioed figure who looked rather like Tom Jackson, once of the Post Office Union, but browner. He was Chand Whig, one of my old officers, and by then a lieutenant-colonel. His greeting was so warm that I felt I must have been a reasonable commanding officer. That night there was an extremely well organised buffet dinner in the Mess in my honour. The new Indian army delights in special occasions at short notice. In this I think they are right for they whip up enormous and spontaneous esprit in doing so. I noticed that the massive pieces of silver of British times were well displayed and in excellent order and I saw the gold medal of my predecessor in command, Bill Beyts, awarded to the champion shot of the Indian army. The custom of presenting silver to the Mess was still observed and there were many new pieces.

It is very gratifying to be given VIP treatment and while I talked to the officers a specially detailed Mess waiter followed me about with an open bottle of beer. It was characteristic of the conscientiousness of the Indian other rank that he followed me with a bottle poised over my shoulder and I could feel him breathing down my neck. Should I take a sip of beer, the bottle was immediately canted into my silver goblet. Hospitality can go no further, but one must be careful not to step backwards – it made me think of Victor Silvester's 'Quick, quick, slow'. A special ADC had been appointed to look after our comfort in the guest suite, though only Major-Generals and above are normally entitled to this courtesy. I felt warmly flattered, but at the same time uncomfortably aware of my own unworthiness.

Next afternoon Colonel Jit Lal came to see how we were getting on and invited me to the Junior Commissioned Officers' Mess that evening. These officers are commissioned directly from the ranks and are akin to, but a little more important than Warrant Officers in the British army. In my time they were called Viceroy's Commissioned Officers, which title has naturally been altered. The Colonel was dressed to play squash and Savile Row could not have set him up better. His rifle green blazer was impeccable with its black buttons; his white shorts were knife-edged by the iron; his socks foamed over his shoes like snow. During this visit we got to know him and his wife Uma well and were able to return a little of their hospitality at the Moti Mahal Restaurant in Old Delhi where we all feasted on marinated, buttered chicken. The proprietor, now a millionaire, was a Hindu refugee from Peshawar City where he had eked out a living running a kabab kiosk. By this time he was sending special dishes by air to America – so he claimed. He met us in the restaurant, knowing that I had just come from Peshawar, and we had a nostalgic talk. I shot a bit of a line by talking Pushtu to him which he knew very well. Uma, her nose slightly out of joint, drove us home at ferocious speed to the accompaniment of faint cries of protest from her husband in the back seat.

It was a great sorrow to us some years later to learn from our younger son who was in the city at the time, that Jit Lal had been murdered after he left the army to take up the job of Secretary to the Tollyganj Club in Calcutta. We had been glad that he had happily settled in civilian life, but a groundsman who had been dismissed by a previous Secretary walked into his office one night when he was working late and blew his head off with a home-made blunderbuss in front of one of his sons. In India, the sun smiles, but there are terribly dark shadows.

We said goodbye regretfully to Delhi, a city I always love, and on arriving in Jaipur at the 3rd Rajputana Rifles' barracks we were escorted to our rooms in the Officers' Mess and an orderly ran off to fetch the Commanding Officer. He came up smiling but stopped short and stood with his head oddly, I felt almost coyly, cocked on one side. He hoped very much that I would recognise him, for he, Lieutenant-Colonel Shyam Singh, had been one of my latest-joined subalterns in Burma, coming a few weeks before I left, as one of the new draft of Indian officers. I completely failed to recognise him and he looked very hurt. This was unusual since I have a memory for faces, but a shocking one for names. I could have kicked myself although Shyam Singh was slightly taller and had filled out after twenty years. I managed to pass it off and there was nothing lacking in the warmth of his greeting, so much so that later in the year we returned to Jaipur to stay with him and his family.

We had a very happy week at the celebrations. No other British officer had been able to make the costly journey and I was given the signal honour of presiding over major occasions, although there were more senior Indian generals present. I felt that this generous, warm-hearted gesture was the epitome of the close and affectionate links still maintained between the old British officers of the Indian army and the new Indian officers. I was asked to meet the other ranks and to award promotions (these of course had been settled beforehand). I inspected the feast provided for the rank and file and felt touched that they waited, poised over their dishes, until I had completed the rounds, over which naturally I did not delay. One morning there was a full parade and I was asked to take the march past. I was, as always, struck by the very high standard of smartness and drill and I looked down with pride at the fine, light-brown faces turned towards me.

The regiment arranged for a well-conducted tour of Amber, the old capital of Jaipur State, for all the guests. The military, which now has a very high status in India, scattered the tourists on their decorated elephants as our jeeps drove thrustfully up the narrow road into the great courtyard of the palace. Blue-rinsed, wealthy American women looked down on us in surprise. From a lowly jeep's-eye view fat legs were embarrassingly exposed.

This was the first time I had seen the great honey-coloured fortress complex which embraces palaces and pavilions with its defensive battlements stretching along the ridges above Jaipur. It is of a particularly pleasing architectural design which seems to me to show strong Mughal as well as Rajput influences, since it lacks the usual heavy over-ornamentation of Hindu buildings in other parts of India. The intricate *jali* screens of delicate stone tracery take the place of windows and in bygone days allowed the beauties of the court to look through at the activities below from light and airy balconies, though hidden from the general gaze. Glass windows were quite unknown in those times (sixteenth and seventeenth centuries) and the fine *jali* work let the breeze play through coolly over the lovely watchers, for Rajput women to this day are known for their beauty, in their wide-swinging skirts and silver anklets.

The tour was guided by one of the officers' wives who was a schoolmistress teaching in Jaipur. She then took the ladies to the famous jewellers of that city which was so splendidly laid out and designed by Maharajah Jai Singh in rose-coloured stone in the eighteenth century. The main streets are wide and on a straight, rectangular grid system, years before its time. Knocking at a side door in a wall, the party was discreetly ushered in. Removing their shoes, the ladies passed a prayer meeting and entered a room with jewellery displayed in glass cases. It was fine and elaborate, but somewhat trinkety owing to the use of rather small stones. There were many rubies, Peggy's favourite stone, but of a watery pink. The jeweller's pale skin was a sickly white, as if he had never seen the light of day. The ladies pored long over his works, bargaining in the leisurely tempo of India. Some ordered elaborate necklaces and earrings. Peggy was as usual short of funds, but was later consoled when Uma told her that the jewellery never arrived in Delhi. Uma herself could afford it as, although the army is not overpaid, she had a job. By then educated Indian women were increasingly seeking employment.

The following evening there was the usual concert party, with many turns surprisingly well rehearsed and more amusing than those of so many British regimental concerts, whose bumpkin humour leaves one embarrassed. A well-known singer sang with apparently great virtuosity. She sat cross-legged on the stage and sang the words directly from a little book held up in front of her face. The songs, without a score, were traditional and the music had been handed down orally. She was accompanied by that instrument universal in India, a piano accordion. Her sari was diaphanous but, incongruously, over all she had put on a thick, unbuttoned cardigan and her plump, bare feet and discarded slippers added to the casual air. But all were much impressed. I felt it was as if Dame Janet Baker had sat down and sung Mahler's Rückert songs. Even I could see it was of that high level. She was followed by a comic turn – teams of light machine gunners carried out the drill of coming into action, using large-bowled *huqqas* in place of the guns; the words of command and mime were authentic and ended in the 'firing' of the tobacco in large puffs of smoke.

In the past, the spur of competition in the ever-present tribal feuds kept the Rajput leaders lean and fit. Feuds took the place of modern sport. Their horses were carefully bred and fleet. Life had a compelling interest, but the rule of the British and their law and order made life lustreless for many of the chieftains.

After Jaipur we were invited by the 7th battalion to visit them at Nasirabad, the old Rajputana Rifle centre. Mapping our way southwards along an unfamiliar road we were stopped by some officers of the regiment in two jeeps with handholds and all salient points brightly chromium plated, and ceremoniously convoyed into Nasirabad, twenty-five miles away. The Land Rover looked odd and unmilitary in this cortège, but it was a singular honour. There we were installed in the rest house near the barracks; it was plain to see that the current occupants had been hustled out ruthlessly. The army has a special position in India, partly, I think, because it has always refused to mix in the political scene and thus is its word law. A quarterguard was posted for our protection and prestige. We were a little embarrassed, but much flattered too and we prepared to call upon our hosts.

We visited the marble war memorial which was later moved to the present regimental centre in New Delhi at a ceremony in which western and eastern religions joined in honouring the dead. Having said goodbye to our most friendly hosts and their lively and very pretty wives, we drove on. It was almost a relief to get out onto the bumpy, dusty road with India's mystery still before us, scarcely tapped.

Having visited the modern military we turned to the past, for we felt we must visit Chitorgarh, the ancient and formidable Rajput fortress whose origins are wrapped in mythology and which was added to with further bastions in the course of time. It is of staggering size, some three and a half miles long, built on one of those strange Arawali hills. The hills are sausage-shaped and lie about at all angles and separate from each other to relieve the monotony of the Rajasthan plains. They still retain their scrub jungle and were ideal sites for the many forts of the ever-warring chieftains. As I looked up at the triple bastioned monster my thoughts turned to Rajput history – a history of unbelievable valour.

Chitorgarh was so impregnable in appearance that I took the opportunity of asking a knowledgeable Indian lecturing an attentive crowd, how it could possibly have fallen in a siege, given the weaponry of those times. He told me sadly that it was untakable to some extent, but that the chieftains having many wives also produced many contenders for their thrones and that treachery was rife – secret passages were betrayed to give the fortress over to capture by stealth.

However, it did fall to force more than once. Akhbar had to crack this stronghold rather than leave the warlike clans as a dire thorn in his empire's side. Gaining little success through either siege or assault, he thought out a way to command the walls, and ordered a huge mound to be built, higher than the highest keep. The work went very slowly as the mound was raked by the defenders' fire. Frustrated, Akhbar offered the workmen one golden *mohur* for each *tasla* of earth deposited on the mound. Workmen died by the thousand, but gold grips men's hearts and makes them desperate. What a reward! A golden *mohur* – security for life from the grasp of poverty for a mere *tasla* of earth, just a flat basinful, smaller than its household counterpart, and the normal head load of an Indian road coolie to this day. The mound was completed, drenched with blood and Akhbar was able to pick off the defenders with ease, for he had a new, long-barrelled musket which outranged them. He is believed to have fired the fatal shot which killed the Chief of the Rewat leaders. An empire can always outbid a petty kingdom and so the fortress fell.

I looked at the various keeps and tried to picture the conditions of a long siege. There would be cattle and horses crammed and cooped up within, and no sanitation for the defenders. The heat, pestilence and flies must surely in the end sap their resolution. But no – in the battle against Akhbar in 1658 one defending chieftain, Jaimal of Bedur, losing both legs in an assault, climbed on the shoulders of a stalwart clansman, Kalla, and both fought on, savagely wielding their swords. When all hope was gone the women, hundreds of them, led by the princesses, went down into a dark, cave-like storeroom and burned themselves to death in all their marriage finery. The warriors, putting on their saffron ceremonial robes, sallied out to give battle and die to a man. Over a period of 260 years the defenders of the time went out three times to commit *Jauhar*, this act of hopeless bravery.

Wishing to steep myself in the atmosphere of Rajput history and valour I paid our entrance fee and just managed to squeeze the Land Rover through the main gate of the fortress, a very stout construction with foot-long spikes to deter war elephants, which were often used as battering rams. We found so much of interest in Victory Towers and ancient architecture that it grew late. Reluctant to leave, we failed to make our exit by closing time and spent a haunted night up on an older and more ruined wing of the fort. A family of quail ran single file across the path – at least a dozen of them. Then the sandgrouse with their strange, never to be forgotten call, flighted in and when darkness fell the devilish yowl of a jackal called the pack to some foetid carrion feast. I really felt I could hear the tramp of sentries and their challenging call from so long, long ago.

Next morning down on the plains I saw the white smoke plumes of a Birla cement factory. Would this modern cement have made a better, uglier fortress, far uglier than the soft purple-red stone of the ancient builders?

As I drove away I felt that I had been privileged indeed to command people such as these Rajputs whose chieftains claim descent from the sun and the moon.

Chapter 9

Gods, Ghats and Gopis

First Indian Visit (1967)

After we left Chitor we decided to revisit a magical place of my childhood. Pachmari, a corruption of Panchmari and a reference to the five polyandrous Pandava brothers of the Mahabharata who are popularly supposed to have hidden there for some years when sent into exile, was a second class hill station: so classed as it provided only limited coolness, being but three thousand feet up in the Mahadeo Hills.

We had difficulty in reaching Pachmari as the Narmada River in central India is not easy to negotiate and lay across our path. We made for several bridges, only to find they had, as is all too common, been destroyed by monsoon floods. It was exasperating as we had actually to drive all the way to the bank each time. It had not occurred to anybody to put up a sign some seventy miles back at the point of take off from the main road to say that the road across the river was no longer viable, though shown on the latest maps. We motored back over and over again, getting crosser and crosser. My beloved India was now assuming her all too commonly irritating mien.

One more try and still no bridge – but a ferry. Determined not to turn back yet again I eased the Land Rover up steeply on to an inadequate-looking ferry boat – just a flat-bottomed scow with two or three men at the oars. It was a sharp roll up and the two planks now raising the vehicle high above the sandy bank were no wider than its tyres. The river was a mere four hundred yards across, but when we were halfway over the boatman began to raise his price. He was in a strong but precarious position. The boat was leaking fast and by stopping in mid-stream in this condition he felt he had the whip hand over me, even if the boat did look like sinking with all hands. I have an explosive temper and I advanced on him with clenched fists, at which he capitulated. But on reaching the far shore I had to back the car down those steep, narrow planks. It was not easy to aim downwards when I could only with difficulty see one of them. Down I went gingerly and just as one plank turned over in the soft sand, I gained the shore. Peggy, usually calm, couldn't bear to watch and turned away, shutting her eyes.

Between the river and Hosiangabad, our next objective, we were blocked on a narrow road by what must have been the largest bullock cart rally I have ever seen. We were held up for another fuming forty minutes as these foot-pace carts filed past, their wooden wheels giving off a dry wail. I suppose I was looking very angry for I heard a bystander (there are always bystanders standing by in myriads) say to another, 'In British times this Sahib would have shot all those carters!' For once there was no nostalgia for the 'Raj'.

We wound up the pretty hill roads which are always in better condition than those on the flat, because they have been properly engineered, For me, teak trees are particularly attractive, with their giant leaves always changing colour and in season a froth of white flowers to surmount the whole. We passed the charming rest house at Singanama, now ruined but holding happy memories of a shooting party years ago on a week-end from the musketry school that used to be on the plateau above.

The haunting beauty of Pachmari with its weird-shaped hills, its black rocks, its steep precipices and its waterfalls was as enchanting as I remembered it. How seldom in life does the present match one's memories! We left the caravan at the bottom of the dominating mountain, Dhupgarh, the Abode of the Sun, and climbed the steep track up its side. The sun sets between the twin breasts of the mountain – hence its name. All was absolute peace and we walked through clouds of butterflies. We felt as if we were all alone until we heard the tinkling noise of a transistor radio. But the offenders, the only people we saw and an assault on the jungle's tranquillity, soon departed.

I remembered as a child coming down from this mountain on an elephant's back at night, but this time we spent the night at the lonely rest house on the summit and got the night watchman to light a wood fire, for it was chilly. The night was loud and wet with a tropical thunderstorm and we rolled this way and that to avoid the drips from the leaking roof. Next day, feeling at peace with the world, we descended and tucked the caravan in among the trees so as not to be disturbed. Beside us was a black stone which made a natural seat overlooking a steep precipice. We could hear the deep, booming call of the langurs, the large white monkeys with black faces and black hands and feet, whose calls reverberated back from the dark sides of the precipices. As night fell the stars were unusually bright and we felt a sense of happiness and release. Then gazing upwards we saw a star moving: it moved across the sky steadily and silently. It must have been a satellite, unfamiliar at the time, and I had a feeling of unease as though an intruder had entered unbidden as an evil portent. We felt a sudden chill and climbed back into the caravan's warmth.

Peace was not long sustained as thousands of pilgrims began to gather in the southern lee of the plateau at the foot of a strange, square-topped mountain, Chauragahr, where in a ravine a cave housed a hideous, black image, some fifteen feet high, all teeth and tusks, glaring eyes and many arms. The pilgrims in their thousands fouled the slopes and drove troop after troop of little, red,

In the Saptura Ranges – Kipling's Jungle Book country.

angry-faced Rhesus monkeys up from their feeding grounds on to the plateau top. This was the land of the big, white langurs, who fell back steadily before this advancing red horde. Leaders of the langurs hurled themselves about among the branches of the trees, tearing them off and belabouring their followers in an effort to make them fight, but they could not rally them and they sat about fearfully, or moved away to give ground. These animals are extremely intelligent and a prey to such fears as we are ourselves. I like the big, gentle langurs with their tremendous acrobatic leaps and always feel a dislike for the small, ugly, red bottomed Rhesus grass monkeys, who moved forward driving the white monkeys inexorably before them. Again, I was uneasy; was I seeing the future enacted by animals?

We went down to Pachmari's little bazaar to shop. It held memories throughout my life in the rare, but well spaced, visits I had paid it. We began our purchases in the tin-roofed vegetable bazaar where our shopping was made pleasant by the vendors' friendly attitude. They were charmed at being joked with in Hindi. Then out and down the street to the egg- and chicken-seller. He, a very old Sikh, had courteous manners, and the forecourt of his dwelling hut and shop was of smooth clay mixed with chopped straw, made antiseptic with cow's urine. The whole area was flat, hard and clean looking. We talked and, learning that we had come through the Khyber Pass in Pakistan, he said that he longed to go on a pilgrimage to Jamrud Fort at its entrance to visit the shrine of General Hari Singh Nalwar, who died in action against the Afghans towards the end of Ranjit Singh's reign in the early nineteenth century.

My watch, the expedition's one timepiece, had stopped and without much hope I sought a watchmaker for my repairs. I was directed up some narrow stairs to a little garret where I met a man who again showed me great friendliness. How I enjoyed these little bazaar trips, meeting warm and simple people. Their simplicity made me also expand, so that I was really made to feel that I was both witty and interesting. The watchmaker was a large, stout Muslim with quiet, pleasant manners. He said that he had had a fine shop in Calcutta, but there was much communal pressure on him. His doctor had told him to seek a peaceful place in which to live as he had a bad heart and should avoid stress. On our second visit next day he enquired much about the world: he was finding the tranquility of his backwater a little flat. Diffidently he asked us if he could invite us to an English breakfast the day after. As travellers we had cooked what we could get and were glad, but curious, to accept. We were served a real English breakfast by his friend who had been the Club cook in the old British days. I remember that there were actually fish cakes, grilled kidneys and eggs and, a rarity in these parts, bacon. Hospitality could go no further, for bacon is anathema to the Muslim. As he served us on India Tree pattern china with good knives and forks, out of politeness our host did not eat though we, a little embarrassed, ate hungrily. He asked us to send him out catalogues of the latest radios and watches when we got back to England: such a small return for so much kindness.

We visited Pachmari yet again another year and we sought our friend, but his kind heart had given out. I am always overwhelmed by the sweetness of ordinary people whom I met everywhere in India and I looked up at his little, empty garret with a feeling of acute loss.

When we returned north again we took the longer way round through Mhow, the military centre of the old Central Provinces, now Madhya Pradesh. I was anxious to visit the general's house from where my father had commanded a Division and where we enjoyed halcyon days of childhood. I wanted to recapture those memories of a fine house with its upstairs terraces which spread out over the central porch and the deep, arched verandahs below. In my childhood's

The general's house, Mhow.

memory the area was as vast as two tennis courts and the heart of the house held a fine ballroom. I remember my father's quarterguard who stood to as he left for office in the morning. How smart the sepoys were, executing the General Salute to the crisp call of a bugle. How proud I was of my dear father. When he had disappeared from view I used to mingle with the soldiers who indulgently allowed me to feel over their weapons – old muskets with permanent bayonets to fire scatter shot to deter raiders by night, while not being too lethal, and modern rifles used by day when thieves were less likely to be about.

I remember the hot, dry nights in our beds lined out on the terrace roof. Although they were under the hard bright stars, they were enveloped in mosquito nets and very stuffy. Down towards the servants' quarters I could hear the soft singing of an Indian mother bathing her child. I caught a bit of the refrain:

> *Ghusli, ghusli mangta,*
> *Tab ka pani tunda . . .?*

I could translate already: 'Do you want a bath, out of a cold tub of water . . .?'

The air was so dry that static lights played over the sheets when I moved and outside it was the time of the fireflies, swarming so thickly as to fill the whole air with soft, rhythmic fairy lights. I pulled up my mosquito net, the better to see and next morning incurred the wrath of Nanny Robinson. She scolded me in well-founded exasperation for exposing myself to dread mosquitoes. 'Master John, I do declare you are the naughtiest of boys!'

How cool the early morning and how sweet the garden. The *mali* (gardener) was already watering it, carrying about square kerosene tins on a yoke. He staggered round with his clanking load to the soft hiss, hiss of the sweeper's brush as he stopped to sweep up clouds of dust, which rose and fell again in the same place. His back was always bent, for his time honoured brush was but a short handled broom. The garden was full of flowers and flowering trees which were opening out to the approaching hot weather. Soon we would be gone to Pachmari. The blossoms had a heavy, erotic scent and the cold-weather, English garden was already wilting. The blight-free roses, the banks of cineraria and strangely hybrid snapdragons still glowed in the early sunlight. O, happy sunlit days of long ago!

As we neared the great house well dressed guests were arriving and so, feeling dusty and travel-worn, we stole away. The incumbent general whom we met later in Dehra Dun would certainly have greeted us warmly, but we would have disrupted his lunch party and so we slipped softly down the road. Perhaps it was better so. Would present reality have been equal to old, rosy memories, which so often stab one's heart?

I have too a memory that is not so happy. Some years before this I had met an Indian army officer whom I greatly respected whose last command was the same as my father's so many years ago and who had lived in this same house. He told me that at the time of Indian Independence he had received a peremptory message from Earl Mountbatten to go to the Holkar of Indore and to tell him to take down the Union Jack and put up the new flag of India on his palace. Mhow lies within Indore territory and was ceded to the British by the Treaty of Mandasor in 1818, being still the headquarters of the Central India command. The Holkar was much affronted and pointed out that he had treaties made between his ancestor, Tukoji Rao II, who sided with the British in the Mutiny in 1857, and Queen Victoria herself, Empress of India. His treaties were not with any government of India. My friend appealed to Mountbatten, but the reply was characteristically bombastic and unfeeling: to go and tear down the Union Jack or be court-martialled. I feel the shame of this high-handed action even today when I meet the Maharajah of Jaipur.

Through the years I have felt that we let the Indian Princes down disgracefully. So many had supported us in the Mutiny and in both World Wars, with treasure and soldiers of their State Forces. We left them to be stripped bare by the new rulers of India. There is always the popular picture of pricelessly rich tyrants who were self-indulgent, despotic and cruel. In modern times we are the victims of too sensation-loving and mendacious media. On the contrary some were astute rulers, governed by the tenets of Muslim and Hindu religion which ensured a measure of rulership and justice that attracted the loyalty of their subjects. Observance of these beliefs prevented many from becoming too decadent in the face of riches and luxury.

In the past the Sirkar had tried to work out a system to ensure the existence of those very large parts of India under princely rule, so that they could continue after the handover of the greater part of India proper. I am afraid the Sirkar recoiled from this almost impossibly difficult task – difficult because some rulers presided over areas little larger than a tennis club while others ruled over millions in areas as big as France; some of them were new rulers and others the descendants of dynasties that had been in power for a thousand years. There were differing religions and differing traditions. The difficult problem was shelved since none could come to agreement.

From Mhow our wanderings took us eastwards to Khajurao and its splendid temples, even though it is a popular and conventional tourist attraction. Temples dotted about in banks of bougainvillaea cover the area. Each is conical in shape as if climbing up the central cone and other smaller cones rise round it, representing mountain peaks to imply aspiration. Each building stands on a high plinth and not an inch of the whole surface is unadorned by deep relief stone carving. There are nymphs and courtesans, kings and princes with rampant lions to represent heroism. The naked nymphs are slant-eyed and sinuous and peer archly round corners. Many figures are entwined in a ritual sexual embrace, but there is nothing vulgar. The whole theme is of gaiety, happiness and laughter in its wholehearted devotion to creation.

For once the entire area was clean and almost deserted. There were none of the small boys and girls, self-appointed guides, who pour out a rigmarole of misinformation and who, if their services are refused, hurl foul-mouthed abuse in English to spoil everything. No, this was a pleasant visit to look into the past of the Chandella Rajputs. What light-hearted people they must have been, but the pace at which they lived could surely not have lasted.

Then our wanderings took us a long way south to see Konarak and the great temple of the Sun God in the form of an enormous chariot. Each of the four faces shows the god smoothly carved in polished green chlorite and each figure portrays a different time of day by its attitude. The massive building is flanked by ornate chariot wheels, minutely carved, and the whole design is as usual of a frankly erotic nature. Again its message is the glory of creation. A party of well-dressed young Indian girls in bright saris viewed this scene of abandon calmly and without embarrassment. Guarding the entrance were two ferocious tigers, each falling upon an elephant. Oddly, the tigers were much bigger than the elephants: hardly surprising as they represent the triumph of Hinduism over Buddhism.

We then drove down to the sea-shore to find somewhere to stay, but could discover no other hard standing than a concrete plinth next door to a lighthouse. Obtaining permission to park there from the lighthouse keeper, an ex-Royal Indian Navy Petty Officer, we hoped to remain undisturbed – Konarak had not been so free of amateur guides as Khajurao. I remembered the huge, crayfish-sized prawns of this coast and asked for fish and prawns at a fishing village

Konarak: The triumph of Hinduism over Buddhism.

outspanned malodorously on the tideless sand. But it was not the season. The fishermen, charred coal black by the sun, wind and spray, went out in the rough seas in canoes with outriggers which were swiftly propelled by a curved dhow-like sail. It was peaceful and we bathed in the shallows where the foam was thick, reasoning that the sharks which are numerous on the Coromandel Coast would not see us through the froth. We did not know anything in those days about the electric impulses that guide them to likely prey! There was, however, a pair of white-bellied sea eagles who live mainly on the very poisonous sea snakes so we were not in any way as safe as we thought. I have never seen such magnificent eagles. In their black-tipped, pure whiteness and size they outmatched so many raptors that I know. The reed beds of the shore harboured wolves, now rare in India, and we were told to be on our guard against attack as rabies was common among them. Truly a shore full of hazards, but the intense blue of the sea and sky and the breaking waves and baking sun were pleasure enough.

Our little host felt it behoved him as a Christian, for he came from Goa and was a devout Catholic, to feed us as our enquiries after fish had been abortive. We assured him we needed nothing, but he brought us daily a glass each of rich buffalo milk as the sun rose. I have always held that milk is the most wretched of all drinks and this buffalo milk was strong-tasting and to me disgusting. Not to hurt his feelings, we choked it down.

The lighthouse keeper said he was a keen sea-shell collector, and often talked of his collection. We made the mistake of pressing to see it, wishing to be friendly and were shown a little pile of assorted shells and sand. It was rather pathetic, for he was lonely, sending back a remittance to his wife who looked after a small plot of land in their far distant home. He diffidently asked us if he could accompany us on a shopping trip to Bhubaneswar to collect a parcel from the station and we were glad to do something for him in return for his milk. It was a picturesque drive along a high, narrow *bund* (canal bank), flanked by marshes gay with white and crimson water lilies. Across the marshes we could see the famous temples of Bhubaneswar – ornate tower piled upon ornate tower terminating in a kind of stone screwtop.

The town itself had a gaily coloured, open vegetable market and as we deliberated upon which stall to start our shopping a voice beside me said, 'Goodbye.' Thinking for a split second that this was a new version of 'Yank, go home,' and that we were unwelcome, I looked up to see a tall figure, big for an Indian, and a pair of friendly brown eyes above a large curled moustache. No, this was meant to be a greeting – a friendly greeting in his little all of English. This big, jovial individual led us round the stalls and haggled for us so that we soon made our purchases cheaply. He called me 'Darling', too and led me by the hand, which normally I would have found disconcerting. It is little instances like this and the warm friendship of the lighthouse keeper which make me like Indians so much, though they can also be almost as irritating as I know I am. Our shopping done, he melted away unobtrusively, absolving us from the agonizing question, should we or should we not tip him?

We bade a fond farewell to the lighthouse keeper and photographed him in front of his lighthouse with his assistants and friends. Then, having promised him a book on shells which we later sent from England, we set off for Madras. The Coromandel Coast was lovely with its backing of *ghats*, or step-like curb of hills, behind the narrow alluvial plain beside the sea. What a fittingly romantic name for such a brilliantly coloured coast! How bright was the gorgeous sun on fields of mustard, broken up by clumps of slender palms that are never quite stiff and have a subtle curve at the top which is all grace. The hard mud threshing floors were spread with vivid red peppers ripening in the sun.

The dark skinned women with their shining white smiles were most attractive. Everywhere in India poverty is taken with a laugh. Their bright clothes and superb carriage, bearing heavy, burnished brass water pots on their heads, steadied by a hand with one breast exposed, added to their natural grace and the pageant.

All the way down the coast we sought the sea. How lovely it would be to bathe again on the golden beaches, I thought. We found however that the coast was so built over that it was difficult to see the sea at all down narrow, winding lanes. We might have been on the Costa del Sol. Hardly a house did not display the hammer and sickle and communist slogans. Any friendly overture on my part was blankly resisted and the weight of hostility threw me back, so we resigned ourselves to making a quick passage to Madras. Even as we set out, our way was blocked in a narrow lane by a carelessly parked Jeep and I had the greatest difficulty in persuading the owner to move it the necessary two feet. There was no Indian tolerance there.

I had been stationed in Madras for a short time during the war and it had left an impression on me. I thought of the great Marina, nearly eight miles long beside the sea-shore and its wide double promenade, overlooked by fine houses built with pride and care, not the flat-roofed concrete boxes of modern India. I felt that the English traders of the past had been great men and ready to spread themselves in India's large spaces. They did not seem daunted by the exceptionally relaxing, humid climate and the ever-present danger of new and virulent diseases which carried off so many of them in their twenties.

I remembered the pretty little Guindy Wild Life Sanctuary and the race-course, bright with bougainvillaea, where we had gambled and lost more than we could possibly afford, the sandy beaches and the large prawns and crabs which we bought cheaply, directly from the fishermen. Then there was a strange little modern house, I fear of concrete, which I rented and to which I got Peggy and John (our first born) down from the north for a fleeting reunion between the war's moves and countermoves. It was painted a depressing dark purple colour. One day, looking across at the next house, I saw gaily-clad young women who appeared much amused at something. I discovered that we were next to the local brothel. Everyone had been too polite to tell us and we had not so far had any misdirected callers. I looked further and was lucky to get a very pretty little house right on the beach. But no sooner was the snatched reunion organised with servants and a going concern, than it was broken up by yet another move and I had to send the family up to the all-the-year-round climate of the Nilgiri Hills where, just by chance, I had learned of accommodation. We were lucky for they could have been stranded in the heat of summer. We were doubly lucky in that the ramshackle little cottage belonged to a local resident – a staunch Jehovah's Witness! Most of the houses in the tiny hill station of Kota Giri belonged to missionaries who came up from the plains in the hot weather to live in their houses which were rented out during the rest of the year. As always,

'Abandoned Wives', as they were officially called, had to live from hand to mouth in a country where no provision was made for them if their husbands went to the wars. Life is full of up-joys and down-sorrows, but there were times when they were almost impossible to cope with.

I remembered the Adyar Club, a lovely domed building with marble floors on the Adyar, a branch of the Coomb River. It was in a splendid position with the backing of the sea and the weekend supper parties were Lucullan even in war time. The box wallahs (merchants) kindly made us service visitors honorary members and they certainly did themselves in style. The building had been erected with loving care by a Portuguese merchant for his son joining him from Portugal. But the young man was killed in a duel at sea a day short of Madras and his broken-hearted father gave the building to the Jesuit order.

So we returned to Madras in our very confined and austere Land Rover with its crochety raising roof and stopped at the Connemara Hotel for a break, being tired of living in our poky vehicle. It had been a hard and hot drive and the small diesel engine had raised its voice above its station. Oh, for a long cool beer!

> And as the cock crew, those who stood before
> The tavern shouted, 'Open the door!
> You know how little time we have to stay
> And once departed, may return no more.

> *Omar Khayyam (d.1022): trans E. Fitzgerald*

We entered the bar to be turned away by a pair of admonitory-looking barmen. I realised, and I should have known it, that Madras was 'dry'. I had heard that travellers could get an alcohol permit and I was directed in the heat to an office some way down the road. Yes, I could have a permit if I filled in two forms, one for myself and one for Peggy. I had to fill in details of a very searching nature, including our heights. We returned to the bar with a new raging thirst and produced our two permits triumphantly. With a broad gesture on the 'Landlord fill the flowing bowl' line I commanded the barmen to bring beer as right had returned to our side. But no – still the admonitory look and it was explained that a record of each drink we had must be entered up. The head barman opened up two exercise books, one for each of us, and wrote in our names and laboriously ruled lines and columns as my eyes followed his pencil thirstily. Then and only then could we have a beer, which alas was hot, for there had been none cooled for the rare visitor with a permit. Hot beer is no beer!

In our early days of long distance motoring we used primuses and here in Madras we needed methylated spirits to light them, so I made enquiries and was directed to Spencers, the time-honoured railway caterers and chemists who had a warehouse complex. Never in India is a simple transaction made easy. It is always tied up with red tape. Armed at last with an authority we were directed from one warehouse to another and back again. Looking into cavernous interiors I could see close-ranked tables, manned by a multitude of clerks. Of their dark, Dravidian features nothing could be discerned but the whites of their eyes and I began to feel that these eyes were pitying in their expression as they followed me. Then a frail old tatterdemalion sidled up and said, 'Brother, you can have half of my ration.' Again that uncalled-for kindness which is the best of India. And what a kindness it was! I suddenly realized – his drink ration! The pitying eyes that had followed us round were merely sad that an apparently respectable, elderly Englishman had fallen so low as to be 'on the Meth'.

Chapter 10

Carpets, Mosques and Jewels

The First Journey Back to England

We went home in February 1968 by the long route through Zahedan and southern Iran, rather earlier than we found advisable in later years, as rivers could be in spate and there were often blizzards in the Turkish uplands. We had to go early to relieve my sister in the half-yearly care of my mother who had become too old to live by herself, as she had done through the many years of her gallant widowhood. We wanted to try out another route instead of the northern one along the Caspian, although this new way was bumpy and the Land Rover broke one of its heavy-duty springs. It was worth it on account of the large-scale, magnificent scenery. The high snow mountains gave me a feeling of release from all that is crowded and sordid in life. I wanted too to revisit Isfahan which had attracted me so much on our preliminary try-out trip in 1963.

Isfahan is a name to conjure with; Persian poets did: Isfahan – *Nisf-i-Jahan* (Half the World). In the sixteenth century the Emperor Shah Abbas made it his capital and it was then indeed a centre whose culture and riches attracted men from both the east and the west.

We drove through the main carpet areas of Iran, past Kerman, Yezd and Nain, but we were too poor to buy their works of art. As we went along my thoughts switched back to the past. In Waziristan, so many years ago, my brother officers and I would sometimes stop a camel *quafila* of Powindah nomads. They were big, fierce-looking men and owed no one allegiance, for desert grass, scrub and thorn bush recognise no boundaries and where they are greenest in season, thither their animals must go. The camels returning from a journey deep into southern India were thin and weary and their owners were eager to get them to the grazing lands in Khost in southern Afghanistan. The camel men would have baled up the left-over rugs that they had not been able to sell in the south and would be glad to get rid of them cheaply to lighten the loads. We knew that at best the rugs were remnants, but a knotted rug of almost any quality is better than a woven one. Although it was a buyer's market these nomads were the toughest of traders. We would make an offer for a whole bale

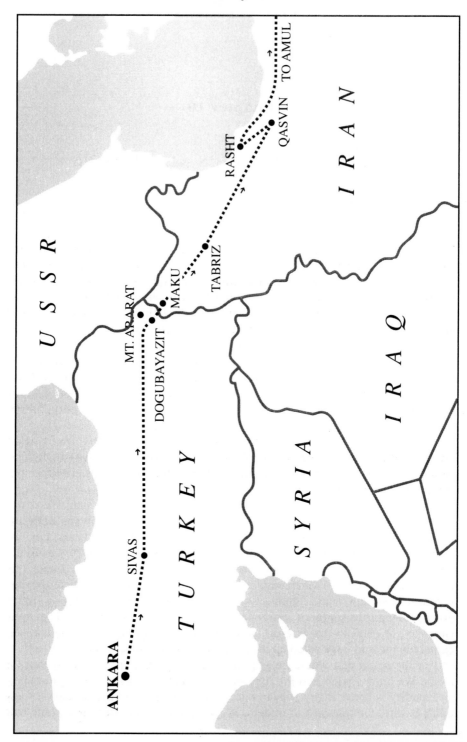

at a time. It would be opened up and the rugs spread out on the ground to be divided amongst us. It was a bit of a lottery, because sometimes there would be a quite good one and that was the fun of it.

Some of these Muslim Powindahs were moneylenders and plied their trade successfully all over India. You may wonder how they got their usurious interest in spite of the fact that they were foreigners who tended to turn up only once a year. Using their ferocious mien and great size they would terrify their debtors into paying up by threats of violence. The Indian shopkeeper is not often a brave man, even if acquisitive, and the money lenders used unconventional methods as well as violence to extract payment. In one case a shopkeeper pleaded that he couldn't pay the interest. He was a fellow member of their great religion; but this did not prevent the Powindahs from threatening to dig up his father's corpse: I am told that good Muslims know only too well that a mutilated body will go on in this state eternally – apparently there are no spare parts in heaven. This ultimate sanction was too much for the shopkeeper.

On arriving in Isfahan we visited Yakoub's shop in the Chahar Bagh Avenue: a shop already described in that delightful book, *A Persian Tea Garden*. I fingered over a few rugs and looked at Persian miniatures, but I did not know enough about the latter to make a purchase. They can, if antique, be very valuable, but I felt that anyone with a fine brush could counterfeit them, and they do. Yakoub shut up shop and took us to his house for tea, but he was a little distrait. Queen Juliana of the Netherlands had visited this great city and the craftsmen, wishing to produce an example of their skill, had made a magnificent round tray of copper alloy, some four feet in diameter. Yakoub had been the prime mover in this venture. It was a remarkably fine bit of work, depicting all walks of life in Iran in beautifully engraved bands. I would have loved to have acquired it. Queen Juliana, perhaps the richest woman in the world at that time did not buy it and hence his sorrow. Rich people only stay rich through being very careful. The tranquillity of drinking green tea in a Persian garden was a little marred.

In Isfahan, Meshed and Herat the period from the fourteenth to the sixteenth centuries was a time of great mosque and tomb building. The use of the squinch, adopted by then in the east, enabled builders to construct fine, circular, bulbous domes, superimposed on four square walls. Earlier these domes had been smaller and pot-shaped, as in Samarkand, but the later ones are exquisite. A more distant tomb, the Taj Mahal, is too well known to describe, but in its white purity and romantic origin, it is my favourite. The dome is the important part of a mosque as it represents heaven inside it, as in the Byzantine church, unlike Gothic architecture which reaches up towards heaven above.

We walked the Royal Square, said to be as big as Moscow's Red Square, and passed through the stone polo posts which still stand there. This great area, surrounded by a double tier of brick arches, is broken on one side by the relatively small Sheikh Lutfullah mosque, named after Shah Abbas's chief minister. It lacks the large open space of the typical eastern mosque where there is room for a multitude to perform the drill-like obeisances. It was built expressly for the prayers of the court ladies and therefore enclosed. They had but to walk across the square from the Ali Kapu or Exalted Gate of the palaces, or, more probably, were borne in covered palanquins. The tiles of the dome of this gem of architecture are basically of a *café au lait* tint which differs sharply from the more famous turquoise coloured domes. Inside, the dome's tilework is in a pattern of regular lozenges and each tier is sharply graduated to give the illusion of greater height and space.

Behind the Ali Kapu with its delicate mural paintings there was once a large area of palaces, now gone. The Exalted Gate itself is but a central passage under a grandstand with its roof supported by painted wooden pillars for the court to watch the sport below. The only palace still standing in the garden behind is the Chehil Satun (Forty Pillars) where huge oil paintings of the court of those days have been precariously preserved.

Then through its silver doors we entered the Royal Mosque, offset from the square in order to face towards Mecca. I must confess that I as a soldier felt uncomfortable at such asymmetry. Its *Iwan*, ornate in a honeycomb intricacy of many richly hued tiles led us under the vast dome, cunningly lit by shafts of light so that it looked airy and insubstantial. I felt a wonderful peace in the great open square outside.

Up in a niche workmen were restoring the tilework. At the time Iran was repairing her ancient mosques. When I spoke to the men they said with pride, 'Say, Governor,' or words to that effect, 'You've got nothing like this!' I replied tactfully that, yes, we had even greater buildings to the glory of our God, but perhaps none so beautiful.

Halfway down the quadruple avenues of the leafy Chahar Bagh we came to a splendid building. Its tilework seemed a little fresher than in other domes and round its base was a broad band of lapis luzuli colour, covered with that most ornate of all writing, Kufic script, in white. We just had to investigate. It was the Madrasseh-i-Madr-i-Shah (The Ecclesiastical College of the Shah's Mother) – how those clerics rolled on in the seventeenth century. It was not a mosque, but a religious school. The grounds were pleasant with trees, but somewhat confined and the mandatory stone pool was the centre of a shrub garden.

The gatekeeper greeted us and I, pulling myself together for a great effort, for it was hot and I was thirsty, greeted him, 'Hail fellow, well met!' in his own language. Sensing my friendliness his stiffness thawed and in talking he asked me, as usual, how many children I had. He capped me boastfully – fecundity is riches where all else is poor – saying that he had fifteen. I turned to Peggy and told her deliberately that he had fifty: fifteen and fifty sound much the same in Persian. He was delighted and threw back his head in a loud, bad-toothed cackle of laughter. While the iron was hot, I asked him, for I was itching to do it, 'What would you say to our climbing up to the top of one of the minarets?'

He stopped in mid-cackle, but his eyes were still friendly. 'W-e-e-ll, if you were to come this way . . .', and he led us to a small side door and up over the roof with its countless little domes or round bumps which marked the anchorite cells of students below, till we reached a narrow door. I have to say 'narrow' as minarets are inherently narrow. As we crossed the roof he told us to keep back from the edge for fear that the mullah who was dozing in the sun below would see us, and object to our presence.

Peggy preceeded me squeaking with eagerness for she is a much more dedicated student of history than I and clambered up the steep, tightly spiralled stairway. I, more bulky, brushed both shoulders on the walls' steep sides and climbed gruntingly. After a great many steps we struggled out into the carved trellis work of a wooden walkway round the minaret. We were at the top but for the stopper-like roof, covered in tiles. The wood must have been very good for there in the full glare of the sun, unvarnished and unpainted, it was hard and strong and yet so slenderly carved.

Dazzled by the sunlight on the high glaze of the tiles I looked immediately down on the great swell of the dome. I was disappointed to see how chipped the tilework was, though so fresh-looking from the avenue below. Sweeping white tendrils curled over the turquoise surface in a coiled design, the *islimi* or snake motif: the very same which is woven into Isfahan rugs today and was so popular in the heyday of Shah Abbas. The design has nothing to do with snakes in spite of its coils, but represents floral tendrils or vines.

I could see the whole of Isfahan from the minaret and beyond it the dark, jagged Zagros mountains that once protected it against raiders from the north. In spite of the great distances there was a feeling of intimacy as we looked down into houses and courtyards. Far below I could see the august mullah still resting in the sun.

Over towards Julfa on the other side of the river, the *Zaindeh Rud* or river of life, was the smooth, modest brick dome of the Armenian Church looking no different from the Muslim mosques save for a small cross on the apex: no tiles there. The Armenians were encouraged to settle by Shah Abbas who greatly admired their industry. Later, on visiting it we found the church big and imposing, the floor covered with fine, sombre carpets largely purple in colour owing to the lavish use of mulberry juice dye. The walls rather crudely pictured the gory atrocities inflicted on Armenian martyrs. How the bloody Turks clobbered these talented people and now, alas, the clobber has begun again.

We then went on to stay with the Waghorns in Teheran. John had established a large plant where Land Rovers could be assembled and maintained under licence in the country: a very good effort indeed. Rovers, then a small firm, had given us an introduction to him on our earlier journey to Iran and Turkey. John was generous with his liquor and the best of hosts. He had the gift of telling stories when he was ensconced in the brightly lit little bar in his large flat.

Ilma, his wife, was one of those competent women with a strong personality. We were to see the Shah's famous jewels, for Cartier had introduced order into the display and done much resetting. I told her rather ill-advisedly that we had already seen a fabulous treasure in the Top Kapi museum in Istamboul and that the monster-sized emeralds and rubies, many uncut, had looked like outsized boiled sweets lying about in unordered heaps – Cartier would have had a fit. Ilma snorted that that was nothing compared with the Shah's treasure which was fantastically guarded by modern electronics and armed sentries. Teasing her, I said that so scientific were modern thieves that nothing was safe from them.

On entering the Shah's treasure house the display of sheer wealth was staggering, if slightly vulgar, and I felt that the rubies, my favourite stone, looked pale and pink. Nowhere, in case after case, crown and tiara in great numbers, did I see a real, deeply lambent, pigeon's blood ruby such as I had seen in Burma as the war ended: too many of these were spinels. After we had driven the Japanese back, men from the Mogok mines offered us beautiful stones, wrapped in the traditional way in tissue paper, for very little money, but I was too exhausted by then to try and extract funds from the Field Cashier and of course had no knowledge of precious stones, so passed up what might have been wonderful bargains.

We were not to touch the cases as this would set off the alarm system. But there was the Shah's state crown which looked like a lofty shuttlecock. I *had* to touch to see if the fine gold filigree at its extremities would wobble when the Shah walked. I tapped the glass case and left: the filigree wobbled. At once a steel screen shut off the Aladdin's cave and steel-helmeted guards, until then concealed by two-way mirrors, were lit up in a series of sentry boxes, all with rifle and bayonet at the ready. We got out just in time. Ilma had slipped away a second before and was looking cross. It was very naughty of me.

I wonder if all this has now gone to subsidise the war against Iraq?

Chapter 11

I Can Never Say No

The End in India of the First Journey, 1967–8 and the Beginning of the Second Journey, 1968–9

Before we left India in 1968 we had a chance of really getting to know the country. The ADC appointed to me when we visited the Regimental Centre was a big, good-looking officer, Mohinder Singh, with unexpected qualities as well as being extremely smart. I was told by the Commandant that in the 1964 India-Pakistan war he, as a temporary officer, had greatly distinguished himself on fighting patrols behind the opposing lines. He reported that he had killed a number of the enemy. His brother officers thought this mild but hefty fellow was exaggerating. 'Oh, come off it, Mohinder!' they said. 'All right,' replied Mohinder, 'I'll do it again,' and, after a sustained fighting patrol, reported back and calmly pulled twenty enemy right ears out of his khaki shorts' pocket in gruesome proof.

Alas, he was going blind. There was a scar on his forehead which he said was due to a blow by a rifle butt that was the cause of his affliction. He said he did so want to be given a regular commission, but hadn't a hope. I felt very sad and thought hard. I felt that the Commonwealth was not much use if brother could not help brother, so I went to the Military Adviser to the British High Commissioner and suggested that if Mohinder paid his passage there and back (I knew his family was wealthy), could he not be treated at Millbank, the then military hospital in London. General Lunt was ideally suited to his role, having roots in both British and Indian service, and was already an established author. He said it would be very difficult as there were so many senior officers in Delhi languishing with crippling wounds from the recent war and hoping to get treatment in England, but he would try.

Mohinder and his father seemed to think this a good idea. His father was Rai Bahadur Hari Chand. The title of Rai Bahadur was given him by the British and held with pride, since as a big landowner and politician he had thrown his considerable weight in on the side of the Raj in times of trouble. Wishing to show his gratitude and, as I felt on meeting him, dying to talk of old times with an Englishman, he invited us out to his estate beyond Chandigarh, the capital of

87

the Punjab built by le Corbusier with such disastrous results. I realised that here was a golden chance to see India deep in its rural areas. I had done recruiting tours in such areas in what is now Pakistan, a very different type of country. But that was all. I hesitated for many reasons. We were in our poky Land Rover and I knew that in the event of damage on rough country roads there were no spares to be had in India; I thought of the long miles back to England along roads still very rough, though improving since our first trip to Iran and Turkey in 1963. I thought too of the crippling customs' indemnity if I could not get the car out. It would run to many thousands of pounds in the days when the pound meant something in real money: some 250% of the purchase price. I felt, however, that it was the one chance I had to get to know what is the best in India – the integrity of the deep countryside away from main roads. I felt too that I must accept for I have always been tender over hurting others' feelings and I reminded myself that my welcome to my old regiment had been both friendly and lavish.

I feared the roads would be horrific, but Mohinder was reassuring, saying they were good and asked if he could travel with me, taking his batman. More weight, I sorrowed, for I always had to carry full bedding, some spares and basic rations in this relatively small vehicle. We formed up to go next morning, but I saw half a dozen would-be passengers with much baggage who swarmed into the vehicle as soon as the back door was open. India always treats a car like a mechanical donkey – to beat the life out of it. Feeling an awful cad, I said firmly for once, 'No, only you, Mohinder, and your batman.'

We travelled north-eastwards at first along tolerable roads, but beyond Chandigarh they got progressively worse. I could see that this fertile land, only moistened by seasonal rain, was extremely well irrigated by an elaborate system of canals which were bringing water brown with alluvial soil to the parched plains from the world's greatest catchment, the Himalayas. British administrators had planned well, but now more and more water was needed as India produced its much loved millions of children.

We were to meet a high caste Brahmin, a Colonel Sharma, at Karnal on the way. We waited hours and at last the gallant Colonel arrived, with no apologies but saying he had had nine punctures. I looked at his tyres, which all showed the canvas. In those days tyres were hard to get in India as imports were restricted and few were made then within the country. You had to queue up on a list and bribe your way along to get a set. We proceeded in slow convoy, the Colonel's Indian-made car lagging behind. He was not going to make it, so soon we avoided looking back, for we were very late, and left him to his fate.

At last we met the Rai Bahadur Hari Chand. He was really a sort of local princeling – a big man, very broad and about sixty years old but, unlike most of his caste, not fair skinned, for he led an open-air, agricultural life. His was an imposing figure, with sweeping white moustaches like elephant tusks, met and bisected by a large nose which was strongly hooked. He had those full eyes you see in Indian idols and in the Indian well-bred, with a lot of white showing below the iris.

It is strange that the younger generations in India, unlike those in the west, do not tend to be bigger than their fathers. Indeed, they are smaller. I think this could be because vegetarianism is on the increase, owing to a greater emphasis on the Hindu religion. Meat is poor in India and so for that matter are vegetables in most areas, lacking organic fertilisers. Stable litter is not spread on the land. It is hard-patted into flat cakes, dried and used as fuel.

We had lunch on a long trestle table in the open at one of the Rai Bahadur's outpost farms where his first and senior wife, mother of his eldest son, lived. Rich Hindus of his generation often have more than one wife, to extend their lands or to have more children. There we met some big farmer contemporaries, all large, fine-looking men. Before lunch we sampled oranges of many kinds. Hari Chand wanted to know if we grew oranges in England – conversation was going very well. He was an extremely dominating, almost crushing, character, so that I was pleased to see that he mellowed towards me as I spoke freely in the Hindi which I had striven to improve. I felt a little diffident, for in the new India I had no status.

As soon as we had finished lunch he suggested we press on to his house as it was getting late. He had come to his borders to meet us. Soon after, the Colonel turned up, having abandoned his car and taken a lift. His son was an unattractive, soft-poached egg, but a friend of Mohinder's; they had met as casualties in hospital. The Colonel said crossly that his son had borrowed the car and run it dry of oil. The son, unabashed, wagged his head in the strange Indian way and said, 'Better you should put dabble kontity of woil in next time, Daddy!' We rather gathered later that Colonel Sharma was stalking the family to make a good match for the poached egg. But Hari Chand, I'm glad to say, pinned the Colonel's ears back every time he spoke.

Soon we were to put the Land Rover to a considerable water obstacle: a broad, sandy-bottomed stream. We hurled ourselves across in lowest four-wheel drive, corkscrewing, sticking and cruelly over-revving. We managed to churn up a steep exit bank. Then we had to do it again. Mohinder was sitting happily with his feet on the dashboard. The floor was awash, but we just got across once more. 'I didn't think you'd make it,' said Mohinder chirpily.

'You said . . .!' and I stopped. What was the use? More deep, sandy tracks and we had arrived. The house was in the highest part of the village, for old villages in India form mounds as successions of mud walls subside and are superseded. We were shown into a guest cell, a small, flat-roofed room with a door and glassless windows, separate from the house itself. I was told it had been specially built for us, but it didn't look new. We asked where the WC was and to our horror were shown a low mud wall with a side drain at floor level and nothing else. This enclosure was looked down into by every house in the village and naturally our every move was watched, as many in this remote place had

not seen Europeans before. When we could hold out no longer we slipped away
into the yard where our caravan was parked. It was very open and with no
facilities, but there was a big buffalo and we dived down behind her motherly
bulk in turn, each keeping a look out. How important mod. cons. are if you
haven't got them, an importance that grows and grows as you travel on.

It is a problem in which Europeans and Indians differ dramatically. Defeca-
tion is performed openly and without embarrassment in India, though of course
change is coming and with it facilities in the houses of the better off. Here at
Bhulan everyone took with him a little brass *lotah* of water and used the
hedgerows a stone's throw from the village. Being healthy and nearer to nature
than we are, the call came just before dawn so it was discreet if most unhy-
gienic. Another contrast is that sex is not mentioned and in the country
absolutely no sexual demonstration between male and female is permitted, even
to the holding of hands. In the towns this is changing and young Indian boys
and girls from the leisured classes wishing to be modern do walk hand in hand.
The modern cinema has now totally broken down this sensibility. Strangely to
me, boys and men hold hands and fling an arm round another's neck – shades of
ancient Greece? Young men do not normally go on a hike or picnic with
unmarried girls. This would be most improper for the girls – as bad as smoking
in public. But again this is changing, especially at the universities and innumerable polytechnics. Still, it seemed strange to see parties of 'boys only' going
out on a spree.

The Rai Bahadur talked much of the old days. He was a worried man, for
factories were drawing labour off from his wide lands. I gathered that politics
were getting a bit hot too. He did occasionally ask a question or two, but it was
mostly monologue, on and on. It was clear that he deeply regretted the passing
of the British. He kept on saying, 'Why did you leave us so suddenly, like little
children in the dark? Loving parents would never do that!' I had no answer.

We ate *mahseer*, marinated in hot spices, from his river which had nearly
been our Slough of Despond. The *mahseer*'s flesh is prized by Indians, but to us
is flaccid and full of sharp bones. We sipped Scotch – real Scotch – and soda. It
must have cost him a great deal. It was then about five times as expensive as in
England and scarce at that; it still is.

I told him I was surprised at India's efforts to become industrialised, when
her fertile lands suggest a concentration on agriculture. Surely that was her
course, as food would soon be the most valuable commodity in the world; but
the Rai Bahadur swept heedlessly on with his remorseless monologue.

We went to bed absolutely exhausted. It had been a long, exacting drive and
to talk or be talked at in a foreign language in its most high-faluting form for
hours and hours had added to the strain, especially as we had all the while to be
careful not to swallow sharp fishbones. Any attempt to spend the night in our
caravan was resisted and to have persisted would have offended our host. There
was a large pepul tree against which our cell leaned. Tired out, we dropped off

to sleep, but the mosquitoes soon put an end to that with their high frequency whine and irritating bites: there were no nets. Then all the little people of the pepul tree slithered down to investigate us. It was pitch dark and something was scrabbling along the beams above, showering dust on our faces. There were soft mutterings and squeaks and occasional plopping sounds. I turned over and my pillow started buzzing and vibrating like one of those trick buzzers you shake hands with as a joke. Then there was a plop and something fell to the floor and scampered away. In my fevered and exhausted mind I felt that if I put my hand down it would be on the irate and inflamed hood of a cobra.

At last the 'dreadful night' drifted away and pale, we took up again our efforts at pleasantries and friendship. There was to be a shoot, chiefly of India's grey partridge, dubbed grey by naturalists, but beautiful in fine black pencilling over dark umber and chestnut. There were too a few of the rarer black partridge. I had to borrow a gun which did not fit, for it is too tedious to get a gun of one's own through the various nit-picking customs *en route*. I found I was knocking down a few birds, but was conscious of being on others when nothing happened. I discovered later that cartridges are skimped of shot or powder, in order to make good profits – this was India. None of the others was taking the birds in the air, I was shocked to see, and as the grey partridge is an inveterate runner, the other guns tended to press on faster and faster, until they too were running. It was all rather frustrating and poor Mohinder was getting very blind indeed – he was stumbling about all over the place. When I did bring down a bird, the gallant Colonel, who had at last arrived, shouted loudly, 'Oh my Gard, the Brigadier has shot a bird!'

Then it started to drizzle and I enquired about its effect on the miles of unmetalled road. Everyone said cheerfully that it would be all right and that the two branches of the river would not swell. It never rained seriously at this time of the year. However, our cell leaked, so in the middle of the night we were rescued and inducted into the main house. This too was handsome as in a high class Hindu household in the country there is as strict *purdah* as in Muslim homes.

So we survived one more night and by daylight I saw some of our visitors of the first one – diminutive little Indian tree squirrels with their long fore and aft stripes. They all looked so innocent. This little squirrel played its part in the *Ramayana* when the monkey god, Hanuman, carried big stones to make a causeway to Lanka to rescue Sita, Rama's wife. The terrible demon, Ravenna, had abducted her to Ceylon. It was then that the squirrel squeaked up and said, 'Me too!' and carried many little, pea-sized pebbles to help build the causeway. Rama picked up the eager, vibrant little body and stroked it and, lo and behold, his fingers drew the dark stripes down the little creature's back.

We took our leave, inventing a pressing engagement. The old Rai Bahadur embraced me warmly as if I were an old and honoured friend, and begged me to come again, which was nice of him. The partridges had been given us, skinned and hotly marinated according to Indian custom. So spiced they stayed fresh for days and were a first-class iron ration.

By then the rain had increased and there was no exit by the way we had come. I was firmly assured that there was yet another road – 'Only a little longer.' We set off vowing silently and ungratefully that we would never come again. What an opportunity to see nice people and how gracious they had been, but I was severely restricted by lack of funds and feared a fabulously costly breakdown in the vehicle. This was a lamentable restraint on my free movement in all this wonderful land. The suggested road was my Paschendaele. We churned in four-wheel drive, often bouncing sideways on, corkscrewing along, the engine revving desperately. There seemed no hope of proceeding and it would be a long muddy walk to fetch slow oxen for a tow. But somehow we won through to the tarmac and away. The Land Rover was never the same again; its gallant heart was broken – its seals leaked. The road was a very, very long detour. I might have known: the easterner politely tells you that which you wish to hear. However, I left careful instructions with Colonel Jit Lal to ensure that Mohinder would contact General Lunt about going to Millbank.

On the Second Journey (1968–9)

The following summer in England was like an exile with its frown of dark clouds and the weak apologetic smile of a pale sun, while the little dove's voice still called, called over the mountains. In my mind's eye it ensnared me in 'A noose of light', so once more we obeyed and set out on our second journey in October 1968 in a new vehicle: the home-converted Hawson delivery van I have described earlier. In November, after a long, bumpy journey through many obstacles, I returned once more to the Regimental Centre and put my name in the calling book – and Mohinder turned up, smiling. No, he had not been to Millbank. He had been cured by very skilled Indian doctors – as indeed they are. I was surprised at this. Mohinder had had a floating retina, probably caused by his wound although this affliction had occurred in other members of the family. I felt rather left in the air and had to apologise to General Lunt.

I was, however, glad to hear that Mohinder had now got his regular commission and was obviously happy. He, with a warm, almost pleading, look in his eyes, asked us to come to his wedding. As I have said, I am always a pushover and hate hurting people's feelings, though I felt at once I had assumed an immense burden which was not lessened when I asked Colonel Jit Lal if he were going and he answered succinctly, 'Not on your life!'

Knowing to some extent what I was letting myself in for I started to make my terms. I would take no extra passengers and I obtained an agreement that I be allowed to stay in my caravan on the banks of the ford where I remembered that there was a little teashop. I pointed out that the owner could keep an eye on the vehicle and I asked that ponies be provided so that we could ride on to the village for the ceremonies and return at night to the van, being under the impression that the wedding was to be at Bhulan. I saw in this plan a chance of enjoying the visit: a simple plan – simple plans are the best militarily and the most likely to succeed, I told myself comfortingly. My second caravan was larger than the Land Rover with good, outsize balloon tyres and a stout diesel engine.

We arrived at the old rendezvous, but waited and waited for our hosts. At last, when we were beginning to feel that all had gone wrong after so long a journey, a little boy who had been asleep for some time hard by woke up and approached us. He produced a letter from the Rai Bahadur welcoming us, saying that he regretted not meeting us in person as he had other guests and asking us to come on using the little boy to guide us. His sons were on their way to meet us. We arrived at the river and there was the tea shop, but no sons. After a long wait we saw them as they took to the flood on a large tractor.

There were warm handshakes from a small man, the Rai Bahadur's eldest son and as such known as the Tikka Sahib (Son of a Prince). His other brothers, or rather half-brothers, were as big and prepossessing as Mohinder who was involved in the lengthy marriage arrangements and could not come. It was a great kindness on their part to devote so much time to welcoming one elderly Englishman when there was so much to do. These big brothers, not being officers, looked more of the soil. This was fine and I asked confidently if the ponies would be coming: but no. They told me the Rai Bahadur had vetoed my plan for he had said, 'What would the neighbours say if I treated an honoured guest so scurvily – to sleep in their car, indeed!' they would add.

The Tikka Sahib asked me if I had a pump as the tractor had a puncture. I had a strong foot pump which I rather grudgingly produced. In India everybody borrows my pump and when I really need it on some snowy Turkish plateau, it is found to be damaged. I pumped, they pumped, we pumped all four, but with no result. The tyre was finished. Bending down, purple in the face, working hard, I inwardly groaned, 'That bloody river again. The pepul (or should I say 'people') tree! Is the buffalo there?' I did hope so. Oh hell! Another car would be maltreated and I was proud of this one – green with a broad, black curved-down medial line and my crest which I had myself put on in gold leaf. And so in the spirit of 'Take thou in charge this day,' I put the bonnet down the long, soft, sandy slope and churned steadily across. The big balloon tyres gripped just enough, but it was rough treatment and the engine seemed hot and bothered, although the river was lower than in the previous year.

On arriving I greeted the Rai Bahadur, embracing him in the eastern manner as between two equals, but he held back because a number of others were watching, sitting round the edges of the patio, having drawn their legs up tailor fashion and dropped off their slippers. I sat down near an imposing Sikh who was by no means friendly – a disagreeable fellow who carried on one-upmanship to trump my every remark. What make was my gun? Oh! his was a

Holland and Holland, and so on. He said that when he was in London as a representative of Indian horse racing, he was absolutely disgusted with the way couples in England kissed openly in the parks. I nearly replied hotly, 'You Indians mess all over the place in the open – much more disgusting,' but I forebore, as all in all I was making a tremendous effort to do a good hands-across-the-sea job.

Next day there was to be a wild boar shoot. We didn't make it. I stuck in a sandy lane and spent hours alone with Peggy digging the car out. My poor paint was sadly scratched by the thorn bushes which could not be avoided. The wild boar wisely did not make it either. I gathered that boars were scarce and he had merely been mentioned to give flavour to a picnic. So we all went partridge shooting, but as Mohinder, an officer with some sense, was not there to organise it the line once more proceeded at a run. The poached egg (Colonel Sharma's son), his belly bouncing before him, was in the fore. The Colonel, suffering from hypochondria, was mounted. I quietly broke away and did a bit of rough shooting by myself, and started building up a nice bag, though I lost many birds. Two skeletal dogs which were brought in couldn't smell anything save their distant meagre dinners and retrieved nothing. Later in the afternoon the Tikka Sahib turned up: a nice little man who giggled fatly at my witticisms. I got out a precious bottle of Scotch and we had a dram or two in a thoroughly restful little session. Apparently the Tikka Sahib returned to his wife somewhat merry, for when the Rai Bahadur decorously conducted the wives to see the caravan they asked me with knowing laughs where I kept my Scotch.

The next morning our hosts announced, 'We're off!' Off where? 'To Jammu, to the wedding,' they replied. As a guest in India one is always left in the dark and often finds oneself unsuitably prepared for an unheralded event. Looking at the over-stuffed bus they were going in on this 240 mile drive, I decided to go in the motor caravan. We would at least have our beds with us and perhaps somewhere we could have some privacy. I made an effort to find out what the plans were and was told we were all to foregather for lunch at the Jammu Tourist Lodge. We arrived at the forlorn and dirty building and were pestered by small, begging children and flies for hours. When we had almost given up hope, the Tikka Sahib turned up and remarked, 'Oh, there you are. We missed you at lunch at so and so,' a rendezvous not mentioned to us. We had clearly missed an excellent Indian lunch and had had to fall back on the caravan's iron rations in the company of the flies.

We were whirled off to a huge tea party for the Rai Bahadur's wedding guests. There were the usual Indian delicacies such as *samosas*, *pakoras* and *shami kebabs*, all fiery and crunchy with cumin seeds, as well as little sponge cakes with lurid pink icing which I remembered from my childhood as proudly produced by our cook. We joined the Rai Bahadur in a side room after tea and found him lying on a *charpoy* (string bed) having his legs massaged by one of his innumerable grandsons. He sat up cross-legged and I realised that

The Rai Bahadur holding forth in the presence of the Most High 'Gards'. (Drawing by author)

through long habit there was no lack of suppleness there. He held forth in his usual way, emphasising the obvious and his tone was somewhat didactic as he discoursed on divorce in the west (very shocking) and the sanctity of Hindu marriage, 'In the presence of the Most High *Gards!*' Duly edified we set off for the wedding.

The question of divorce in this context was far too delicate for me to embark upon, for I had come as a friend. I reminded myself that the Rai Bahadur had solved his particular problem by having more than one wife. In India this practice among the well-to-do used to be above reproach. Now new legislation has legitimised divorce, though at present the very small upper class appear to be the only people to avail themselves of this chink in the door, but a chink can swing wide to let in a strong blast as has happened in the west.

We were all to go to the bride's house where we were seated under *shamianas* (marquees) at long trestle tables. There were many guests, all male and mostly at the tables for non-meat eaters. Peggy, as usual, was an honorary male. Our fellow guests passed the food, but were glum, shy and tongue-tied. High class Hindus do feel defiled by westerners and I have no doubt that our plates and some dishes, for I had passed them round, would be destroyed later. You can imagine how shy I felt. It was agony, but I went on smiling until my face cracked.

The Rai Bahadur had grandly said that as a sister of the bride had already married one of his sons, no dowry would be demanded: just a merry celebration. We were introduced to the bride's father and supporters as the Brigadier and his wife who had come twenty thousand miles to Mohinder's wedding – a slight exaggeration. They were bowled out in one. The home side had no one to put in to bat and looked crestfallen.

I had an opportunity to look down at the town, for the house commanded it. There below, all was bustle, for it was the wedding season and there were several going on at once. The propitious day for the ceremony is chosen by the *pandits* (holy men) who consult the parties' horoscopes and for some reason, possibly connected with agriculture's off season, is nearly always in December. These weddings are done in every detail by contractors. There is often tragedy at their hands, for where liquor is permitted some lethal and cheap concoction is produced which kills large numbers of the guests. One reads of this all too often in the Indian papers. Sometimes even spirit-based varnish is provided. Such is the habit of the cut price, pinch penny, small businessman.

At Mohinder Singh's wedding, an exclusive, high class affair, alcohol was not permitted. There was a desire to keep the wedding on a spiritual level. In India once alcohol is present there is seldom any restraint at all and so there is some wisdom in the custom of prohibition, but good regulations often produce unexpected results.

Down below I saw a strange effect in the thronged square. It seemed to seethe, for the crowds were being criss-crossed by long threads of bobbing lights and I realised that coolies were carrying twin lighted petromax lamps on their heads at the usual shock-absorbing, bent-kneed trot, from one wedding to another. It looked as if electric chains were weaving bright patterns through the darker mass of the crowd. Their trotting gave the chains a strange pulsating appearance and the effect was fairylike. The contractor was rushing his well worn paraphernalia from one venue to the next, late, lost and bewildered. Chains of other coolies were staggering along with rolled up *shamianas* on their heads. As usual the contractors had taken on more than they could honour – hence the lateness and the frenzy. Here and there, there was a bone rack of a white steed. These poor racks, long unfit for the shafts, looked incongruous in their loose-fitting, gaily coloured, sparkling harness and head plumes. Nuptials were their last job.

Later I saw Mohinder looking magnificent in a long-skirted, cream satin *atchkhan*, intricately brocaded in gold thread. His flame-coloured turban, tied in the Rajput fashion, had many twisted rolls down one side over his ear, the other balancing side showed smoother silken folds, and it was, as is customary, surmounted by a jewel-pinned egret's feather. This lopsided turban has a very dashing effect. He wore tight-fitting jodhpurs of fine cotton and embroidered shoes curled up at the ends. At his side was a jewelled, curved scimitar or *talwar*. But hold, what was this? His steed, the famine horse from the apocalypse quartet, hung its weary head to the ground, its knees puffy and bent. In India the fall from the sublime to the ridiculous is steep and sudden.

We were not to see the wedding ceremony – Europeans are seldom invited: a disappointment after so much effort. We did, however, see during the bridegroom's arrival some sort of mock wrestling match between the Rai Bahadur and the bride's diminutive Dogra Rajput father which looked very funny for had it been for real I would have put my money on the Rai Bahadur. A red cloth was cast down on the ground between them and I think it symbolised the bride's virtue. I tried to confirm this, but replies were slightly evasive. Perhaps many things are best left a mystery. When there is embarrassment, one does not press and I never have, so I have not learned much.

There were fireworks, and bands of traditional entertainers, rather like buskers, preyed on each wedding to collect a shower of small coins, cast grudgingly on the ground, as they sketched a sort of dance. They didn't give much and they didn't get much.

Next day the wedding was over, all unseen, and we made the long trek back to Bhulan, but decided to spend the night on the near shore by the tea shop. We had had enough turmoil and tucked the caravan in among the shrubs where no one could see us. 'Oh, what peace!' I thought, 'And a good night's sleep,' in the sweet scent of the bushes. But then the wedding bus arrived and stuck in the river and our peace was shattered. There was revving up and a good deal of shouting. Unworthily, I felt some satisfaction at the bus's plight, for our hosts had so often brushed aside my anxiety over the crossing.

The entertainment after the wedding.

The following day there was a concert and clowns too. We delayed tactfully as we felt our hosts had had a restless night, but when we arrived at the village the party was in full swing. We were invited to sit on the ground with the Rai Bahadur. I noticed that as they arrived sons and near relatives, and there were many, stooped and touched the old man's feet in respect. I thought then that India was still dominated by the old and middle aged. A son will not smoke in his father's presence. Father's word is law as he holds the money bags. A very wealthy business man with whom I once stayed in Delhi said he treated all his sons very liberally and was not at all despotic – I had manoeuvred the conversation that way – 'Everything,' he said, 'is free and easy.' Then a hard note came into his voice and he went on, 'If they step an inch out of line, I chop them!' This was said with a sharp downward karate sweep of his hand, and he had already done so with one son, cutting him off with the proverbial penny. In Bhulan I felt the old Rai Bahadur was king of all he surveyed, but there was a brasher, younger world in India close on the old man's heels.

The concert went on for hours and hours and our limbs ached insupportably. But the company sat comfortably and at ease cross-legged, while the outer periphery squatted behind. Indians have mastered both arts and can rest for hours sitting in either posture. Indeed it is quite normal to see someone squatting for ages on a narrow post, like a bird.

The singing was of the high pitched, nasal style – oh yes, worse than pop singing – the finger placed in the ear to get the sharp pitch exactly. The damsels would sing a verse or two, then stamp round, bouncing the clusters of bells on their ankles. Then another verse and so on endlessly. Did I say damsels? Not on your life. The dancers were powdered and rouged youths, and some stringy and not so youthful. I have been told that they are generally eunuchs. It is thought improper in good village society to watch female entertainers, but I thought these dancing boys got up as women were downright obscene.

There was a long break for some slapstick comedy, which also went on and on. The buffoon took the part of a Pakistani and he wore a *kulla*, or pointed Muslim cap. Secularism is not very strong in India, in spite of the government's claims. Whenever there is social stress Hindu attacks Muslim and *vice versa*. The armed Provincial Police do not hesitate to fire on the crowd and, regrettably, large numbers are killed in the most casual manner. The wars between India and Pakistan have not helped matters.

The clown was repeatedly slapped for his foolishness – with a slap stick. I had never seen one before. Then on and on with the singing and, as is the custom, money was handed to the singers. This was often a matter of ostentation and was given, not at the end of a ballad, but at any time, so that the song or dance was broken off for the entertainer to walk over prostrate legs to reach for the proferred note. There would follow a little song of praise – a monotonous little song – for the donor, or someone he wished to honour, time and again. I was singled out more than once by the Rai Bahadur's friends who rewarded in my name.

The entertainment was perhaps not very superior, but for villagers miles from the nearest cinema it was a rare treat in their hard-working lives. All the men and the children were there while the women watched from the housetops with enormous enjoyment. The Rai Bahadur was sufficiently sophisticated to know that this was a very bucolic affair, but it was his feudal duty towards his villagers as their part in the wedding festivities and it was to be followed by a feast for them all.

We took our leave exhausted, but I felt that we had done our stuff. We were kindly asked to come again, but I thought, 'Never!' Then we stuck in the sand and there, far from the village and help, had to dig the car out, using branches torn from the road side. I thought that I was getting a bit elderly for all this mole work. Now that the years have passed I think affectionately of that vital, rural family. But its centrepiece has gone. The splendid old Rai Bahadur was murdered by a political adversary soon after our visit.

Chapter 12

A Spun-Gold Wedding

India 1968–69: The Second Journey

We had been disappointed not to have seen the actual ceremony at Mohinder's marriage but on our return to Delhi we were delighted to get an invitation to a wedding in the cantonment, where we would be able to watch the whole ritual. We arrived on the appointed evening as strangers at first and mingled with the guests. It was still December, the propitious marriage season and Delhi was bright with many weddings, often two or three a night. Maroons were detonated on all sides and fairy lights were threaded in a myriad of tiny, coloured bulbs lined on flexes to look like bright showers. Brass bands burbled enthusiastically: Indian brass does just that. The large garden was shut in by *shamianas* (marquees) printed in bright designs. Although Delhi is generally cold in December, often uncomfortably so even for those from the west, that night was a freak one as if a threat of fiery days to come. The *shamianas* shut off the air and the bulbs heated it. Those little minced buttons of spiced fire, *Shami kebabs* were handed round. I found them delicious, but I had not realised that although it was a military one, this wedding too would be 'dry'. I could find only a syrupy Coca Cola to quench my thirst – the last one.

Peggy joined the queue to go and wish the bride good fortune and found her sitting cross-legged on a bed, looking rather bored as friends drifted past. Some of them unostentatiously left paper-wrapped parcels, but present giving is not generally the custom at Indian weddings, though how the bride's parents bleed financially!

Soon the ceremony was to start, so I chose a pair of chairs for us at a good vantage point. But I was hailed and joined by a strange figure. He was dressed in a long-skirted, navy blue *atchkan* with its high military collar. His bandy legs were in tight fitting, white cotton trousers, through which his dark skin showed. He had not quite secured the neck of the *atchkan* and a blue and white pyjama collar had escaped and lodged under one ear. On his head he wore a conventional fore and aft Gandhi cap, but this, oddly, was of ginger cat's fur – a cat that had seen bad times in life and after. He definitely lacked style. My friend, for that was how he declared himself, plumped down beside me and

101

began to eulogise the British, for he had been a minor official in the time of the
Raj. Though I was prepared to go along with him, his flow was like a torrent.
Times had changed for the worse, he said, and corruption was everywhere. You
even had to dicker and bribe for a car licence. I tactfully said that all things are
mellowed by the mists of time. He said what a wonderful man Churchill had
been. I could assuredly agree with this, but not for the reason he gave. He
declared that Churchill had shown the ultimate generosity in standing aside
after the war to allow the Socialists in. I rather doubted whether that was how
Churchill had viewed it.

His voice rambled on. He had a face rather like a bullfrog, as do so many
Indians who follow a sedentary, clerical life, or is it a hereditary type which
goes in for clerking? Protuberant eyes peered at me through small-lensed, tin
spectacles, bright against his dark skin, but lost across his broad nose. His thick
lips were red as were his teeth since he had been chewing *pan* – he looked as if
he had just come from some Dracula meal, yet his countenance was genial and I
felt some sympathy for him as he seemed to have been unable to adjust after the
changeover.

I tried to talk to him, for to get close to incomprehensible India was my aim.
But in conversation many Indians tend to shut their ears. Like the Rai Bahadur
they like to pontificate and listen to nothing, so there is no conversation, no
delving into interesting ways and customs. On and on he hurpled, as usual
stating the starkly obvious, as if bringing enlightenment to the moron. Cliché
followed bromide and in my stress I felt I saw these in a dance of ephemera,
round and round his head. I was most anxious to watch the colourful ceremony,
but to emphasise his 'new' truths, he kept on banging my arm to drive in this
spate of instruction. So I did what I always do in such circumstances: I ran off a
sort of cassette strip of, 'Yes, indeed!' – 'You don't say so!' (with emphasis) –
nod, nod – smile and laugh if he smiled – and if he laughed, I slapped my thigh
and laughed all the more – 'Incredible!' I murmured – 'Just fancy that!' and
shut my mind off.

There before me sat the bridegroom in a pretty little bower, all in sparkling
gold tinsel and marigolds. He was resplendent in a cream and gold *atchkan*. His
turban, not so stylish as Mohinder's, but big, bun-shaped and cerise coloured,
sported the usual jewel and an egret's feather. Soon he was joined by his bride,
brilliant in an orange-red sari (the bridal colour) and the light caught a foot
wide, gold tissue border, for a fold was pulled down modestly over her face
which was further concealed by a heavy gold fringe. Her two attendants,
daughters of friends, wandered in rather casually. One, Madhu (Honey) was the
pretty daughter of an old officer who had served with me. Her sari was royal
purple, but set ablaze by intricate embroidery in bright gold thread. What
colour! All the guests promenaded round the bower in every beautiful hue –
Indian dyes seem brighter and fresher than ours. The young women were
wearing tight bodices which left bare a broad midriff. What a lovely colour

their skin was, almost matt gold. But I focused on the bride – graceful, a gorgeous splash of colour in this bower, and I thought of a Fabergé singing bird in a golden cage.

This uninhibited colour was pure joy to me, coming from a drab, conservative land. I heard a jarring note though. Passing girl friends leant into the bower and talked loudly or said to each other, 'Oh my dear, at our wedding we did it *quite* differently!'

Silhouetted against the blaze of gold knelt the officiating pandit, incanting endlessly in Sanskrit. Contrasting starkly, the holy man had scorned the comforts of this life. On his head was a threadbare, brown felt pillbox hat and round his neck was flung a woollen scarf, not very clean, as if come from a muddy rugger field. His worn slippers were cast off behind him and revealed the soles of his feet, deeply cracked as in those who walk much barefooted. His acolyte was a shabby, skinny youth in gaping plimsolls.

The ceremony went on – a lengthy one. As each rite was performed I tried to ask my friend about its significance. But he, looking into the distance heard not and trundled on. Oh, if I could only concentrate! The bride was feeding the bridegroom from little bright brass bowls on a brass tray. How slender her hand was as her long and supple fingers bent backwards. Then I saw that her sari was tied to his coat and, thus appropriately united, they circled the little fire. I assumed the god of fire, Agni, was welding the alliance. Then the father, a most distinguished general, much liked and admired in my day, was to wash the bridegroom's feet. There was a pause and all looked embarrassed. 'Where's the damned water?' the general seemed to cry. There was much shouting. '*O Bhisti, pani lao*' (bring water), but as always, lowly servants were slow to hear.

At last the *bhisti* (water carrier) arrived in the ring of light on matchstick legs at a decrepit trot and banged down a bucket with a loud clang before his master – rather resentfully I thought. But no – everything is banged down in India: playing cards are smacked down, plates and glasses are dumped before one with a clonk.

The washing did not proceed. The general was getting cross. He must have been muttering, 'Damn it, where's the blasted towel?' More shouting, '*Toelia lao*! and a *khitmagar* (table servant) rushed on with a towel with a large curry stain on it. I have to describe this. It was all quaint, lovable India – as usual, sublime to the ridiculous with a jerk, but it had something special for me. It was the prettiest and nicest wedding I have ever attended in any country and we were privileged to be asked.

A young man who had lived on a diet of the national press which always runs the west down, tried to impress on me that this wedding with its spirituality was so much better than the 'carnal weddings' of England which 'always end in divorce'. I countered mildly that our weddings generally take place in church in the presence of God and do not as a rule end in divorce. I added that the wedding I had just seen was charming, but the underlying theme was a commercial contract while the actual ceremony was far more ritually materialistic than ours. We left it at that. Did he listen? As a young journalist he should have. I, proud of our past, tried not be depressed and irritated, for I know that I am jealously over-critical. Although, as I have said, those who served alongside the British have retained a warm regard for them, they are growing fewer and the Indian press delights in impishly criticising its former 'masters', partly, I feel, by young men testing their wings as do all young men, and partly because of the need for the new India to assert its individuality and build itself up against the overpowering influence of the west.

There followed much photographing of the principal guests and they wanted me to be taken with the attractive bride and bridegroom. I demurred slightly out of deferential modesty, but an old major of mine, a relation of the general, grabbed my arm and almost jerked me off my feet, so eager was he that I should be in the picture. I think they wanted me to give the wedding an international flavour. I was then introduced to many young generals, already veterans in border wars. I say 'young generals' because in India's fine, expanded army many had not even been commissioned in my time, which made me feel old and a back number in spite of my hosts' courtesy.

On that second journey to India we visited a friend of mine, an Indian officer, early in January 1969. He had a wealthy background and when he had been on a course with the British army had taken all his servants with him because he could not do without them, and occupied a whole floor of a leading hotel in London. He seemed to feel this to be quite normal for 'an officer and a gentleman' – after all, his wife was rich.

Now his daughter was to be married and he had to put up the dowry. I could see that he and Suresh, his wife, were anxious and I felt that he was under great pressure from the bridegroom's family to produce a lavish settlement. The daughter, still very young, sat about moping, torn between getting away from Mum and embarking on an almost unseen marriage. There had clearly been some very hard bargaining and an exercise book, crammed with manuscript notes, was being thumbed through by the distraught mother without much cooperation from her daughter. Suresh was exasperated: 'We haven't bought the tea towels,' she cried in despair.

I listened to a description of some of the items of the dowry. Apart from cars, European-style suits had to be produced for a surprising number of male relatives of the bridegroom.

The dowry is the curse of eastern society, although officially it is no longer allowed in India. Families have to save and scrimp for years. My friend certainly had not and was getting to the bottom of his barrel. The birth of a daughter can be regarded as a disaster, yet there is another side to it. If you manage to get your daughter married into an influential family, they could see that you prosper, for nepotism is a way of life too.

In the national newspapers and others, daughters of good family are advertised for marriage in a special column for that purpose. Vital statistics are given and above all a fair complexion is emphasised and that the girl has some educational qualifications. A main topic of conversation among Indian mothers is the constant enquiry after eligible men; in the upper middle classes names and addresses are passed round – rather like hostesses' lists in Edwardian society in England and with the same end in view.

While arranged marriages are the cultural custom of Indian society, it is also the custom that girls move to the families of their husbands, not *vice versa*, but perhaps girls who have grown up in England could never be happy in India. They know what they would be up against, should they transfer. In India, on marriage a girl fits into a precise niche in her husband's family, even if the young couple do not nowadays always live with the family. If she joins an old-fashioned one, the niche may be in a big one-house establishment, incredibly noisy and over-full. In any case she walks into what to us westerners would seem a very difficult life. Even if she is the wife of the eldest son, she has rather less position than you would expect, for over her head loom mother-in-law and possibly some elderly widowed aunts – always disapproving, always expecting to be waited on. Mothers-in-law are not a joke in India. It is a general assumption that they rule their young daughters-in-law with a rod of iron and often with endless nagging. A highly educated and capable Sikh woman once asked Peggy seriously, for she had three young sons herself, whether she did not give her son's wife 'a bad time?' It was quite obviously an accepted attitude, so it is not surprising that so many young couples are breaking away and are trying to loosen the geriatric bonds.

Chapter 13

Bad Language

The Third Journey (1970–71)

We spent the winter of 1969–70 moving house and providing a firm base for the youngest member of the family during his last year at Cambridge, so when we set off in October 1970 our longing to return to India was most insistent. Still in the Hawson we decided to visit Goa, that picturesque mixture of east and west which has the quaint prettiness inherent in Portuguese building, but we did not get very far. Our route from Delhi took us through Gwalior, Nasik and Poona where I had once served, whence we set out for Belgaum. On this stretch I was chiefly conscious of the general lack of colour in the countryside in the dead season of winter and the dust set up by vast herds of scrawny cattle and buffaloes which came out of the towns in the early morning and returned in the evening to the soporific clonk of cowbells. To our western eyes this is very strange, but it stems from the days when the cattle were an easy prey for tiger and even lions, both so plentiful in earlier times that they were regarded as vermin. This forced the herdsmen to seek the safety of the various cities' confines. They still continue to do so, although the two predators, now so scarce, are themselves far more in need of protection in the face of man's innate fear of the wild which lingers on in spite of India's tremendous effort to preserve her natural heritage. In any case, cattle in India do not graze in pastures, but browse in the scrub jungle from which their agile herders chop down every leafy branch from top to bottom. Driving through this dust-covered land the millions of unemployed and under-employed with their terrible poverty in their low shanties seemed to be laid bare to the western traveller's eyes. In the rainy season India clothes her trees in flowers, fruit and foliage and seems thereby to render her people less naked to alien eyes.

After passing through Kohlapur we swung round a corner on the border between Maharasthra and Karnatica, short of Belgaum, and saw a long line of stationary buses with a few policemen standing about. Travelling in the east I try not to close with a crowd but, assuming it was one of the numerous *octroi* barriers where local taxes are taken from commercial vehicles, I drove up. We had to stop because by then there were people all over the road. No sooner had

106

we halted than some of them started swarming up the sloping bonnet of the camper to paste red posters on the windscreen. Others began rocking the vehicle. Realising that the crowd, waving red flags, was not particularly friendly, I felt that drastic action was necessary – and that very quickly. Their next move would be to overturn the caravan and then, having gone so far, to assault the occupants as they scrambled out.

In the early days of our travels I used to take a formidable-looking .45 revolver with me. But as I had no intention of waging war with the people I had come to meet and whom I loved, however exasperating they might be at times, I had had the firing pin removed and so the .45 was merely a threat and no weapon at all. Looking fierce, I drew this threat and pointed it at our assailants, who fell away rapidly. Brandishing it, I cleared the road, and swung the vehicle in a tight U-turn and departed. I roared reproaches out of the window as I wheeled away, and, as so often happened, felt a bit mean as the rows of light brown faces looked crestfallen. They had been having so much 'innocent fun'. I think many damaging riots start comparatively innocuously and only get out of hand as excitement mounts. I had then no idea of the cause they supported though I thought the trouble had perhaps had something to do with a factory we had just passed. I only thanked my stars for the big vehicle's forward control which made it as handy as a saloon.

Still intending to make for Goa, we examined the map and saw a way to by-pass any troubles and get us back to the main road, but this by-pass was a monsoon-scored bullock cart track and almost unmotorable. On and on we went, my anxiety mounting, for as always I feared for the vehicle and on our remote track no form of help could be possible. When I could take my eyes off the ground for a second, I saw men going our way pushing cycles decked with *blue* flags. We passed little knots of 'the Blues' and I thought they looked very cross. We bumped and thumped on and on along the track; it was leading in the wrong direction in spite of the map. While entering a mud-walled village we saw two policemen running as though their lives depended on it. They shouted, 'You've got two minutes to turn round and get out – they're coming!'

Then, far from offering help, they leaped into a jeep and drove off madly. There was I, confined in a narrow place, for the village enclosed us, and 'they' were coming! I tried to turn my unwieldy vehicle round once more, but there was no room. I twirled the steering wheel madly back and forth – yes, I had got the bonnet round four inches. Backward and forward we shunted and more inches were being won, when 'they' swarmed round the corner. 'They' were a large body of men waving clubs and blue flags and still running in their thwarted efforts to seize the policemen. They were all shouting and by the sound of it they were not pleased. With five yards left for them to overwhelm the caravan, I managed to swing clear in the narrow passageway. I felt that the back bumper shrank away from clutching hands as I pulled my tail between my legs.

Having motored some distance to be clear of any stray Blues, I pulled up to reshape our course. The charm of a caravan journey is that one can change plans at a few moments' notice. I then saw that the back of the van was still plastered with red posters, so the Blues would have slaughtered us. Earlier I had removed the posters from the windscreen on getting clear of the Reds. To my annoyance, the rear ones were stuck on with some substance which removed my paint as well.

We decided to go to Mahableshwar, the little hill station above Bombay, which is near Partabgarh, a stronghold of Sivaji, the great Mahratta leader. We stopped for a few days in this pleasant spot and sought a little peace after our adventures. We edged the caravan into a thick strip of the remaining jungle and felt that we would not be discovered by inquisitive local inhabitants. We had come to see India's peoples and learn as much as possible about them, but we had not reckoned with the teeming millions of the present day. So here we were, hiding away in this lovely piece of dense forest – or so we thought. But we heard a giggle and we were soon the victims of bright, prying eyes. Out of the thick, concealing bushes numbers of young girls collected round the car. They were as usual tending cattle which browsed the jungle away to provide a meagre supply of foul-tasting milk from their skeletal bodies. However, the cows had melodious bells which helped the herd girls to keep touch with straying animals. They would not go away, but retreated giggling, their bare feet thumping on the hard-baked soil as they ran from my assumed scowls. Did Krishna pursue such as these? They closed in again, smiling and giggling. There was no shaking them off. Krishna dealt with these *gopis* more effectively than I.

We needed food so we drove to the attractive bazaar and soon found ourselves talking to a nice looking Parsi and his wife who had a Sunbeam Alpine, modified, he said, for rallying. He was fascinated by our home-made Hawson and I was equally interested in the fact that he and his friends were prepared to rally on India's exacting roads in light, imported English cars which must have cost a king's ransom. It was the new 'in' thing in Bombay where they lived.

The Parsis emigrated from Persia (Fars, hence Parsi) some twelve hundred years ago as Zoroastrians to escape Muslim persecution by the invading Arabs who overthrew the Sassanid empire. Few in numbers, their enduring spirit and religion, symbolised by the eternal flame of Zoroaster, enabled them to survive, as many refugees have done – it is the very trials of their exodus that seem to harden them. Later they were protected by the British from more relentless Muslim persecution in India so that there has always been a close affinity between us and this prosperous merchant community who threw in their wealth to help us in both world wars.

Sam and Dinas his wife invited us to a meal in their Parsi hotel. The owner sat at a table overlooking the dining room keeping an eye on it – a very good arrangement that could well be copied in England. How many unusual people one meets in India; and it would take a thousand years to describe them all. Here was sophistication, but the day before we had been among the timeless *gopis* of mythology.

Before we left we had to get a boost to our cholera inoculations – and what a fierce boost you get in India – so we called in at the local health office. Talking to the doctor in charge and probing as usual I asked him about the population explosion, because at that time every mud wall of every village had a crudely executed poster showing two parents and one child, the ideal family represented by an inverted red triangle. Much coveted transistor sets were being given as a reward for those who submitted to vasectomy, thus replacing one menace by an even worse one. The doctor said the operation was often unsuccessfully carried out and patients, not knowing this, failed to come for a check-up. When a patient's wife subsequently became pregnant, it was immediately assumed by her friends and neighbours that she had been promiscuous, so the operation had fallen into disrepute in many quarters. He himself had just been in time to save the local milkman's wife from a beating and total ostracism by intervening and explaining that the milkman was one of those whose vasectomy had failed. He went on to say that mass vasectomy and sketchy hygiene had brought many side effects so the campaign was not going smoothly.

He added that he felt the best way to control the growth of population was to ensure that more children reached a healthy maturity. If parents no longer relied on large numbers of children, only some of whom might survive to look after them in their old age, they would be more ready to attempt serious birth control. The best way to achieve this survival would be in better medical care, but one great difficulty was in educating the predominantly peasant population to break the habit of breast feeding until the next baby arrived and then abruptly transferring the first one onto adult and unsuitable food, which was a recipe for a high mortality rate. There was another increasing menace in the promotion of bottle feeding which had been taken up eagerly by the slightly better off who often failed to observe basic hygiene. Besides this the baby lost the immunisation given by breast feeding, so essential in disease-ridden India.

In parting from the trim little doctor with his crisp, curly grey hair cut in the western style, I felt a glow of happiness that here at least was sanity. It is so characteristic of India that when she is in her most zany mood, you suddenly encounter good common sense.

It was then that we learned about the quarrel between the Blues and the Reds. The central government had decided to re-draw the boundaries between Maharasthra and Karnatica on linguistic lines which was strongly resented by the people on both sides of the original border who regarded each other with hostility. We learned too that we had been in distinguished company as the refugee Dalai Lama had also been held up at that point.

We then decided to move and took the steep road down towards Bombay. I have seldom seen such beauty as that of the forest flower- and creeper-clad slopes as we dropped quickly down Fitzgerald Ghat. We stopped the camper below the fort of Partabgarh and walked up the five hundred steps. There was something special to me about the history of this fort. It was the scene of a strange action by a leader who, although illiterate, had studied the methods of warfare recommended by Kautilya, minister of Chandragupta in India's dim past. Kautilya had maintained that unless a general could be sure of winning in 'open fight', he must use 'treacherous fight' – that is bribery, stirring up factions among the enemy or luring an adversary out of a strong position. Sivaji, leader of the dramatic Mahratta revolt against the Mughals, the hero of folklore and ballads so greatly needed by India to establish her national identity, used these Hindu methods against Muslim overlords.

The action at Partabgarh was not against the Mughals, but early in Sivaji's career against the forces of the independent Turkish/Afghan kingdom of Bijapur which had seized his ancestral lands in an earlier invasion. The motivation of his uprising was initially the regaining of his birthright and it was only later that it expanded into an attack on the Mughal empire.

The fort being held for Sivaji was invested by Afzal Khan, general of Bijapur, with an army some ten thousand strong and far too great for the burgeoning Sivaji to take on in 'open war' as he came to raise the siege. Acting on what he had learnt from the distant Hindu past he set the scene for a deed most dire. He proposed that he and Afzal Khan should meet between their two armies to make terms. They were to be unarmed, wearing only the billowing muslin robes of leisure. They advanced and embraced. Afzal Khan dropped dead, to the horror of his supporters – it was quicker than the sudden silence that ensued.

After their champion fell the Muslims broke ranks in a turmoil of dismay and Sivaji's Mahrattas, though fewer in numbers, cut them to pieces as they ran hither and thither. Afzal Khan's inexplicable death in plain daylight horrified his followers and indeed it was horrifying. Sivaji embraced his opponent and used an unexpected weapon – the *Bagh Nukh*, or tiger's claws: a set of four steel claws attached by rings to the fingers of the *left* hand. Pinioning his enemy with the claws as he embraced him, Sivaji stabbed him with a dagger on a further set of rings on his *right* hand, folded back along his forearm so long as the hand was clenched. All he had to do was to press the dagger in with his open hand. The left hand weapon still exists at Satara, further down the Ghat, together with other treasures and arms belonging to the great Mahratta. His treacherous action was lauded by minstrels in India, but for the John Company the *Bagh Nukh* (mispronounced *Wagh Nakh*) became synonymous with sharp practice.

What was the secret of Sivaji's pre-eminence when so many petty chieftains rose and fell like bubbles in a boiling cauldron? Why were he and his state more durable? I think it was because he departed from the established rule of leadership and control of local rulers' armies in India. In short, he insisted on physical fitness which led to lightweight cavalrymen, lightly loaded – the Mahrattas are small men. They still have a fetish for fitness. I remember seeing remarkable feats of strength and agility carried out on a strange device, the *malkan* pole. This is a long pole with a polished wooden knob at its head. The participants in the exercise climbed, balanced and held themselves at right angles to it: a strange acrobatic routine which followed prescribed forms and needed great physical strength. I have not seen anything of this nature anywhere else.

As far as possible Sivaji paid his men directly and mounted them himself instead of recruiting them on the *sillidar* system. This latter has been given the honorific of feudalism but, knowing India a little, as I think I do, I would regard it as a contractual arrangement whereby men and horses were supplied for an agreed fee by petty chieftains and landowners. The men provided tended to be unprincipled ruffians and their cut price steeds unfit even for the knacker's yard.

He drew his rank and file from the *Sudra* caste: the peasants, whose many sub-divisions did not weld readily in society. Knowing this tendency to fragment, Sivaji disregarded the sub-divisions and treated his men equally as a whole. It worked so long as they were in his army and there were no discrepancies over pay through unscrupulous officers. He preferred to collect funds through centrally controlled tribute, rather than in scattered loot which always leads to squabbles. He put his fist firmly on the lid of the money box.

Sivaji was unique. His successors quickly degenerated and power was seized from them by their ministers, the Peshwas. The Mahrattas continued to play a part in India, but more as brigands than liberators and were eventually cut down to size by the British under General Lake. Modern India hails Sivaji as the first 'freedom fighter' against the alien Mughal rule. This is perhaps overstating the case, but the movement that began as a fight for personal rights did with success inevitably develop into an attempt to establish a Hindu kingdom, based on Maharashtra. Heady success impelled Sivaji to take on Aurungzeb, the emperor. I would not, however, regard him as a liberator of India. He was fighting against Indians, some of whom were also Mahrattas and he had Muslims and men from other parts of the land in his own ranks. I am sure he was trying to establish a Hindu state of Maharashtra in opposition to the Mughal empire which had emanated from Kabul, but I do not think he had any vision of India as a national whole. The idea that he was the first nationalist is a little hard to substantiate. We British tend to regard the sub-continent as a whole – it seldom was.

Peggy and I fought shy of going into vastly expanded and horribly crowded Bombay, perhaps the most modern and progressive city in India, where you must now boil your drinking water for twenty minutes before it is safe, because the city has thrust up into the twentieth century with all endeavour directed towards the sky, not downwards, so that a proper city-wide sewage system does not exist. Cancerous high-rises face the Arabian Sea standing in their own

ordure, for the buildings drain into their own gimcrack soak-pits. This horror
has long been apparent in Teheran, another brash city, and is now appearing in
New Delhi. In the latter fair city it is hard to keep one's vehicle on a straight
course when driving past the Golf Colony, so solid is the bludgeon of stench
that comes in from the left as I take my chance in a big caravan down the Lodi
Road, and yet the Golf Colony is the abode of the rich and successful.

We skirted Bombay on the north, making for Ahmedabad where we wanted
to see the famous Sidi Sayd mosques and shrines with their quivering minarets
and beautiful perforated stonework. I am a bad man at viewing dry masonry in a
warm climate and I fear all too soon my thoughts turned to iced beer. The *jali*
work was a wonder of fine stone carving, but rather hard to find and I felt we
had seen finer in Jaipur. The best has been looted out of Ahmedabad and is in
England in the Victoria and Albert Museum. Murray's otherwise splendid
handbook and the indomitable Fodor describe old buildings in hyperbole, so the
dingy reality is disappointing. They have scales before their eyes. The real
wonders of India are magical, evanescent, not of stone and hard to pin down,
but the magic is there, it is there!

In a teeming eastern city I felt we must base ourselves on a hotel or be
swarmed over. It took us a long time to find one through the narrow, winding
streets. In India if you ask for directions you will never get a clear answer.
Usually the man from whom you enquire will wave a limp hand vaguely down
the way in which the vehicle is already pointing, as the underlying attitude is a
reluctance to undertake a new and lengthy description. The feeling is: it's all
too hot and I haven't had a square meal for a week anyway; and at the same
time he is too polite to say that you are going wrong. Presumably you'll get
there somehow. So we got ourselves in a thick traffic congealment with high,
foetid tenements on all sides. The impasse was caused by a Muslim funeral and
we had unwittingly thrust our bonnet into this sad occasion. I thought wildly
that this was the sort of incident when the crowd gets nasty with the beastly
foreigner. In any case, Ahmedabad is always a flashpoint. A Hindu pig has but
to grunt to start a Muslim over-reaction. If the Muslims won't provide a
provocation, the Hindus start hitting out at each other in disputes over caste
rights. After all, Gandhi preached civil disobedience on the banks of the river.

I salaamed reverently towards the corpse borne on high and doffed my hat.
To my relief, all was smiles. Great pains were taken to clear the throng to
enable me to get the caravan free – the passage of the car was momentarily
more important than that of the bier: just another example of Indians' wonderful tolerance in a sea of intolerance, for they can be warmly understanding to
foreigners in spite of the xenophobic abuse in their papers.

We found the best hotel at last – a sad and scruffy place with a depressing
dining room. Of all colours it was painted dark blue, ceiling included. We
squeezed the caravan into the forecourt garden among neglected flowerbeds of
hot-coloured marigolds – sacred and much beloved. I am always sensitive to

bright colours and these indomitable little flowers cheered me up. And now for a cold drink, for I had not by then learnt to fight shy of India's beer which was preserved with glycerine – death to one's liver. No, there was no beer, but there was a strike – yes, of all the hotel servants; we might have been in England. One of them on the steps came up to the car and pushed a pamphlet through my window. Hot and tired, I angrily crushed it into a ball and threw it back. I regretted my temper, for pay in India is only one point above starvation and he must have hoped to see a helper in me.

We hired a taxi and the hotel provided a very good guide who brushed aside the mosques and their pure carving as 'those empty old buildings,' and showed us with enormous pride, square austere block after block of government offices and other municipal developments. Such was his pride that we played along with him. It was clear that the capital of Gujarat, the centre of the Marwaris, was prospering and there were people here who, together with the wealthy Parsis of Bombay, were go-ahead in a country where lethargy and graft so often prevail. I felt encouraged for here India which I love was not just a tottering scabrous giant.

The drive up from Bombay had been through pretty, sylvan country for the most part, but the road hit back at my van. India suffers much damage to her roads in the monsoon and has little or no plant with which to repair them, but she has ant-like millions to take its place. On this road stones were brought up by slow bullock carts from a neighbouring river bed and broken up by hand for metal. The fetching, carrying and spreading were done by women, who as usual were taking on the heavier tasks. Often they were mothers with small babies, dumped bare-bottomed on the sharp stone chippings. There they learned early to suffer discomfort as they sat uncomplainingly playing with sticks for toys. Looking down at times I felt touched as they looked up at me with sloe eyes, lovingly encircled with *kohl*.

Tar was being heated over a stick fire under a standard-sized barrel whose upper side had been torn open so that garden watering cans could be dipped into this hot, bituminous cauldron. The tar was then 'watered' through a flattened spout over the macadamized surface of the road. Before it was quite cool, more women with their delicate hands spread it smoothly with a swimming motion to make a strangely patterned surface. Much of India's arterial system is still kept going in this way. So slow is the process that the road would be ready just in time to be steadily eroded in the next monsoon. It is a wonder that India keeps communications going at all and is able to attain a semblance of a coherent whole, a whole that is still underpinned by the far-sighted British railway system. Before that it never was a whole. Not even the Moghuls could subjugate the entire country with communications regularly destroyed by the monsoon.

I noticed that the labour force took time off to sit round a *hookah*, that most companionable of pipes, and that tea was brewed whenever stocks allowed. The coolies in their countless numbers cannot be driven beyond a series of short spells of work. They simply do not get the calories to supply the energy. This did not deter their gang leader from standing on a mound of chippings and hurling continuous exhortations upon the bent backs below him – exhortations that increased in force when his superiors approached. But I could see it was all invective that bounced off the heedless bowed bodies, who had not the stomach to go faster.

There were times when I felt that touring India by car was too rough going, for no car springs could insulate us from hour after hour of pounding from potholes, which robbed us of the zest we had had for exploration. In spite of this we had been to Ellora, Ajanta, Hampi and Sanchi among others – places described far better in tourist guides. Unfortunately the wonders are far distant from each other and we found it a tremendous slog. It is clearly better to use internal air services, but although you may have booked your place on a plane, you will have to fight your way on board. I often considered putting an end to it, longing for some deep jungle bower away from banks of inquisitive crowds. One only had to try and buy a dozen oranges for hundreds of villagers to collect. They were friendly, but they would chatter and giggle so that it was difficult to make oneself heard and I felt the inert weight of India's millions who had nothing else to do. I once actually paid for some oranges with a note passed under a camel's belly whose owner had come up to join the fun.

We then set our course for the Jain temples of Dilwara, high up on Mount Abu, and were at last climbing up into the coolness. Mount Abu is an abrupt, freak mountain rising nearly four thousand feet out of the lower scatter of the Arawali Hills. It is really a four thousand foot pillar of rock with vegetation clinging precariously to it. It has not great breadth or depth and a short walk in any direction will take you to a precipice, but there is something fairy-like in the ascent through the beautiful tree-clad slopes with here and there a rocky bluff with steep precipitous sides. It was once the hill station for the government of Bombay and there are the remains of the nineteenth century barracks and a small cemetery where Honoria, the wife of Sir Henry Lawrence, lies buried.

I have always been interested in the Jain sect who believe that everything alive has a soul, even an insect – and why not? But whole books can be written about this ancient belief which was founded at about the same time as the movement started by the Buddha in the seventh century BC. The Jain priests wear a muslin band across nose and mouth for fear of breathing in and destroying even a gnat.

For once, I was not disappointed on entering the temples, for the marble carving is magnificent. It is cut out behind to give it the translucency of alabaster and the detail is so fine that none but a dedicated craftsman could have given his creation the time and patience. The story is that each man worked on a separate panel and received a bonus in silver equalling the weight of marble chippings he removed by back-cutting and hence the dedication.

In order to go in we were made to take off our shoes and other leather had also to be discarded. We said to each other that we would have to burn our socks after a tour round the 'usual' eastern temple. How wrong we were and we felt hardly clean enough ourselves as we watched the acolytes compulsively sweeping the floors. Everything was spotless: not an ant should remain to be crushed under foot. The Jains certainly make things very difficult for themselves in grubby India.

An acolyte advanced to place a holy mark on my forehead as he had done to other tourists, but I waved him aside. I felt afterwards that this gesture of mine had struck a jarring note in this abode of peace – it was a meeting of religions and a place of no religions.

In each elaborately carved niche was an image seated cross-legged, almost Buddhist in appearance. These figures, known as Jinas, have staring eyes with much white showing round the irises, and I felt that they had become very stylized. But on leaving the temples I saw a little boy with eyes and features exactly like the Jinas: perhaps a real case of 'nature imitating art'?

Later, we sought lunch and were directed to the Bikaner Palace Hotel. The building was one of the palaces used in former times by the Rajput warrior princes who sought relief from the hot plains here in the summer. Some of these buildings are castles out of fairyland. One of a rather lurid pink is a mass of weird turrets and arches: perhaps Rapunzel lives there still? We ordered a curry lunch, for there were no other guests and by the generally seedy appearance of the place, business was poor. The lunch was excellent and while it was being prepared we toured the dark, gloomy rooms where furniture had been stacked hugger mugger. The dimly lit walls were covered with photographs of hunting trophies, dominated by the tall, princely figure of the former Maharaja of Bikaner. Why do big game hunters always put a foot on the dead quarry? Haven't they violated it enough, or is it the ultimate act of triumph? There must have been photographic records of hundreds of splendid tigers. What a waste of such magnificence, but India's dwindling habitat could hardly support them all now. There was no other form of picture.

We asked the manager, a trim ex-engineer of the Royal Indian Navy, if he could recommend anywhere we could camp, for on the way up we had found the old military cantonment shabby and depressing. He suggested a little wild life sanctuary at the very top of this pillar of a mountain and there we found an excellent parking place under a banyan tree below a little *bund* (dam) containing a rocky pool of about two acres in extent. On the *bund* there was a small gazebo with *jali* windows and a plaque stating, 'For the recreation of my princely friends and other gentlemen.' Below this was the name of some petty rajah. It was a place of sheer peace and we walked about the little sanctuary, but saw no animals, for there were none. But the great, round black rocks, a feature of much of India, and the cactus and flowering shrubs had an aura of enchantment.

We had been alone for a day or so when we were visited by a party of youths, resplendent in voluminous, cerise-coloured turbans and clean white clothes, with gold rings in their ears. They had carried heavy cans of milk up the steep slopes for some twenty miles, sold them in the bazaar and then done a day's work for the Forestry Department. Having thoroughly inspected the caravan, which they told us they had passed in the early morning while it was still dark and we were asleep, they boiled a kettle on a twig fire and began to make a sort of tea with leaves they picked green from a bush. We offered them a packet of our tea and some biscuits, and they told us they were returning by the same route to their distant village, taking only a short pause before beginning this long walk. I was full of admiration, as always, for the hardiness of the yeoman farmer and liked their handsome, light russet-skinned faces. We went on talking and they asked whence I came and remarked that their fathers had said that the British times were better than the present ones. They asked, 'Will you not come back?'

I said, 'No,' and felt sad, but pointed out as usual that things looked at from afar assumed a rosy aura, though I had little inner conviction.

Chapter 14

The Terai Conquered

On our third journey (1970–71)

After we left Rajasthan and Gujerat we decided to spend the rest of the winter in Corbett National Wild Life Park which we had briefly visited on our two previous journeys when we had fallen in love with the place. I have never felt so happy as when wandering in Indian jungles. I always remember motoring through them as a child in my father's old Model-T Ford and I had so much wanted Peggy to see them. As a child she had been mostly in Simla. With this end in view we took up a long-standing invitation and turned off short of Ramnager in Uttar Pradesh, the base town for the Park, to visit the Puris. The quiet Park and its animals called us onward, but we liked Bani Puri with whom we shared a common love of fishing and bird life, so after meeting him in Delhi we took up this chance of getting to know the more sophisticated youth of India – a chance I should not miss.

As so often happens things did not go smoothly. We had the greatest difficulty in finding the farm and so failed to arrive in a relaxed frame of mind. The Puris preferred to have no sign on the main road for fear of molestation and robbery and it was at the height of the campaign to abolish the use of English in the province in favour of Hindi, so signboards written in English had been smashed by enthusiastic reformers. Although we moved backwards and forwards up and down the road none of the locals seemed to know, or would tell us, where the Puris lived. At last we followed a rough track and in the distance saw the house, but the camper's paint was hideously scratched by a narrow avenue of blossoming peach trees. This was the last straw after a journey over a main road which could have been designed for a motor-cross rally. We were met by two very shabbily dressed old people and thought they belonged to the usual collection of servants. I was, I fear, a little testy for our hosts had clearly not preceded us from Delhi as arranged and I was anxious to clean the vehicle and change into fresh clothes.

The couple were shocked at our efforts to fetch water. 'The servants will do that,' they cried, but I have found to my cost that Indian servants are rough with car paint, so I declined, perhaps shortly. It gradually dawned on us that the couple were our hosts' parents, now a little miffed, though I must say in self-justification that Bani, their son, had never told us that his parents lived there when inviting us. They were no more shabby than I am when I garden. My fault but, as is so common in India, no warning of our arrival had preceded us and we appeared as surly interlopers.

Dr Puri, once of the WHO, was then over seventy and was to live on, I am happy to say, to a great age. Bani's mother, was the driving force. It was she who had organised the clearing of their land, but her personality made the atmosphere uneasy. Bani and his wife Apu were very handsome and had not, as is so often the case with the Indian well-to-do, degenerated into fat. Her jet black hair, swept back into a large bun, accentuated her long, slender neck. Her mother-in-law had completely taken over the small granddaughter and Apu was not allowed any normal contact. This hyper-possessiveness by grandparents is all too frequent in India – perhaps to compensate for advancing age. We felt she did not like us, which is not surprising under the circumstances. Returning another year we found that poor grandmother had died of a mixture of heart trouble and diabetes, the two modern killers in India – probably due to lack of physical exercise and a high animal fat diet in the shape of the *ghi* (clarified butter) used so lavishly in cooking, exacerbated among men by chain smoking. Though a vegetarian, like so many, Mrs Puri ate clarified butter in many forms including sweetmeats. When we saw Apu that year she had her child back and was much more relaxed.

Bani and Apu's marriage had been an arranged one. I was a little surprised, though, when they said they were in favour of such marriages, for they were rather modern in general outlook and, for what it is worth, Europeanised. Bani had been educated at the Doon School, India's 'Harrow', founded by the British with British masters. At least they had been allowed to meet before marrying and there is always an understanding that either party can opt out. To do so, however, would cause quite an upset as Indian marriages are really most practical, if mundane, being based, as I have said, on an accompanying strong business contract for future security. To have broken off would have caused ill feeling between the families since a large number of prior arrangements including the fixing of the dowry and a lot of careful planning would have gone for nothing. Both parties have to be of the same caste and social background and in this case mother-in-law was very religious and spent much time visiting shrines, so I am sure there was an intricate web of horoscopes and omens behind everything. Apu confided to Peggy that she was terrified at the first formal meeting, fearing that Bani would not like her – what an ordeal for a girl, any girl! I felt her fears had little foundation, as she was both beautiful and sensible and she and Bani made a most handsome, happy couple.

The Puris had other visitors as well and my heart failed me. Staying with Indian friends is always difficult. They do things at a slower, rather haphazard tempo, and you never know what is going to happen next. Bani was very proud of the house which they had just had built – so far removed from their original pioneers' shack. It was architect-designed in fired brick and would have fitted in anywhere along England's south coast. Naturally we made haste to praise it, but the house was already as full as was tolerable. The other guests were a Sikh garage owner and his family of wife, son and a large, not ill-favoured, blonde Scottish daughter-in-law. The wife was immensely fat and never moved from her chair. Not unnaturally, she complained of ill health and was as hostile as Bani's mother. I think she and her husband were a little irked to find that other, equally favoured, guests had arrived before them.

The son, a schoolmaster, recently dismissed from the Doon School by the English Headmaster and smarting under it, was a pain in the neck. He was called Cuckoo – the name speaks for itself, but apparently pleased his fond parents. As a history graduate of Edinburgh University he took a great deal of trouble to read passages to us out of some book running down the achievements of the British in India that maintained that they had left no mark on the country. I forebore to get dragged into an argument, although much of the book out of which he declaimed was pure gibberish. I did, however, point out mildly that at least we had left red pillar boxes everywhere behind us. I could have embarked on a long description of how the British had brought India into the twentieth century and had made the country into a coherent whole, mainly by linking the far corners by the efficient railway system and by establishing a uniform system of law and administration, a postal system cheaply available to everyone, a valid currency, an organised police force, a national army and so on and so on. To crown it all we had moved out graciously leaving her all these assets as well as splendid buildings.

What sort of life would his Scottish wife have, for women's lib. had not gone far in India? Luckily for her, her fairness was of the kind much sought after among Indians who like to introduce a light skinned strain into the family if they can and as she was very stolid she looked as if she could absorb much punishment. When she appeared for the evening meal dressed tawdrily in what she must have believed to be the correct wear for perhaps the King's Road her big blondeness drew a whispered 'Wah' Wah'' of admiration from round the room. Fair is high-class Aryan, dark is low caste, but I was unable to understand a word of the girl's broad Scots accent, though Cuckoo's indifferent English was comprehensible. The party was talking the usual unconscious mixture of English and Hindi known as *Kitcheri*, but I still couldn't get on a level amicable keel.

We went on a well organised picnic. The food was good, but we all sat on chairs at a table brought out by the watchman of the Forest Resthouse where we had stopped above a great gorge, looked into by rough-barked evergreens with a pretty little temple at our feet – they could or would not say what god it served, but it was very holy. It had the unexpected charm one so often finds in India, perched as it was on a narrow plinth cut out on either side by a stream. I felt that the priest tinkling a bell in the hope of alms would dislodge the whole into the stream below if he rang too hard.

The Puris' servants served and it was all rather artificial. The Sikh father, when replete, cast himself down on the hard ground in his dark town suit, all amongst the feet of the rest of us and the chair legs and dropped off to sleep immediately. Conversation was difficult – he snored so loudly.

He did not like the British either – many Sikhs do not. Others, for they are astute traders and fine soldiers, have mixed with us and there can be a close rapport. This Sikh complained to me that on Partition the British had let the Sikhs down. Sikhs certainly feel that they were owed a debt by us for they sided with us in the Mutiny. What could I say? I had always felt that the Partition of India ninety years later had come far too precipitately. It had been bedevilled by widespread slaughter and suffering and was a botched-up job. I replied that on passing through Pakistan the Pakistanis had said to me that Partition was unfair to them. On entering India, Indians had said it, and now the Sikhs said so too. I suggested that as all had equally criticised the British, they must clearly have hit on a fair middle way! He ground his teeth and loured.

I felt some satisfaction at my adroit riposte – how often have I had the perfect answer, but hours after the event. Later my thoughts were tinged with regret at my levity. The problem was his, not mine. I was just a visitor, he had to live with it. These outstanding people felt we owed them a debt and yet we had cut their lands asunder: about sixty per cent to India and forty to Pakistan. We had ignored the fact that the Sikhs regarded the five rivers of the Punjab as their own property in an undeveloped desert that they had turned into India's great granary and that control of the waters had been handed over to two central governments. The Partition was the signal for the bloody exodus of hoards of frightened people across the new border. The slaughter of Muslim, Sikh and Hindu had been played down but I have had it at first hand from friends in the former Indian army after it had itself been split between India and Pakistan who were trying to keep order in 1947, that the death toll was far greater than has ever been admitted.

I have met so many people north and south of the Partition line who crossed over, leaving their lands and businesses behind, to face destitution. The old hatred between Hindu and Muslim would not have broken out in such widespread violence, but for the years of propaganda and counter-propaganda by the Muslim League and the Congress party – all exacerbated by the very suddenness of the Partition, the volatile nature of the people and the general feeling of insecurity. Although there was much hatred fanned by fear and widespread slaughter, this was not always the case. One of my friends told me that when the Muslims had to leave his Hindu village south of the new border, the Hindu elders lined the road to bid them farewell and helped them to carry their baggage to the distant railway station. They were all in tears. So many others too have told me of this sorrow on parting.

The challenge has often brought out the best in the refugees. Numbers of the people I have met are more prosperous now than before and the Puris also were refugees and had succeeded in an area torn from the teeming and malarious Terai (high water-table jungle) – an area once deemed too unhealthy to live in. Other farmers in the Terai told me that tigers were so common in this thick belt of jungle which their parents were clearing that when they were small they vied with each other to sleep in mother's bed as they were terrified by the roaring. The hut in which the Puris first lived was frequently attacked by wild elephants, who were not necessarily attacking men, but were light-fingered, or should I say light-trunked, in search of titbits. No one in the area realised that to clear this jungle was to bring about the near extinction of elephants and tigers through the loss of their habitat. The Terai had provided such a large reserve of game that there was a comfortable feeling that it was inexhaustible. It was a shock to find that the animals had gone for ever in the space of a few years.

Animals or no, the Puris had hacked out their farm and were prospering with cash crops and herbal pharmaceutical oils. They had little encouragement to grow staples as Indira Gandhi was trying at the time to split all farms up into little plots, unworkable by tractor. Like so many refugees, they had been given a really large farm area by the central government, who perhaps cynically thought that they would make no more of this land than all those who had gone before and that they would succumb to the malaria mosquito and so no longer be a problem. By the time of our visit, the Uttar Pradesh government was bringing pressure to bear on these former refugees to break up the prosperous farms, which were far larger than would originally have been allotted by the provincial authorities. The Puris who were parcelling their land out, if in name only, to many close relatives, had apparently survived governmental interference and still do. Mrs Gandhi's aim of settling untouchables on land obtained from farmers has not succeeded everywhere. There was naturally a tendency for them, lacking any influence in the area, to be allotted the poorest soil that had not been worked before, too far from irrigation and too hard to be ploughed by oxen which were in any case too costly for them. Now, many keep small herds of pigs on their inhospitable plots, tended by a member of the family, and continue to seek service in the more unpleasant jobs of house sanitation or leather tanning, so that they are only marginally better off, though they can now proudly say they are landowners. Even a dry briar patch has given them some little status and a few handfuls of Mother India's dust to make them feel that at least they are part of her, not entirely outcast. But this does not really amount to very much and the cruel grip of the caste system on the lower orders causes much suffering. The palliatives of the central government have been able to do little to improve India's image. It cannot destroy the caste system – an apartheid far more fundamental than that of South Africa.

We visited our hosts' cousins in neighbouring houses. They were all charming but their chief interest appeared to be playing cards, which they loved. I hate cards when there is beautiful sunshine outside, turning the eucalyptus windbreak to blue steel. The game, unfamiliar to us, had something in it of poker which I had been forced to play out of sheer boredom in Burma during the war. As hand after hand was dealt we began in all our innocence and with the help of a cousin or uncle to win quite a pile of banknotes, protesting truthfully that we didn't know how to play. The game ended and the Sikh father slapped down notes and said scowling that he did not mind losing at cards. Next day the same thing happened, only more so, but the party decided much to our relief and at our suggestion to waive the money!

The night which should have been so peaceful, deep in dear India's bosom, was rent by a banshee-like yell every twenty minutes. This was only the night watchman, just to show he was watchful, for burglary is even worse than in England. In New Delhi householders subscribe to a Night Watch who patrol the neighbourhood in the suburbs all through the dark, tapping staves and blowing whistles. Why don't we do it in England? It is so comforting in the small hours.

Dr Puri's driving was something to experience when we went as part of our entertainment to Ramnagar's famous sweet stall. He just charged about in the narrow street as if he thought the lower castes expendable. Mere pedestrians and a quite respectable minor clerk jumped for the high pavement, the latter displaying yards of skinny brown leg from his flapping *dhoti*. His face was venomous, his eyes glared through pebble-lensed, tin spectacles and his bad, bloody *pan*-juiced teeth snarled. Surprisingly we arrived at the stall all in one piece.

Best of all the sweets were the *jellabies*, which are fine coils of tubular, golden dough boiled in thick syrup. With a practised wave the shopkeeper drove off a black garnishing of flies to reveal the feast below. We protested some indisposition to refuse the banks of sweets. Our hosts and the Scots wife ate freely; you can achieve immunity in time – if you live long enough. The Sikh garage owner seized the opportunity to get his car serviced cheaply while the rest of the party hung about for hours and hours, munching sweets in the narrow, malodorous street. I could not understand why his own garage had not set up the boss's car for his rural weekend. Such patient waiting is a feature of India, though it was torture to me, just hanging about and doing nothing.

Next day we left the farm for Corbett Park and as we drove towards it I thought about this visit. I had been prepared to make it a happy one but I found myself quite unable to relate to these nice Indians. If I criticise them I must criticise myself. I had arrived in high hopes of cementing friendship with a country and people I loved, but felt I was too regimented and they were too relaxed for us to mix easily. I am intensely proud of the record of the British in India and all their efforts, so that to find it was all lost made me jealous. In spite of this we always remained in friendly contact with the family.

In the clear daylight we could see some of the highest Himalayas as a serene backdrop to the flat fields stiff with sugar cane and bright with mustard: the same mountains at which I had gazed as a small boy from the hill station of Ranikhet (Queen's Field) so long, long ago. Parts of India have stolen my heart for ever and I find little solace on our foggy shores.

Chapter 15

'To Be a Pilgrim'

Our Third Journey Home (Spring 1971)

We spent the rest of the winter in the Park, walking soft-footed to love and forge some link with the wild animals, but the time was all too short as we had to go home on account of our half-yearly care of my mother. At least I could tell her stories of the Queen's Field (Rhanikhet) and other places she had known and loved so well. I knew though that to travel early in March, before the optimum season which I was beginning to discover, was to take a considerable risk because of snow and, worse still, the pack ice in the high mountain passes of Iran and Turkey. The professionals had snow chains, but were not free from total disaster as the ribs of wrecked monsters proved, lying wheels up and twisted, down some chasm thousands of feet below the road. They would certainly be barging about and packing the snow into ice with their weight. Chains were useless to me. Who would hang up a hank of rusty metal in his elegant little flowered-curtain living box just for a few days' emergency? Repairs done in those high mountains had already suggested to me that to put chains on at that altitude would be to die of cold. The bottom of a vehicle sucks in any icy draught as you lie under it in the snow.

All went well till we got to Islam Qila, the Afghan border post where the inevitable official delay assumed a strange form. It was so cold that the customs officer was in a coma, crouched over the dying coals of a sulky *bokhari* into which he gazed with a drawn, sad face. I saw in him the epitome of Afghan pride trying to transcend near-starvation. I prodded him from time to time. 'What about our forms?' I asked gently. At last he heard me and dealt with them, but said, 'You can't go, anyway!' and pointed down the road to a gorgeously ornate truck which had blocked the one and only exit to Iran and all stations beyond, having foundered askew in the snow across the narrow track. It looked like an old, beshawled, childhood memory of a drunken hag with her bonnet awry. My nature demands that I press on, so I put the handy Hawson at the mud lip of a half-frozen irrigation canal beside it. Up went the bonnet and for a sickening moment we teetered over the ridge like a see-saw, and then the front wheels banged down and we were across.

124

There were other trials ahead driving through snowy uplands. Knowing that the Bojnourd Passes lay between Meshed and the long fall down to the Caspian, I enquired from the owner of the petrol station near the airport, for there was no one else to ask, if the passes were yet motorable since on our last journey home in the spring of 1969 we had turned sharp left for Teheran, between the Elburz and the Salt Desert, through Nishapur, Omar Khayyam's burial place, to avoid the snow.

> Dust into Dust, and under Dust to lie,
> Sans Wine, sans Song, sans Singer and sans End!

> *Omar Khayyam (d.1022 or 32): trans*
> *E. Fitzgerald.*

Omar Khayyam's tomb, Nishapur.

I knew this roundabout route would be free, but the road was so bad that medicine bottle tops undid themselves with the vibration, and camera screws came out. The proprietor breezily said it must be OK because the first of the pilgrim buses were beginning to come through. That was the best answer I could get and, I thought, a good one.

So, bonnet down, I made for Bojnourd direct, not without a little sinking feeling in my stomach because some of the gradients in the passes beyond were as steep as a wall and with that irritating potholed approach which prevents one from making a good run at them. We filled up in the cramped yard of the petrol station at Bojnourd town just before the first pass and my heart quailed as I looked up at it as it lay immediately ahead under thick snow. However, there were tracks of many cars so I pulled out and started the long ascent against a darkening sky. We were nearly over the first stage when we met a total block of snow. The labourers clearing it said we could get through in the morning and the snow-plough was working far, far up above. So we had to return to the town, since darkness was coming on and it was getting colder and colder.

I edged into the narrow petrol yard since I knew from previous experience that the police didn't allow casual parking in the town itself. We were joined by other vehicles, including one of those cigar-box shaped Mercedes saloons. Its owner set about sticking layers of newspaper inside all the glass – clearly he was a survivor – and he settled down miserably for the night. I invited him into the caravan where we had a Tilley stove which was just tipping the scales against internal frost and offered him piping hot soup off our cooker. He turned out to be a Filipino band leader who had spent a season in Kabul at little profit and was now bound for England where, he said, he had heard he would be welcomed with open arms. He was a delightful companion and we pressed him to stay to supper, after which he retired behind his newspaper curtains to suffer out the night till the pass should open.

I woke to the rumble of vehicles coming thump, bump, down into Bojnourd and found that the Mercedes had departed without so much as a toot. I said he was a survivor but I hate someone going one better than me!

We set out ourselves and made tolerable progress, but as we approached an intermediary crest we were forced to make room for a heavy lorry coming downhill much too fast – no right of way here: might was right. In making room I got my wheels into the soft snow of the verge. I could not avoid it and was unable to get moving again. A broad bus following us could not get past and the driver was extremely huffy for he had a schedule to keep even under these conditions. I reasoned with him and explained that neither of us was likely to get anywhere if he didn't turn out his passengers to give me a push. He saw the sense of this and bundled them out before they had time to object. They pushed us back into the middle of the road and we carried on ahead of the bus. It tried to get by where the road was a little wider but, mindful of the reserve of manpower behind me, I failed to give way.

At last we reached the highest point of the passes with the wind playing on the packed ice to make the road as slippery as soap. Zig-zagging fearfully I topped the crest and there, just below me, was a bevy of fat buses, bunched like a herd of anxious musk-oxen at bay, their headlamps looking like apprehensive eyes, to block the road on the further side. It is the universal habit on these roads that if something sticks others will try and squeeze past only to stick themselves and form an even greater obstacle for everybody. The vehicles were only a hundred yards from the crest, but their wheels could not grip. This was infuriating. Walking up to them I saw the occupants, the women shrouded in modest *chadurs* and the men in city suits, sitting miserable and supine. They had paid for the trip and therefore the bus had to get them through, though by what means was no concern of theirs. Remembering our reserve of hearties in the bus behind me, I tumbled them out, though they came reluctantly. City gentlemen don't soil their hands. How the oncoming buses got over was no concern of theirs either. By boarding and haranguing the other buses I got their male occupants out too to push and inch by inch we got bus after bus over the top. As is the custom of the east they called in a regular chant upon God and mythological giants to come to their help. I too took up the popular cry, calling upon Allah because I felt connections were good with nearby Meshed, the goal of their pilgrimage.

As they saw the end of their predicament they congratulated me excessively and thumped me on the back, but when I saw out of the corner of my eye that I had achieved the object of my efforts – a caravan-sized gap in the huddle, I leapt up into my cab and drove quickly through. Even the hosts of Islam could scarce forbear to cheer, though they were a little surprised at my sudden desertion.

Chapter 16

Bother on the Border

Our Fourth Journey (1971–2)

Our next journey was in the big truck caravan which I designed and had built for me. We planned to spend the whole winter in Corbett Park, which gave us all we could desire, having had our fill of bumpy roads. We left home in October 1971, although there was news of mounting tension between India and Pakistan over the struggle in Bangladesh, then East Pakistan. On our reaching Peshawar it was obvious to us that war might break out between the two states very shortly. We remained there for three weeks hoping that the situation would clear up, Then, when it seemed almost certain that there would be war, I talked things over with Peggy, feeling terribly responsible for her. She was eager to continue the journey for she said that we had come so far, it would be a pity to turn back and I thought of the threat of gathering snow behind us. So we started for the border, motoring fast, and crossed the Attock Bridge once more. In Islamabad we got our passes to cross to India with unusual ease; everyone seemed rather distrait and a Secretary murmured that it would be then or never.

We pushed on to Lahore which we reached that evening, driving through the much beloved, eroded Salt Ranges on our way. *Shisham* trees along this hot road provided some shade and at intervals natural halting places had been created by planting banyan trees whose spread of aerial roots had gradually embraced a quite big area in which tired travellers could rest, often by a small spring. Obviously someone had had some sense in the past.

Next day, as was then the rule, we crossed the border into India at Husseiniwalla, well to the west of the old Grand Trunk Road through Amritsar, which had been closed for many years. Once in India we were routed round Ferozepore through which we had been accustomed to travel; it was obvious that there was a considerable body of troops there near the Pakistan frontier. We had seen none in Pakistan, but had been told that the armour had left Nowshera a couple of days before, moving fast southwards.

After we arrived in Delhi there were rumours of impending air raids and there was a good deal of confusion, since war had not actually been declared. We had got over with only hours to spare. When sirens went off that evening there was a general panic. Cars showing too much light were slashed at by the crowds, using staves. We could see it all from a high balcony in the Ashoka Hotel where we were enjoying our usual two days' relief from caravanning. No planes ever showed up, but everyone was obviously enjoying delicious thrills of fright. Disliking this general atmosphere of hysteria we stocked up with stores as quickly as we could and set off eastwards along the bumpy road to Corbett Park, through Moradabad, Kashipur and Ramnagar, keeping a look out for the serene snows high above the Terai. How cool and welcoming was the jungle after all the turmoil. I always relaxed with a sigh as it closed behind me in a leafy embrace, for I had come home.

We spent the winter as we had planned – fishing, bird watching, encountering the occasional tiger and studying wild elephants on our long walks in the *sal* glades. For the first few weeks we had the Park to ourselves because of the war and our welcome was warm in acknowledgement of our effort to get there through thick and thin. But it was not an entirely idyllic existence because we were anxious about being cut off. We had achieved perfection, but this is forbidden fruit and anxiety nagged daily with an insistent little voice. If we could not take the vehicle out of India after six months we might have to pay a swingeing indemnity or get a six months' extension on our carnet: an extension that was not readily granted, for the Indian customs did not really understand caravan tourists and made hard conditions.

Before we left Delhi we had arranged with the Consul at our High Commission to let us know if the road home was to be re-opened. We took particular pains to emphasise that we would regard it as a special favour, somewhat beyond his usual brief. He answered with a smile that it would be no trouble to him at all. At the end of the winter's stay we learnt through a stray remark from a new arrival to the Park that the border was to be opened for one day only, towards the end of March, to let stranded caravanners across; no message however had come from the Consul. Hurrying back to Delhi, we checked with him to see if any papers or documents were necessary, for eastern borders are paper-crazy. He told us that there were no formalities: 'You just cross, old boy!'

As there was only one day on which to cross, the next day, and it was already late, we hurried northwards. Spending a hot, mosquito-bitten night on the edge of the factory area of Ludhiana – and how it smelt – we reached the border early next morning at Attari beyond Amritsar, a newly appointed crossing place on the old Grand Trunk Road.

We were stopped short of the border at a barrier and were told we were not on the list of those allowed to cross. This was the first we had heard of this list. There had apparently been an announcement in the papers by the Swiss embassy telling all would-be travellers to register with them. They were in charge of proceedings, acting for Pakistan; and the announcement had presumably not been noticed by the Consul. All in all he had not been of much help; in my long experience consuls seldom are.

Our way was barred by officials of the Defence Ministry and when I asked them if there was to be another crossing day, they said happily that they had no idea. There was a large number of caravans in a line beside the road. Some were on the list and some were not; others had come up a fortnight before on a false alarm and all were very angry. I think their morale must have been very low, since they had let themselves get scruffy: a great mistake when dealing with officialdom. We were held up well short of the border and there were no facilities for such a party and less shade. It was a very hot day.

The presiding official said, 'No,' he could not let us cross – he had no authority. On being pressed repeatedly he said he would phone for instructions to Delhi. A tall, swaggering Sikh brigadier arrived, attempting to cut a dash with the western girls among the caravans. There was much gaiter slapping with a swagger cane. Then I contacted him and told him I was a retired brigadier and, seeing he was a Sikh, said I knew the Maharajah of Patiala, name-dropping hard. I had in fact met him many years before. This didn't work. The brigadier replied, 'He is not of an old family. I am of a much older one.' He then promised to help us get across and departed, but we did not see him again and I learnt later that he had gone off to play golf.

Much to my chagrin the small number of vehicles on the 'List' was then allowed to cross over. No one had ever stolen a march on me at a border before. I damned that Consul's eyes. The officials still refused to let the rest of us go, although we had filled in elaborate forms at the crossing point. Frustrated and angry, I caught sight of the man from the Defence Ministry again and asked him if he was obtaining the necessary authority to release us. He said no, he could not get through on the telephone. I gained the impression that he, like so many small men given a little power, was thoroughly revelling in our discomfiture. In any case, like all Indian officials, he lived in terror of his superiors and dared not take a decision of his own; I think he was afraid even to ring up his boss on a Saturday morning. He was difficult to pin down. He *had* phoned, he had *not* phoned, he was doing everything humanly possible to get our clearance. How was the clearance coming? He did not know.

Fully mindful that for some reason only one day was allowed for our crossing, although a cease-fire had been declared, I pressed this elusive little figure hard, growing more and more angry. Hostilities could always start again and then where would we be? The day was getting hotter and hotter and our caravan with the wherewithal for tea making was held up well down the road – we had walked up to the barrier at the border. I felt I had to stay up there to dominate it.

The earlier reference to a telephone was worth following up. Where was the telephone? I was shown a field telephone – one of those with a handle to wind – at a nearby military post. I looked at the line running along the verandah. It was mended roughly in several places, even on this short stretch, but it was no worse than in the equipment of the grossly neglected British army of those times. There seemed little hope of getting Amritsar exchange and through this the Defence Ministry in Delhi. The telephone system is much improved in India now, but then it was quite a feat for one person to call another in Delhi itself, though people were always trying. I wound the handle a hundred times, but the line was dead. On pressing still harder I was told that there was another telephone at the police station near where we had left the caravan. I went there and asked if they were in touch with Amritsar exchange. They said that they were.

After about an hour I managed to get the exchange, having been cut off over and over again. I asked to be put through to the Defence Ministry in Delhi and after much effort got it. I explained my predicament, only to hear the receiver hastily put down. Someone else would take no responsibility. The same thing happened again and again and when I at last got hold of someone, Amritsar would cut in. The hours passed as I reached out for a faint-voiced wisp of hope, getting hotter and hotter and more and more exhausted. At last I got a voice which seemed receptive. I told my tale, already told a thousand times this doleful day, at which I was asked to speak louder. I raised my voice higher and higher until I was reduced to shrieking into the mouthpiece. Then I was cut off. Still no one would understand.

Repeating the same hopeless quest, being cut off, cut into and not understood for another hour, at last I heard a cultured voice – I felt it was a chance in many thousands. Someone in authority had happened to pick up the phone on a Saturday evening. How had I got past all his secretaries? Looking back it seems a miracle. I explained our trouble once again, trying to be calm and lucid and the voice said, 'Yes, of course you can cross, old chap!'

I said, 'Will you *please* order your official who is at my side to release us?' and I thrust the receiver hastily into our tormentor's hand, feeling that every second was precious, for Amritsar would be certain to cut in yet again. But no, the little man took up the receiver with a look of terror on his face and words such as, 'Oh, Protector of the Poor – Prayers of the Poor – Honoured Sir,' quavered from his drooling lips. He was even raising his hand to his forehead in a salaam across the great distances to Delhi and his knees were shaking. He crouched lower and lower and his palsied head waggled as his distant senior officer railed at him. At last with a sweet smile he turned to me and said, 'See what I have done for you – You may go! The Secretary for Defence says so.'

Why I did not batter his head to a pulp with the receiver, I do not know. I went back to the caravan, avoiding any show of haste for I did not want to precipitate a rush of vehicles ahead of me and I intended to be in the pole position and get through quickly. This could mean a gain of many hours as each vehicle's papers would be laboriously scrutinised on both sides of the border; I had learned a thing or two about border crossmanship. Swinging my vehicle out onto the crown of the road, I shouted to the huddle of other caravanners that we were through. They had done nothing but sit and moan. So I led the throng to the border and triumphantly signalled the sentry to open the gate. But no, he would not. For a second I considered charging the barrier, but the sentry was a hefty brigand with a .45 revolver and a bandolier of dum-dum bullets. The officials wanted to record all our details and cancel our carnet all over again, for they had torn up the forms I had given them earlier in the day; however, I was at the head of the queue and none could pass me. I sat fuming with impatience, but at last we were across. It had been my fear that the Pakistani border officials would have closed down by then for it had never been a round the clock service and it was evening now.

Pakistan was still in business, and friendly too. Getting special treatment since I spoke the language, we were given chairs. I said I was tired and, hoping for ready sympathy, said that the Hindu so and sos had held us up all day. The Pakistanis, glad to assume a role of rectitude said, 'What could you expect from the Hindu pigs?' and shook their heads sorrowfully; then they offered to fill in the forms for me themselves and green tea was brought.

One official was an old friend from Husseiniwalla to whom I had promised my driving gloves if we ever returned safely from India. I kept my promise, but as a thank offering gave him a new spare pair.

Then on to Lahore and we decided to go to the Intercontinental and, to make up for a really bad day, book a room instead of the hot park in the grounds as we had done so often before. Oh, for that hot bath we had promised ourselves as we left the hated border! The water was stone cold and the air-conditioning was out of order!

Chapter 17

The Rim of the Frying Pan

The Fifth Journey (1972–3)

In 1972–3 we decided to expand our trip to India to a whole year instead of six months and spend the hot weather in Kashmir. Sadly, my mother had died in the autumn of 1970, and we were now quite free. With infinite labour I got an extension for the caravan's carnet. The authorities delightedly dangled me on a string before I got it, but my eloquence in Hindi won the day after I had trailed from one dusty, obscure office to another. I don't think many extensions were granted – few applicants would have persisted so long.

I was anxious to recapture those lovely days in the past when we had pitched our tents up among the tall, resin-smelling deodars, where flying squirrels planed from tree to tree, or under walnut trees when, tired after a day's hard scrambling over a lengthy fishing beat, the evenings were soft and aromatic round a camp fire of fir cones. I thought of the wonderful trout fishing which would cap the excellent sport I had found for myself in the Ramganga River in Corbett Park where I had persuaded the *mahseer* to take a fly readily. What a year of sport it would be! In times past we had lived on lovely carved house-boats on the lakes with their attendant *shikaras* – the Kashmiri equivalent of gondolas – and we longed to see them again.

We arrived in April in pouring rain and the Vale looked sloppy and uninviting. The rain continued throughout the month and into May – surely there was more rain nowadays, or had I forgotten? I was soon to find the fishing very poor because extensive and ruthless deforestation had shorn the beautiful lower slopes of the valleys I had known. The press and nibble of a vastly increased population and the huge influx and settlement of Gujars, a horse-trading people with slightly nomadic tendencies, had caused the forests to be cut back even more savagely to provide grazing for ill-bred ponies and rank smelling goats. The sum total of this rape was that rainfall, no longer absorbed by the former trees, swept down the mountains and hurtled through the valleys in torrents into the fishing streams which now remained thickly browned with mud, and unfishable well into the season. The old camp sites had been ploughed up and put under rice and there was no place to park so much as a mini-caravan in the

133

narrow valleys. Even the water was fouled by the waste of the greatly enlarged villages. On the floor of the Vale, which is a series of lakes and waterways, I looked eagerly up the banks for the bright red pomegranate blossoms, looped and threaded by the dipping flight of golden orioles, but all were gone. The shores of the great Wular Lake were narrowed by more *bunds* and more mud-walled rice fields. The pheasant-tailed jacana no longer trod with spidery feet on the rimmed lotus leaves.

My daughter and her husband had suggested a summer holiday in India with their small daughter. Knowing that India proper would be too hot, I proposed that we jointly took one of the ornate houseboats on the clear, spring-fed Nagim Lake near Srinagar. This with Nasim was the best location. The old Dhal Lake and the Chenar Bagh, under giant *chenar* (plane) trees, the venue of our parents, had by then become aquatic slums on dirty water, loud with transistors and fouled with waste.

What better, I thought, than to seek out my old houseboat, the *Triumph*, for the owner was a wonderful cook. We did a tour round Nagim, which was relatively unspoilt, away from the clank of the occupying Indian forces and from the barge and bump of countless people. We saw a magnificent houseboat across the lake and as we were paddled over I could read the name, the *Triumph*! I counted the gabled windows and could see that it was a good boat. Three gables meant three bedrooms and French windows showed a pantry, a dining room and a drawing room with an elaborately carved, open prow deck. I realised that this was not my old *Triumph*, which, though good, had not been so big and fine. We were hailed from the large sun deck roof, which was half shaded by a cloth canopy with scalloped edges. The voice was familiar and there was something in the expression of my caller's eyes which I knew. Time went backwards for a moment as I looked up. This fine individual with a neat grey Astrakhan fore and aft cap and baggy Muslim trousers was an imposing figure, strong nosed and bearded to a clipped point. Then time caught up. He was not the old owner, but his eldest son, A'hmed whom I had known as a callow, but handsome eighteen-year-old youth when last I had gone house-boating. He greeted me affectionately, though I had always fought tooth and nail with his father over charges in the past. By now father had died, but A'hmed had a large and thriving family – sons popped up everywhere and his wife peered out of the cleanly *doonga* or attendant crew's family *cum* kitchen boat, as fat as a queen ant.

Before the days of skiing, now established in Gulmarg in the winter, the Kashmiris had but a short season in which to squeeze the visitor. In this they were adept. Every little addition or service soon became an extra to be paid for. The weary new arrival was in no fit state to put everything down, cut and dried on paper. But this time I set to, to lay down terms of a contract for a month's stay for our party. Charges were heavy, but possible for our combined families, though I had hoped to beat A'hmed down, pushing sentiment and for old times'

Houseboat 'Triumph'.

sake, blah, blah! I knew I was up against a past master. He riposted by pointing out that as the best boat on the lake (it was) he could ask anything he liked from Birla the multi-millionaire and others of the same opulence. But he did give way a little and remarked, as though to cover his weakness, that his Indian guests who ate of course with their hands, would wipe the curry off on his lovely, embroidered curtains. These curtains whose delicate, well chosen blend of colours was not fast would naturally be ruined.

Things went well for our young family. My one failure was that Kashmir was so staggeringly new to them that I would have done better to escort them round, but I held back to give them freedom. However, there were shopping trips to buy the country's very artistic wares. There were lake and river trips on large boats propelled by strong rowers with heart-shaped paddles. The food, however, though adequate, was not of a high standard, for it was unimaginative. Duck, which abounded, were poor and would remain so until the rice had been harvested and they could feed on the scattered grains washed down in the rivers. There remained the Kashmiri sheep whose meat was strong and goaty in flavour, and rather stringy chickens. Beef was barred as it always had been in a nominally Hindu state. Everything, I realised, was geared to quick turn-round, modern fly-in tourist holidays, so that the same menu was repeated monotonously every three days. The excellent fruit season was yet to come. Gone were the days of culinary distinction. In the past there had been one or two widowed memsahibs, British officers' or officials' wives, who had settled in the Vale and by example and instruction trained a number of quick-learning, local Kashmiri cooks so that in its heyday food was outstanding. Our dear old cook, Musa, had been one of these. Even picnic baskets were painstakingly prepared and the contents neatly packaged and tied up with cotton thread, for they (the picnics) were brought to a fine art in the time of the Raj. Never was the salt forgotten. But now luxury vegetables such as asparagus and globe artichokes were no longer to be had – they were no longer grown. How standards had fallen!

Wild birds were fewer and floating gardens were pressing in from the shore to squeeze out the lotus beds. The floating gardens are based on rafts of water weed packed solid. Earth is put on top and in no time at all there is a new bit of 'land' encroaching on the water. However, some of the old pleasures remained. The flower boat came round every few days, almost hidden by its masses of brilliant blooms for us to choose from to make the houseboat gayer still. An idle hour could still be whiled away bargaining with jewellers, carpet sellers, embroiderers and woodworkers, who also brought their wares round by boat.

Kashmir had still kept its individuality. It struck me that in no aspect was it Indian, nor for that matter Pakistani. It was essentially Central Asian and the majority of its inhabitants wished fervently to side with neither Pakistan nor India, but to remain Kashmiri. Outside influences on their craftsmanship have come from China and Iran. From whence did these Muslim river and lake people derive? I believe they too came from Iran. They look like Persians and they think like Persians. When asked they are vague, but definite that they descend directly and rather appropriately from that intrepid boatman, Noah or 'Noo'.

Life on the houseboat had changed. A'hmed, probably in reaction to Hindu overlordship, had become stridently religious. He held prayers on the *doonga* at, we felt, an unnecessarily early hour, chanting from the Koran with his weighty family coming in loudly with responses. It went on so long and with such insistence that I felt the deity would certainly give way and grant any request. Another innovation was for the sons to turn up at 'sundowner' time on the fore verandah. Whether they did this from politeness or through boredom or curiosity I do not know – in any case they did not drink. Once upon a time I would have got rid of them, but I thought they felt they were acting as hosts – indeed package tourists would probably have expected to be entertained.

Peggy and I were so disenchanted with Kashmir and the difficulty of finding anywhere except Nedou's Hotel grounds to camp in the motor caravan, that we decided to return home as soon as, all too soon, our daughter's family had departed, for we could not afford to houseboat on our own. Nedou's Hotel was a delightful garden and verandahed haven – nowhere was its sprawl more than two stories high. It was run by Colonel Harry Nedou of a crack Indian cavalry regiment and of mixed Russian and Kashmiri descent, together with his wife Salima, daughter of one of the great Muslim houses of Kashmir, descended from a saint. Harry Nedou was the epitome of a gentleman and a devout Muslim. He showed us enormous friendship which I feel we little deserved. One of the features of this great religion is hospitality and he offered me a shooting holiday in Kashmir the following year as his guest. What a tempting offer, for the winter duck shooting was still outstanding. A friend of his, an official of Air India, made this offer still more attractive by promising that he would arrange for as many cartridges as we wanted to be carried free of charge. But I no longer wished to kill and was reluctant to be beholden even to such a good friend. Soon after this he died suddenly and I felt extreme loss.

We were aware that we should have to motor in great heat, but we set off, notwithstanding, in June 1973. Pressing northwards along the broad Russian road from Kandahar to Herat the car was setting up a rhythmic clonk from one slab of concrete to the next. A following wind was cutting down the drag of the bluff-sided caravan so that the engine was pulling smoothly and gave me a feeling of great well-being. I was going as fast as I thought prudent in this relatively low-powered vehicle, but fortune's smile was false. I noticed that the temperature gauge needle was too high. I said to Peggy that we had only got two miles to go to Girisk on the Helmund River and then we'd investigate. This was a fatal decision. As we slowed up at the filling station the following wind blew up the fumes and steam from the engine behind and below us, with a stench of oil, burning oil which I can smell to this day on a bad night. Steam was forcing its way through the header tank with a loud trumpeting noise. The pump attendant stepped out into the fairway and waved us away, thinking that we were a fireball to blow up his pumps. The engine died and we both got out rather quickly – our lathered steed had foundered. We were unable to restart after a cooling period. The mechanics in Girisk who swarmed eagerly onto the engine, aided by small boys who could wedge their way in, the only way they could learn, were unable to achieve anything beyond further damage. There were some well dressed travellers sitting on a verandah who offered us hospitality and suggested that I get a tow back to the workshops of a famous mechanic, Reza Khan in the Hajji Khayya Serai in Kandahar.

The thought of a seventy-mile tow back to Kandahar made me quail, but there was no alternative, so I settled terms with a party of Pathans, armed to the teeth and sitting on the back of a small truck. Their charge was very small and I said I would pay on arrival. They fished out a coil of stout telephone wire full of kinks and knots. I eyed it dubiously. In the wilds of Afghanistan in those days no sooner was a telephone line set up than the tribesmen cut off lengths. It was so useful for tying up bedding, cows and so forth. After all they were putting it to some use, for who would want to speak on a wire – it just didn't make sense.

So we set off, but they could not keep an even speed and either jerked forward or slowed up suddenly. They were clearly an irresponsible gang of braves. Bereft of power-assisted brakes, I was hard put to it not to charge my rescuers when they slowed, but managed desperately to use my good hand brake which worked on the transmission to check my rush. I had to snap it off, oh so quickly, when they shot forward to tighten the wire too suddenly. It parted several times, but my helpers seemed to have an inexhaustible supply. In high good spirits, not to say mirth, they would set up another tow. One turned to me and asked where I had learned Pushtu. Knowing that the Pathan has an ironic sense of humour, I replied, 'When I was shooting up your Daddy!' This remark was repeated to the others and made them all fall about with laughter. I was relieved at this because with these cut-throats, or should I say angels of mercy, we were very isolated and alone.

The wire finally parted in a shower of sparks as we swung into the Serai. Still having some way on I rolled towards a shop entrance where a man was beckoning. This was Reza Khan. I paid off our cheerful brigands with a generous bonus as their charge had been ridiculously small.

As usual the Serai was a stout fortress-like enclosure where camel convoys had once staged, rested and sold their wares outside teeming Kandahar. Next morning I looked round this spacious place and saw that the outer wall embraced shops with their backs to it, opening out in large arched doorways in a ring round the courtyard. This was full of lovingly painted, ancient trucks gorgeously decorated with pictures of improbable snowy mountains and tigers. Little did the owners realise their riches for here was a vintage collection beyond price. The drivers regarded them as a burden and a failing asset as they could only keep them crawling along the roads sustained by crude and ingenious home-made parts. Imports were restricted for there was no foreign currency to pay for them. The archways housed workshops and sleeping quarters for travellers to throw down their bedding on the floor. Each workshop plied its separate trade. One wound armatures, another made springs, a third cleaned out radiators and so on. There was no central organisation.

Reza Khan had the engine out next morning with much shaking of heads and undertook makeshift repairs to get it working again to some effect, but the engine sounded very sick. He could do no more. As a good Muslim he had given me, the traveller, pride of place and all his attention.

We stayed by the car for a terrible week in the breathless enclosure, for it was our home. We sat on a bench and watched the work – so slow – the grinding of valves done by hand, the radiator sent to the radiator cleaning shop on the back of a coolie, and so on. At first the bench was in shade. As the sun moved up it, my eyes followed the edge of the shade with fascinated horror. When it reached us at the end of the bench whither we had squeezed ourselves, we were in insufferable heat. Reluctant to leave our possessions we struggled to the Kandahar Hotel daily to seek a WC and tea. The WCs were revolting, but there was no other sanitation except for the outer wall of the Serai where everyone squatted down indiscriminately. It was too hot to eat, but the tea was good and I saw a ticket hanging from the pretty little Gardener teapot – Liptons. I am no teabag man myself, but now I venerate the name of Lipton.

Reza Khan's charges were absurdly small and he refused any more, but asked if I would give him my straw hat in which he looked very dashing. I did give his willing helpers a very handsome tip, a thing unknown in that land.

We set off in some trepidation and by the time we reached Farah Hotel and filling station on the road to Herat we were using a gallon of oil every hundred miles and I had to have more. I *had* to have it, but the attendant refused it to me since it was so scarce. In the end after much altercation I bullied enough for a top up out of him at an exorbitant price. We clattered through historical Herat, picking up more precious oil and twenty miles out on our way to the Iranian border we had a puncture on an Irish bridge – so called because flood water goes over its concrete floor rather than under. As I lay under the car removing the wheel the wind was blowing stinging pea-sized gravel in my face and it was then that I realized we must go back to Herat for further help.

I was told of the two Hajji brothers who had a big workshop. There again we stayed for a week in dreadful heat. The two dignified owners had done the Mecca pilgrimage and hence their honorific 'Hajji'; one of them was making car parts with great finish on a home-made lathe. He had been trained by the British in Quetta. The brothers cobbled our engine together with a copper solution where cracks had appeared in the cylinder head and put Mercedes rings into our pistons – these nearly fitted. Daily, beggers filed through the shop picking out the small change put out for them. As usual they gave no thanks for they were helping the donors to acquire merit in the hereafter.

We struggled on over the border, travelling by night because the engine tended to overheat again. It finally collapsed on the shores of the Caspian just as I said to Peggy, 'I believe we're going to make it,' forgetting the huge mountain passes yet to come. I arranged for yet another tow by a Mercedes International bus, old and no longer plying regularly but still very powerful, to get us up the 270 miles to Teheran including the forty mile climb up the winding Haraz Pass, in the dark, to a height of 10,000 feet from just below sea level. This offer of a tow was a once in a lifetime chance and the charge was very small, but first we had to find a towbar and, after a long search, a slender rod was found whose rings were attached with silver solder. I groaned to Peggy, 'That won't tow us a yard,' and it didn't. As soon as it took the strain it fell to the ground with a clatter. The sound fuelled my despair! Much later, after another long search, a massive towbar was produced fit to cope with the heaviest truck, but it had a right-angled bend in it – the mark of some horrific accident. No one had the implements to straighten it so we had to make the best of it. As we set off this bar forced me to follow our tower jutting dangerously outwards on the off side as we pottered away like a wounded crab. As we began to climb the pass I could not see the bus as it nipped round the endless hairpin bends in the dark. I had to twirl the wheel desperately in pursuit and use my handbrake over and over again so as not to bump it. Fortunately at night there was no traffic on this perilous road.

Next morning at the edge of Teheran I paid off our kind rescuer and gave him a good bonus over the agreed price. He wisely said he couldn't go along like this in the torrid Teheran traffic. I thoroughly agreed with him as authority would have seized upon our curious crabwise progress. I secured the help of a local breakdown team to take us to a workshop nearby. City slickers, they charged me the earth. I was so tired by then that as I finally got out I staggered and fell into the open *jui* or drain. God, how I stank! We went into the workshop and were greeted by the owner who ran a bus depot there too. He took over the camper and an intelligent-looking mechanic who said he had trained with Mercedes in Germany took it all very calmly, though I was smelling like a polecat. I knew by then we had to get a new engine somehow and there was a Bedford agent in Teheran, whose existence had given me some hope as we crawled up the pass, even though when I said 'Bedford' everyone immediately tried to direct me to Ford.

The mechanic took us to Bedford's. I felt it was certain that we would not get a petrol engine like mine as all transport had changed to diesel, but I pressed on after this slender hope. Being a dogged character underneath, though you would not believe it as I am given to stamping and fuming rages in adversity in contrast to Peggy who is always calm, I was determined to find an engine. The Bedford depot said, 'No': they had not got a 214 petrol engine. I began to fume, though I hadn't started stamping. A long and turgid life has taught me never to take 'No' for an answer and I cried angrily that there just had to be one in their store. An agitated underling reminded his boss that a number of packages had come from England six months before and had not yet been opened.

'Open them!' I almost screamed, though I was sure they would only be more diesel parts. We opened the package and slowly, part after part of a 214 petrol engine emerged.

While the engine was being repaired we slept in the car in the yard – sanitation there was a hole in the middle of the workshop floor – and found our way daily to the Marmar Hotel, much used by British businessmen. It had a dartsboard and tolerable draught beer. The bar was full of these businessmen complaining loudly about the Iranians' unbusinesslike ways. The barman, who spoke English, was probably an informer to the secret police, as is the custom in eastern countries, and must have reported their every remark. The businessmen preferred this cool pub to going out into the streets to do business; how we ever sold a thing I do not know. Our own trials were lightened by the kindness of the workshop owner who took us out one evening to an open-air restaurant high above the city, followed by a night in his villa.

Repairs completed, we made for the border, anxious to get the car out before our carnet expired. After a while it was clear that the engine was still running very hot. On the way I had suggested among many things that the thermostat was not working. All the mechanics maintained that the radiator had become constricted. They knew nothing about thermostats, never used in these hot countries, and firmly dismissed my suggestion. Climbing the high pass above Erzincan in Turkey the water started boiling away so we had to stop to let it cool down. This took hours so we boiled water on our cookstove to top up the radiator and decided to travel by night only, sitting the deadly long day out on the road in the diminishing shade of our vehicle – what a bore!

The last approach to Ankara is very lofty and steep and the temperature needle started to rise slowly, even though it was night. In the dark it was very hard to see, as it was but dimly lit, and I crouched over it, gazing at it with fascinated horror. I found the car ran more easily in third gear when it was possible, but I had to feather the accelerator, oh so lightly. Even the slightest extra pressure set the needle mounting before my horrified eyes. All this added to my exhaustion, but Ankara, where there was a very big and modern Bedford depot, beckoned.

I thought we were over the mountains, but at night distances expand. Rounding what I thought was the final corner, I saw far above me a string of red lights like rubies in the dark and realised to my horror that these were the tail lights of traffic into Ankara. By then I was beyond normal exhaustion, but managed to potter on to surmount the last pass and down the long slope into the capital. I pulled in at the first petrol station I saw, got into the back and fell asleep. I woke to a banging sound and thought, 'Oh, that engine playing up again!' But no, it was a stout Turkish corporal who firmly said that I could not park there as it was near the gates of a military barracks. I tried reasoning with him, but the good corporal knew his job and as an old soldier I had to curb my annoyance and obey. I drove on another half a mile and stopped at the next petrol station and went to sleep at once in the same manner, only to experience an exact repetition of what had just gone before – the same bang on the door, the same corporal who said it was a military zone and no parking allowed anywhere on it. I pointed out that the petrol station was a civilian one – Shell. I fear my sense of discipline had now left me and I was very rude to the good corporal, but had to give way and moved on into Ankara, stopping for the rest of the night in front of the Bedford depot.

When it opened I sought help to find out the cause of the constant heating. Here I again raised the question of the thermostat and the head mechanic said, 'We always take them out.'

'Then take mine out!' I almost screamed. It is in fact very difficult to get out in that Bedford and I had not been able to reach it, being very broad and constricted by the confined engine cover.

We took it out and driving through Germany the engine suffered more from cold than heat, particularly as an extra large fan had been put in in Teheran. On reflection I think that with the undue heat my thermostat had been sticking from time to time in the closed position, thus shutting off the flow of water except for a little through a small by-pass. Though I am no mechanic I think I was the victim of a rather freakish fault. To service this vehicle one needed the arm of a fiddler crab and the body of a dwarf.

Chapter 18

It's No Adventure

Our Sixth Journey (1973–4)

Next autumn, still in 1973, we planned to stay at home for the whole winter to recover from our adventure, but the pulsating call from India came louder and louder. There was no resisting it. The fatigues and agonies of our return journey were soon forgotten and with little time, having arrived back in the summer, we planned for yet another winter in our 'demi-paradise', Corbett Park. There were so many items of food and medicine, unobtainable in India, that had to be taken with us for a six months' journey, even to burnable paraffin and, of course, meths for the primus stoves. Apart from this we needed visas, carnets, insurance, inoculations and other formalities connected with such an expedition across ten different countries to our destination.

I have often been tempted to settle somewhere in India, but such a step would have so many disadvantages as to put it out of court straight away. It would mean never seeing our children, grandsons and granddaughters again. In retirement one would have absolutely no status whatever and would be fair game for the wily Indian tax man. We would also miss the excitement of driving there across high mountain ranges where the difficulties lent spice to the journey.

Our journey out and stay in the Park were uneventful, though we experienced feelings of extreme happiness. Just to be in the midst of India's fast dwindling natural forests and animals was all I have ever craved.

As usual we returned through Delhi and visited various friends. When I suggested that to drive out from England to India had elements of adventure, my hostess, who had come out in a swift Range Rover and had been lucky to strike good weather all the way, said rather dampingly that it was *no* adventure and really rather boring. She was a women of great ability for she could pour cold water on anything.

It is an adventure if you take your home with you and stop in strange, wild places. With a camper, you travel at less than half the pace of a car and the odds are that you will meet bad weather somewhere on the way. At times it is just a long drive out, however entrancing and one can say casually at a party, 'I'm driving over to India tomorrow.' But this does not take into account the two evil

143

spirits that dwell, one in the Caspian and the other in the Black Sea. Should either of these be in a bad humour, then look out. We were shortly to prove it when we were returning in the spring of 1974, an optimum period. Through the years we had, so we thought, learnt our lesson as to when to travel – a very severe one.

As we drove homewards through Iran there was a drizzle near Amol which stands back from the Caspian at the foot of our old adversary, the Haraz Pass. I drove up and up from sea level round the tight corners and horseshoe bends, craning my neck to look out of the window upwards to see what would be swinging down the wet road towards us. Within four kilometres of the top I turned to Peggy and said, 'Thank God, we're over!' – fatal words. The witch of the Caspian heard and her brow darkened. In two minutes daylight had turned to blackness and the drizzle had become a blizzard. The snowfall was so heavy that it shut out all the light. I kept the vehicle going, though the snow was being packed hard by the big transporters up ahead. Suddenly the lorry in front of us stopped in the fairway on a narrow bend and as there was no way round it, I had to stop too. On a steep slope you cannot go forward again on pack ice without chains so there we were in the middle of the road with a monster likely to surge up into view at any moment from behind. Visibility was down to ten yards with all lights on. I had to get off the crown of the road as the transporters with chains on them were still coming up big and blind. I let the vehicle slip slowly rearwards in a controlled slide backward and outward, but very carefully as there was no wall at the edge and a sheer drop of a thousand feet. I counted on a small pile of chippings to stop my slide and it did. So there we were, just off the narrow crown, with the juggernauts bellowing past with but inches to spare. The vehicle which had stopped us set off again, but our less powerful one could not grip the surface.

We spent an uncomfortable half hour. Then at last the darkness began to clear and snow ploughs from the head of the pass arrived on the scene and started towing stranded ducks like ourselves over the top. They demanded payment, which was probably irregular as they were part of the maintenance and rescue service, but seeing ourselves in a dangerous position I agreed to the steep price without demur. We were hitched up to a crude tow wire which was secured by a large plumber's spanner. The plough driver set off very fast although I shouted to him to go slow. The spanner snapped and I saw the head plunge into the snow on the bank. Using a strong tyre lever to anchor the loop we tried again and off we churned, too fast once more. The driver was in a hurry because there were other fat ducks to pluck. We were whisked round a corner and swung out and out to the precipice edge. I was yelling for the plough to stop. Now we were near the edge, so near that I could look down into the dark depths. It seemed as if we were going to be killed, and we would pull the plough down too on top of us for we were in a heavy vehicle. I yelled to Peggy to jump out, for she was on the inner side. Then the driver looked back, saw the danger, with Peggy half out of the vehicle, and stopped. After a great deal of sideways pulling and a good deal of urging by me, we were drawn away inch by inch from the chasm. We had been no more than a hand span from it.

Soon we were over the pass and rolling gingerly down towards Teheran. A day of no adventure, you might say, but I was a bit pleased with myself. If someone hurls a brick at your head, you duck. You don't have time to tell your companion to do so. But in a split second I had got Peggy on her way to safety, though for the second time in our travels she could not bear to watch.

We left Teheran behind. What a fantastic drive it always was through that thronged city. At times a nimble man could cross the double carriageway on the roofs of saloon cars, for the traffic moved at glacial pace. I have always loved driving through this traffic, for it is an art form: to be in perfect control of a machine, to stop or pass with but an inch to spare, to be in the right gear at the right time gave me the same feeling that Sir John Barbirolli must have had conducting the LSO. I was right-hand drive, but it was difficult as the others were all wrong-hand drive. The initiative must never be surrendered. Bounce forward into a gap: no 'After you, Sir!' – to give way is to be swamped and stopped. Driving is opportunist. There is no code of manners. Keep a constant pip, pip going with the footling little standard horn and dominate that slippy little taxi trying to push you into a fourth lane where there are only three. Rock him back on his haunches with the three-trumpet wind horn – the Doomcracker – a mighty GER-R-ROUT! Lean your flushed angry face out and say sorrowfully in Persian, 'O, thy mother!' or worse, 'Only a mother!' Yes, he'll be as rude to you, but will not fall into the error of taking you for a decorous *farangi* driver.

But Iran had the last word as we set out into open country, bonnet down to Takestan, our sheltered night stop. The evil weather brewed up blackly from the Captain Sea was smiting the vehicle on its right flank – unseasonable weather, for by now it should have been warm. The traffic was moving at a snail's pace over crunching, dish-sized lumps of ice, nose to tail. Where there was a gap in the traffic the snow looked like a fast moving, unusually white roller towel, driven across the road with hurricane speed.

I felt my heart leap into my mouth – was that a slight falter in the engine? Gradually it failed to a stop. I had been too clever. On the previous disastrous journey, I had, as I have said, replaced the fan by one with extra blades and now the carburettor had frozen in the cold. The replacement was a fairly sound idea if one did not have to cope with the witch of the Caspian and her fickle ways, but was obviously a mistake in weather as cold as this. There we were, no engine, so no heat, and thousands of trucks, tractors, buses and barouches were stumbling past dismally over the piles of broken-up ice. We were exposed, as it was now dark and the snow limited visibility. I climbed out of the cab and waved my red triangle. The wind was bitter, so bitter that had the doctors told me in those days about hypothermia, I would certainly have died of it. Trying to put on a windcheater, it streamed out and I had to haul it in, hand over hand to pull it on. No one heeded me. My voice shouting, 'Help! Give me a tow, I have money!' was carried away in the roar of the wind.

Then I saw a faery vision: a large American-type, traffic police car hove up. It was all flashing blue lights and in the lights I could see two fat, well fed police officers. I thrust the red triangle toward them. But they just smiled indulgently and drove on. The nearest policeman, but a yard away, waved soothingly to me with a fat, beringed hand in a sort of blessing gesture. *Pace, pace,* but there was no peace for me this dreadful night. Time dragged on and I was so cold, that I lost the power to think, but still held the triangle aloft, shouting in Persian, 'Help! For I have money!'

When all seemed lost, a large commercial truck piled high with bales of cotton stopped. My numbed wits told me that I was dreaming. But no: two figures calmly hitched us up with one of those excellent, stretchy nylon towing straps and I blurted out that I wanted to get to Takestan, four miles on. They towed me there – it was easy to follow without running into the back of my helpers because of the give of the strap. On each journey a mug like me learns. Now I take a nylon towing line with the proper fixings.

We pulled up at Takestan and I fished out my money, gabbling thanks. They would take nothing – just two more knights of the road – and they drove off to my shouted words of thanks and praise.

We stayed the whole of the next day at Takestan, waiting, thoroughly disheartened, for better weather which soon came as it should have, smiling warmingly on us. We whiled away the time by making a radiator muff and drinking Turkish sludge coffee with friendly transporter drivers. The Turks among them were running a thriving black trade at the restaurant in gold cigarette lighters and *gallon* bottles of Johnny Walker.

There is no love lost between the transporter drivers and the fast, bullying buses. I hate them too, for they pay no attention either to the rules of the road, or to safety. They all have names painted on the cab. The favourites in Turkey are, '*Yilderim*' (Lightning) and '*Yildmaz*' (Thunderbolt). Revving their powerful diesel engines to ninety miles an hour they give way to nobody. A blond Turkish driver told me how one of them had at last overdone it and turned over onto its back on the icy road. 'They were all keeled!' he laughed.

The Iranian truck drivers had probably saved our lives, for even then some years back we were just a pair of crazy geriatrics, though five years later we were still doing this sort of thing. There was perhaps 'No adventure', but it was April Fools' Day.

Chapter 19

Near Paradise

1971–1979

Between 1971 and 1979 our winter-long sojourns in India were chiefly spent in Corbett National Wild Life Park. This and the following chapters are the distillation of our happiness, though I have already picked out some of our adventures on our journeys to and fro.

The Park was named by India after Jim Corbett, the famous killer of man-eaters and in recognition of his deep knowledge of jungle lore. Few now realise the terror of whole communities in whose neighbourhood a man-eater stalks. Man-eating tigers and leopards have killed villagers in great numbers – one leopard killed over six hundred before Corbett accounted for it. He hunted it on foot on its own terms, after more conventional methods used by other experienced hunters had failed, owing to the animal's great cunning. Villagers did not dare to bring in their crops, or to leave their huts at night to answer nature's call. Life came to a full stop in the whole area. So notorious were some man-eaters that they figured in headlines in the English press at the time. Corbett's stories gave atmosphere to the Park, for it forms part of his happy hunting grounds. His books are still printed in India, though now, alas, difficult to find in England.

I like to think of this Park as a secret valley which is enhanced by the Ramganga River, a salmon-sized one which swells to a broad torrent in the monsoon, hurling down torn up trees on its way to join the Ganges. The river is the centrepiece of the main valley: the Patli Dun, which is flanked on the north by tiers of ever-rising foothills climbing up to the highest Himalayas. In certain lights these foothills, each one lapping the next, look paper thin, like a theatrical backdrop. Apart from the grasslands beside the river, there are tall, dark forests of *sal* trees which meet overhead like the arches of a cathedral and their bark is rough to the touch. Perhaps there are more beautiful places in the world but I have not yet found them. Even though sometimes the Patli Dun's clothing is drab, at other times it is magical. The hills marching up towards their big brothers over the false crest turn purple every evening – a purple that darkens almost to black if there are storm clouds gathering. In sunlight the forested

147

slopes make me think of a rich fruit cake, for rich it is, with a thick sprinkling of purple-red Barclay trees and splashes of gold where the *sal* is turning, for the fall is in springtime here. Here and there the sun penetrates through the forest into bright clearings where the dappled light plays on the speckled flanks of herds of spotted deer. Here was paradise. I wished for no more.

The principal camp of this wild life sanctuary is Dhikala and its focal point is a large, colonnaded house, once the headquarters of a Rohilla general. Later, the British drove back a Gurkha invasion and took over the area. The camp is designed to accommodate tourists and, besides the servants who look after them and their quarters, there is a large staff from the Uttar Pradesh Forestry Service to administer the Park. For us, returning there each year, was as if we had come home and when they came over in a wave to greet us they were like our own family.

The Forestry Service showed me much friendship and more consideration than my cranky nature deserved. I can never give India up and I find myself still holding onto it with both hands. I was given little privileges, which I valued greatly. I was allowed to park my camper under my favourite *haldu* tree and did not have to go into the often noisy official park. When I arrived I had but to plug into electric sockets of crazy Russian make which were already screwed into my dear tree and put up specially for me. Through the years my vehicle under this tree became a landmark and people visited me as a kind of Guru, though no Guru walked or fished as hard as I. Gurus tend to be inactive – that is their attraction for the idle.

I remember an evening towards the end of one visit when almost overnight it became so hot as to warn me we must soon be going. The camper's windows were wide open and at last a breeze rustled the round *haldu* leaves – what a relief! I looked down at the lake newly formed by a dam across the river below the camp where by day ospreys and fishing eagles hunted. As the huge moon came up shadowy nightjars performed silent acrobatics, the white roundels on their wings flashing as they turned in the air, often onto their backs. They would perch immediately outside the window and keep us awake with their churring calls and the loud thwacking of their wings – the most evocative of noises in the jungle night. In the hot, still dawn we woke to the strident mewing of peacocks and the shrill crow of the jungle fowl, no different from that of the bantam, its descendant and on the ground round the caravan little spotted doves cooed comfortingly.

Peggy and I were allowed to walk wherever we wished for the staff thought I had sufficient jungle craft for us to be safe. In order to pay homage to the tiger and elephant, who have a nobility of their own, I felt it fitting that we should go on foot and Peggy agreed, but she still wanted to go up and stroke tigers. She has an empathy with animals that they recognise – up to a point. To go on foot, and not on a tame elephant's back or by car as was the general custom (and I think a bit of a cheat), was to get the feel of both animals' majesty and the elephant's lofty might. For those who have ears to hear, these and other potentially dangerous animals make a low, but warning noise of one kind or another if you get too close to them. When I heard this I would withdraw at once. The animal had used tact and I must respond.

I said 'a cheat' above because wild animals regard a riding elephant as an elephant pure and simple. They do not appear to realise that men, the great enemies, are riding on it, however brightly they may be dressed, so long as they do not make a noise. The motor car is not regarded as a direct threat, nor does it seem to be connected with the enemy, except that some elephants do take a very poor view of buzzy little jeeps and attack them.

Alas, the Park has been spoiled by its success. Now, far too many bus parties and noisy trippers in chattering diesel jeeps and trailers run about its paths. The reservoir formed in the Ramgunga River has swallowed up the best fishing pools. In this oblique way man has encroached once more on the forests and reduced the wild animals' habitat in a park that was never very big. It is all too easy to turn Corbett Park into a holiday camp for forestry officers and their families and for them to invite the railway convention which buys *sal* wood for sleepers, the hydro-electric board which built the dam and others on a cheap 'swan' to cement good relations. The Park is comparatively close to Delhi and regarded by the central government as an excellent place in which to entertain foreign VIPs and statesmen with the attendant pomp and ceremony that flattens everything. It was so easy to send busloads of noisy schoolchildren to work off their exuberance in a sylvan setting. In theory this was to teach them about the wonders of the wild. In practice they were just turned loose in starling-like flocks and little effort was made to interest them. All they seemed to want was night-long bonfires and sing-songs and never a thought for the animals, for their eyes had not been opened.

I told myself that there were still a few quiet walks along which we could study elephants, tigers and the birds in some peace. But they were becoming more harassed by shrill sight-seers who had not yet learned to love them and still regarded them as a kind of threat as did their ancestors, although I am bound to say that the Indian government has done extremely well to increase and extend existing sanctuaries and develop new ones. I think and hope the day is not far off when young Indians will learn to appreciate their few remaining wild animals. We have met one or two families who have shown a keen and knowledgeable interest in their great but dwindling heritage and Indira Gandhi and her son Rajiv gave unstinting encouragement.

For convenience the responsibility for wild life preservation was first foisted on the existing structure of provincial governments' forestry departments. The development of Project Tiger as an independent, centralised organisation came later. Forestry departments tended to be ambivalent and their masters, local politicians, were at the beck and call of an electorate chiefly interested in getting hold of more land and exploiting it. Foresters were trained to regard the forests commercially, to be cut down and replanted when necessary. The *sal* tree fortunately is self-perpetuating. Naturally animal preservation would take second place. Until the care of all wild life can be put in the hands of trained specialists with power to enforce protection, animals are in danger both outside the parks and in the parks themselves, where they will inevitably be trampled over by the weighty visitations I have described above. Beyond this the preservation of wild life was almost a personal concern of the Gandhi family and there is no guarantee that their successors will be equally dedicated.

In our time the officer in charge of Dhikala camp was Narain Singh Negi, a Gharwali of the foothills. Like so many of his hill people he was tall, slender and handsome. He had their Mongolian cast of features and his high cheekbones and slightly slanting eyes gave him an elfin look which suggested a man of the forests. On our earlier visit, before the influx of tourists, life in the Park was more tranquil and quiet, so that we could wander for miles together on elephant back and learn a good deal of jungle lore from him. Then in the evenings in the cosy glow of the camper I would get him to tell stories of the forests. But as the years went by he became more and more occupied in administration and construction – for part of a forest officer's training is a course in simple building. He really liked the development side of the Park but, as he became more absorbed, so our little expeditions and stories became less. Our friendship never diminished though his responsibilities took him away from the Park so often. In this life, experience of near perfection can never be repeated.

Of good yeoman stock, he was left with four younger brothers to provide for. His dying father told him that there were insufficient resources for the whole family, but that he, Narain the eldest, must fend for them as best he could. 'Climb up the mango tree, my son. Only you can go, but when you are up see that you shake down the fruit for the others.'

Narain, already well educated, had joined the Gharwal Rifles on the clerical side under British rule. I think he found the indoor life irksome and accounting tedious and dreary, for after a while he left the army and joined the big and well-founded United Provinces Forestry Service, later to be called the Uttar Pradesh Forestry Service. He was clearly not getting up the mango tree fast, for to break seniority in one government service and transfer too late to attain the senior ranks in another was to debar him from its highest fruits. Yet, with all these disadvantages, by selling a little land – so hard a step for a petty yeoman to take – and by saving and scrimping he saw to it that his brothers were well educated. By then two of them were high up in the UP Forestry Service. One was a District Forest Officer and likely to go higher. The other was already a Conservator of Forests – a very high rank indeed. A third brother was a respected schoolmaster and the fourth looked after the joint family land and cared for Narain's wife and children while the latter were at the village school level. When they grew older they simply moved over to the charge of the schoolmaster brother. Always the younger brothers and their wives, women of a more sophisticated background, on greeting Narain touched his feet in the time-honoured gesture of homage and respect for the head of the family, though he was a comparatively lowly Forest Ranger. Again, when the wife of one of these brothers joined her husband who was on a forestry photographic course in Holland, it was Narain who had to escort her to Delhi and to see her off on a plane. A respectable married women would not have gone alone, but had to be accompanied by the head of the family.

To fish in the Ramgunga had all the elements of paradise. The water, devoid of silt in the dry winter months, was so transparent as to be almost invisible. The lovely river offered the conventional sport to the multi-hooked, plug and minnow spinner with his slipping clutch reel and hefty rod: surely a mechanism that was too clumsy and an affront to the setting. However, Narain Negi persuaded me to spin, as indeed was the custom of all anglers there. We were fishing for *mahseer* – a powerful, streamlined, riverine carp which had become a legend as a fighter and I hooked a twenty-two pounder which launched itself into the air like a bar of gold. Then all I had to do was to winch this wonder yard by yard to my feet. The heavy tackle gave it no option but to come, well hooked by the plug in its thick lips. It lay on the round, grey stones – a thing wrought in beaten gold. I would surely catch bigger fish with this tackle and compete with my stories over evening 'sundowners', but I was dissatisfied. So on an impulse I gave Narain my stout spinning rod and reel.

Next morning I realised that I had more or less burnt my boats as I had come thousands of miles to fish on this our second visit to the Park. The clear water tempted me and I felt increasingly that it was ideal for fly fishing. I knew of no record then of the fly being used to catch this great fish, except for a brief reference in one of Corbett's books, but I had on board a stout rod and reel and some nylon as well as flies. Why not go for light tackle, finesse and quick action rather than use the bludgeon of a heavy plug or spoon? I went down to the water with a nylon cast, steeply tapered down to a 5 lb. breaking strain, and mounted a wet loch fly with a touch of silver in its body. It was about half an inch long. I expected the fly to be scorned and in any case, if taken, I would surely be broken. I had tied all the knots with many extra twists and tucks in. Perhaps the flexibility of my rod would give to the shock of a fish taking.

I fished in the bright ripple at the edge of the fast water, where trout would lie, but there was no response. So I pushed into the swell of the river's core, leaning back hard against the flow and slipped the small fly through the surface. Then, oh then, my fly was taken with a tremendous punch, the point of my rod grabbed down to the water, but it all held and I had remembered to let my wrist give at the shock. It was a *mahseer*. The characteristic attack was more exciting than that of salmon or trout. Though my knots held I had to let my reel run on a light check of the brake and the ratchet screamed. Getting out of the deep water, stumbling over slippery boulders, cursing my slowness, I made the fine-pebbled shore and set out at a sprint after the fish, which seemed to be making for the

A typical mahseer.

sea! Sprawling over big, round bruising boulders I still maintained contact down a fast, shallow rapid with the fish cutting a bow wave which splashed up the line. Into the next pool it dived – lovely, light green water of some depth. The fish bored down and I had time to wind in a hundred yards of backing which was humming in the air. Now level with him, I put a sideways strain on, and so a long battle waged. I gained a yard, the fish took ten in short rushes. After hours I saw his golden side as he lost his balance and I felt I would have him. The sideway strain was aimed at tiring out his pectoral and anal fins, designed for balance and weaker than the great orange flukes of the tail, which would not tire.

I was just below my quarry by now, making him breast the current, but I knew that if he dashed down the river his gills would be closed and breathing would cease so that he would tire more quickly. I got above him and encouraged another run down the pool. This was a mistake because he got into the rapids and down, down into a bigger pool. Falling heavily, cursing, I closed again, but could not feel the thrum, thrum of the flukes of a fighting fish on my line. I saw the line stretched over a boulder in the rapids. Wading and risking being washed down into the pool, I seized it and eased it over the boulders, suddenly to feel the rhythmic drum of a big fish still fighting for its life. I had hooked him at mid-day and now it was dusk. A very large tusker was bathing across the stream. In the sunset he squirted water over his back. The spray made a white frame against which he looked as black as ebony. He paused as if interested, but it would have been a scramble for him to cross over and pester me, so I ignored him. Now I was winning more yards than losing them and at last beached my quarry, all burnished gold and about 15 lb. Light handling and flexible tackle had beaten him. As if concluding the show the tusker swayed off thoughtfully.

Such was the sport so often repeated until the dam ruined the river. I wore rubber shoes, cotton shirt and shorts only, since waders would have been too cumbersome. The going was too rough and distances too far for anything but the lightest wear. I was to catch many more fish in this manner, leaning back with all my sixteen stone against the icy torrent, often looking longingly at the warm, sunlit bank, often losing my footing as the fast water washed the gravel from under my feet so that I disappeared below the surface to come up spluttering.

When I could stand the cold no longer, I sat on the bank stark naked to dry my clothes, for the sun was warm – the water from the great mountains icy. When I was warm again I fished on all day and every day in this manner, the weather being that of a perfect English summer. In the evening I carried my fish on a pole with a co-opted helper some miles to the road end and the camper. This was elemental sport, needing strength and stamina. I was fishing like a wild, primitive man and though moving all too fast towards my seventieth year, I grew stronger every day to attain a toughness beyond that of my youth. It was paradise untrammelled, as enjoyed by a wild hunter.

Then one day, fishing, I felt a heavy thrust in the small of my back and nearly jumped out of the river. My subconscious was always alert for a crocodile, for there were crocs there. This time it was only a large bundle of paper grass which the cutter had sent down in this easy way – easier than carrying it on his head. Slightly startled, I swore indignantly at him, breaking the spell of paradise.

I had to use my jungle lore to decide whether a pool was safe or not. Generally I avoided rocky ones with sub-aqueous caves which crocodiles use as larders, but once I was shown a monster up a shallow side stream. After that I was always a little nervous since they can move very quickly and I would be wet, cold and slow, slithering over the round, polished stones.

Corbett Park – the Ramguaga River crocodile and gharal pool – watercolour by author.

When I fished one lovely curved pool which would have been a classic in Scotland, along the bank above it came a thin trickle of men carrying fascines of bamboo on their heads, so that I had to cast a quick fly when there was a short gap in their ranks. They received my bellowed curses calmly – just another mad Sahib!

The forest guard nearby in his humble hut was much afraid of wild elephants and would keep burning the tall grass to keep them at bay. In this he was doing no more than his duty because the coarse grass was burnt annually to encourage green shoots for a greater than natural concentration of spotted deer: the tiger's food. But the guard never seemed to get the grass going and was always lighting up in scattered places so that I had to break off fishing and move the camper up the difficult track to save it from destruction.

There were many otters in the Ramganga, but in the balance of nature which the wardens were so keen to maintain, there were enough fish for everyone. But the otters resented my fishing. They didn't think there were enough fish and I would be surrounded by mustachioed little heads, looking for all the world like cavalry majors in a club smoking room, hissing disapprovingly. I suppose they, like the crocodiles, could have been a threat, for a couple will gang up on a big python, taking a bite at its neck from one side, then the other, until its head is nearly severed and it is killed. When they left the water all together and closely packed, they flowed over the round stones looking like an expensive fur coat being dragged along the ground.

The long drive back to camp in the dark down seven miles of track, nursing the caravan over appalling bumps, was a magic time. I had to give the jewel-eyed nightjars, dazzled by the lights, time to fly clear. Little Here-here, the hare, seemed anchored to the beam of light and would zig-zag ahead of us. He was always there at the same place, hence my name for him. At the same time I had to keep a sharp lookout for wild elephants going down for a late bathe. They sometimes got aggressive if they had their children with them, so had to be given time to cross the road.

When we arrived back at Dhikala there would be a rush of camp servants to the camper, for we gave all our catch to them, as there was little protein in their usual diet. As far as we could we kept the distribution on a strict rota, but they were fair and would remind me if someone was on duty and could not get his share. To add to a perfect day's sport, I felt I was catching food for those who really needed it.

Towards the spring a little silver fish with black spots (*Barulus bolar*), erroneously called the Indian trout and averaging two pounds, took the fly readily and was good eating. Having often caught this size of trout I could compare their fighting qualities and *Barulus* was the better. It was not unusual to catch a hundred in a day and I caught as many as I could because of the camp staff.

I had not thought that fish would be so popular, but when I emptied out my basket on an early visit, an onlooker had murmured, 'I could do with a nice fish

Corbett Park – The Tiger Pool – watercolour by author.

like that!' I gave it to him gladly. Next time people came up saying, 'Here's our fish!' After that it was a case of 'Where's my fish?' and 'Why aren't you going fishing?' if I had not gone out. There is a Hindi proverb, 'If you offer a man your hand, in the end he will take your arm.'

When I got back to England, each day increasingly I forgot the irritations of my secret Patli Dun and I reproached myself for being angry with the coolies since I was no longer 'The Sahib'. I forgot the starling-like flocking of visitors. I forgot the pall of smoke that pervaded the camp from the burning elephant dung in their lines and the firing of the coarse grass down the valley. I forgot the pestilential and multi-lingual jungle crow. I remembered the joy of long walks in the jungle and all the soft noises which told me a sweet story and called me insistently. I remembered the distant roar of a mating tiger at night and the incessant thwacking of the nightjars in the full spring moon. How I longed to return again!

Chapter 20

Elephants I Never Forget

Elephants have always intrigued me, for there is so much more to be learned about them. Zoologists rave about the fidgety chimpanzee who with his short thumb can clumsily poke for food in a hole in a tree with a stick. 'Ah,' they say, 'It's the one animal which can use a tool.' The elephant, although it has a trunk and a tail, both of which are articulated to a surprising degree, also uses a tool when it wants to. I once watched one of the Park's tame animals waiting to move forward after having transported a party to a tiger showing. She picked up a stick with her trunk, broke it to the required length and then scratched the corner of her eye delicately. Next day, halted at the same spot, she found the same stick and carried out the same action.

An elephant can easily pick up a coin as small as a penny with its trunk. It can twiddle a juicy branch and turn it round in its mouth with great dexterity. It can gather a sheaf of long, dry grass with a deft twist and with the toes of a forefoot dig up its deep roots, pulling the while with its trunk so that the whole sheaf comes up with a ball of earth attached to it. The animal then bangs all the earth off on its forelegs till the root is clean. It then uses its trunk to roll up the sheaf across its mouth to the correct position so that it can nip off the sharp, spear-like seed husks which it rejects. The banging of the roots makes a herd of grass-grazing elephants sound like a combine harvester at work. The noise is almost identical and gives the herd's position away to me when I am looking for it. I did learn a little about tracking from the two very cheerful official trackers and after a while I found myself telling *them* where the elephants were, rather than the other way round. It was one of their jobs to locate the herd so that the short-stay tourists could, regrettably, embus to see it. I think the trackers felt I saved them a lot of unnecessary bother. Later still, when I found the herd I told no one, because that only started a rush of cars out to see it and considerable harassment for my rotund friends. Then it was just me and them for happy months.

When feeding off a leafy tree an elephant will strip off a few branches and then push the tree down with its forehead to eat the leaves and bark at leisure. When it browses like this it is terribly untidy. If I find trees fallen this way and that – some of them over eighteen inches in diameter – I know that the herd has been there. One of the trackers told me that two or three males will push over a particularly big tree working all together. He described how they did it. Pushing from all sides with their foreheads, they loosened the roots and when they heard one give with a crack, they all went round to that side and forced the tree down. Though I have not seen this happen, I have seen some very large trees they have knocked down. The same tracker said that when the tree fell the elephants would all raise their trunks in a bellow of triumph.

I saw elephants do this myself when two tame ones were made to haul the wildlife warden's jeep up a bank down which it had fallen. After pulling it up on the road, both elephants raised their trunks and cheered. However, one of them was but newly purchased from a neighbouring *nawab* and, feeling that car recovery was against the rule of her union, she remembered the palmy days with the potentate and slipped off to her old home. The *mahawat* (driver and keeper), an idle man and fat – most mahawats are small, lean and wiry – had been day-dreaming. He went up to the warden and chipped in, 'Please Sir, – er, – er, I've lost something.'

'Look round in the grass, you fool,' said the great man testily, thinking he had lost something unimportant.

'Oh, but honoured Sir, I've lost my elephant.'

'Your elephant?' the warden almost yelped.

It took twenty-four hours to track and recapture Phul Kale (Flower Bud), who was well on the way to her old home.

Wild elephants survive through their herd organisation. When a cow calves there is always another calfless female to come and help. The calves are kept enclosed in a compact group hedged round by a protective wall of massive cows. The compactness of formation is essential as a tiger will cut in like lightning and snatch a very small calf, which to it is as tender as a sucking pig is to us. The newly born calf walks under its mother's belly to be within easy reach of her teats which are placed forward on her chest. When a herd has had to take to hasty flight, I have seen a mother snatch up her very young baby in her trunk and dash off with the rest, lest the baby be left behind or trampled on. They must have caught my scent because the whole herd disappeared in a flash as if at a signal. The wind in the valley is always capricious. Later in the year while I was fishing I saw a herd crossing the river. A mother and a nurse elephant supported a baby over it with their trunks. Motherhood seems extremely important to the cow elephant and I feel sad that the tame riding elephant cows in the Park are now denied this experience.

Indian elephant cows have no tusks, or occasionally only tiny ones, but an old cow is leader of the herd of cows and young bulls. I say leader because her authority is permanent. From time to time a big tusker will join the herd to mate and will protect it with his goring tusks, but even then he stands off from it. At other times he is just as likely to be off with another tusker in a small 'stag' party – how Indian. A tusker near a herd can be a real danger, or shall I say threat, to a tracker. I have never stood my ground with one to see what he would do. Would you? Sometimes wild elephants are aggressive, at other times evasive – not so fierce as their African cousins, but always unpredictable; therein lies some danger. When I am on foot I feel very small if a tusker swings towards me and he looks as tall as the Empire State building. Moreover, while I am watching the herd closely, he can circle round at a distance and outflank me. In one instance, hearing a crackle behind us, I realised that we had been out-manoeuvred. We slipped away down the remaining track and a big jungle leopard, finding things a bit close, said, 'I'm coming too!' and he did.

It is an old cow who bosses and leads the herd, as I have said. No wonder an elephant remembers, she has so much to pass on. She knows where the bamboo is most tender up on the lower slopes of the hills and then, when the jungle dries out and the bamboo grows tough in the winter drought, she knows where to go. She leads her charges to feed on the big leaves of the sub-tropical trees, where they crunch the greener branches noisily and use the smaller ones to swat flies and insects all over themselves, for their skin is surprisingly tender – again, using a tool. They strip off bark neatly and pass the tenderest part to the calves. Then they go where the elephant grass is thick and high enough to hide the herd and provide roughage for the elephantine gut.

Trying to add to my hard-won knowledge of India and its jungles I asked a forest officer the name of the tall grass. Forest officers have to learn the botanical names in English and Latin and are generally knowledgeable. The officer replied blandly that the grass tall enough to conceal an elephant was called elephant grass and that which concealed a deer was called deer grass and so on. Really, I was getting nowhere in my search for jungle knowledge. How far were we to descend? Presumably mouse grass would be as close as an English lawn. It is so often like this in India.

But I fared better than a senior forest officer many, many years ago on his first visit to the rain forests from the scrub jungle of Central India. A junior officer was taking him round his range, a carefree individual who had not done his homework. His senior asked him the names of various trees and plants and he readily gave a name to each, being determined not to be stumped. It is said to this day that some of his names, which were odd, have stuck. I have always wondered if the lovely, soft purple Barclay tree which sounds so improbable is one of these.

The old cow knows the salt licks which clean parasites out of the intestines. She knows the quicksands, so dangerous to the elephant, who must nevertheless have a daily bath. She knows where the lollipop stands are, for the jungle has them in the wild orange, the mango trees, the sweet figs and other fruit stalls. She and the other nurse cows chastise the calves with their trunks to keep them from wandering. Their protesting squeaks sound like toy balloons being rubbed together and I know at once if there are some small baby elephants to watch. They are great fun, as they romp and spar like puppies.

The leader knows where to find the cooling earth with which the herd can cover its back as a protection against heat and insects. Mud is both a cosmetic and a shield. With their highly articulated trunks the elephants press the mud into a little ball and then throw it dextrously over their shoulders.

What an animal! It has to have a brain to control four monstrous legs, a trunk that can do almost anything and a tail with a bottlebrush end so exactly controllable that it can fastidiously clean its most intimate parts. It has a cooling system too. The large ears are full of veins and by flapping them the elephant cools its circulation. I have noticed that zoo elephants in England have much smaller ears, presumably atrophied through lack of use. The pale grey colour of the animal commits it to nothing, for the bright light casts sharp shadows which break up its great surface, but the constant flapping of its ears gives the herd away. It looks black when wet and red when covered with sand.

I have seen elephants in big herds as if gathering for a convention, but they then tend to break up into little family groups. When a small group rejoins a herd I have watched it stop some distance away to be identified. One of their number goes forward to greet the leader of the larger party. This latter will accept her with a brief touch of trunk to trunk. It reminds me of the military procedure: 'Advance one and be recognised.' These gregarious animals settle their pecking order early in life after a good deal of skirmishing. There is no communism in the natural world or artificial levelling down to a proletariat.

Few people know that if it must, an elephant can deal decisively with a marauding tiger. It seldom uses its trunk and is chary of its being clawed, so it tucks it away between its forelegs, since it is very, very tender, although it feels like old bark. A great deal of training is necessary to teach a tame elephant to stand firm in a tiger drive. The wild ones will do this in order to protect the herd if attacked, but the fear of the tiger is always there. Their main weapon is a really hefty football kick with the forefoot, killing the tiger, or sometimes a man, outright. Twice while I was there a dead tiger was found in the Park and, when examined, it was discovered that although in both cases the skin was intact, each had sustained multiple internal injuries as if from a terrific blow. I lifted one tiger's head and could feel the neck was clearly broken under the skin. The only tracks in the area other than those of the tiger itself were those of an elephant and only a kick could have effected this bludgeon-like destruction. The foresters and trackers who were there all agreed. An elephant can also deliver a kick with its hind leg, somewhat less powerfully, but unexpectedly in a sideways direction. I have seen this when a senior riding elephant puts a younger newcomer in her place in the hierarchy. The rear foot kicks at right angles, rather like a karate blow. However, if a tiger is actually cornered between two elephants, one of them will try and kneel on it. The trunk is used for smaller adversaries, such as man, in a lightning swipe, followed up by trampling.

Tuskers fighting each other do primarily use their tusks. I once examined a sizeable one that had been pierced fore and again aft as he had turned away, so deeply that he had been killed on the spot. There was no blood trail. There he lay, already somewhat decomposed, looking like a grotesque, blown up rubber toy, the legs sticking up stiffly and of course he stank terribly. It was an awful smell and an awful lot of smell. It is not very common for one tusker to kill another, for more often the weaker breaks off, conceding victory. The head-on clashes frequently result in broken tusks, so that animals with one whole tusk and a stump only are common. This one had only one whole tusk, so presumably his last battle was not his first. Low caste sweeper Babu Lal had the job of hacking the tusk out and was given a whole bottle of rum with which to fortify himself against the stench. So thrifty is the forestry department, that any tusks so retrieved or any deer's horn cast seasonally are sold on behalf of forestry funds.

Elephants are capable of a fair variety of calls and sounds. A piercing trumpet, as loud as and similar to a bugle, denotes panic and an odd noise is created by banging the trunk on the ground – a loud, hollow plopping sound. This is an anxiety signal when one smells a tiger – the nearest equivalent to a human's wringing of hands. They also have a particularly hoarse roar, quite unlike a tiger's. It generally indicates irritation and means a threat. A variation, more like a bellow of great depth and volume, is used when friends meet. The tame elephants in Corbett Park, all females, form special friendships. Phul Kale and Sheikna are great friends and will rush towards each other in the morning after having been in separate stables all night, bellowing mightily as if they were going to fight, but these are cries of joy. When they meet, each touches the other softly with her trunk. I have often wondered if perhaps they are mother and daughter, captured separately in their long lives?

The most remarkable sound they make is a burbling purr, sometimes loud, sometimes so soft as only to be audible to an elephant. It can sound like the exhaust of one of those splendid old racing Bentleys, but signifies friendship and is companionable. The sudden switching off of this low purring noise by one elephant and then another until the whole herd is silent is a kind of negative warning signal of danger. Then they will vanish into the tall grass in one motion. When an elephant is making this noise you can feel it in its throat, as you can a cat's purr. Don't try this on a wild one.

The tame cows I have mentioned above all have characters of their own. I found them soft and feminine with their brown eyes and long black lashes. It is essential to an elephant's health, whether wild or tame, to bathe daily. I was returning from a long trip on Malan Kale (Flower Bud of Malan) when she began complaining continually in a high-pitched whine. She had seen the others off duty, bathing happily, and she felt hard done by. Malan Kale was my favourite – big and fat and always eating. She was hopeless on tiger stalks since she made so much noise tearing down branches for food, but we loved her dearly through the years. She always came confidently up to me, and her own *mahawat*, Bashir, told me she remembered me since years ago I had given her a large basket of coarse brown sugar balls. Oh, I do hope that Flower Bud of Malan is still padding the paths. It could be so, for she was not old.

Another of the *mahawats*, Sharafat, told me a story about her which demonstrates her steadfastness and intelligence. A *mahawat*, or more often his assistant, has to go out with an animal and chop off a big load of green branches for fodder for the elephants. Whilst cutting high up, Sharafat slipped and fell to the ground. Picking himself up with difficulty, for the fall had been very heavy and he was alone, he climbed up onto Malan Kale in the normal way, walking up her trunk whilst grasping both her ears. An elephant trained in this exercise slowly raises her trunk and head so as to enable her driver to deposit himself on her back without difficulty. Sharafat, badly hurt and in great pain, fell unconscious among the greenery already on her back. They were some five kilometres from base camp at Dhikala and but one from Kinanauli forest bungalow in the other direction. Malan Kale chose to carry Sharafat away from Dhikala to Kinanauli. What made her do this is not quite clear, but she apparently sought help from the nearest place, although she had seldom visited it and Dhikala was where she lived. It might have seemed that her first thoughts would have been for home where she would have her cool evening bath in the river and could have expected some large wheaten cakes to make up for her lack of grazing time. Did she reason that Sherafat needed help as quickly as possible? It would seem so. She attracted the attention of the watchman at the bungalow, who at first could not understand her agitation, but eventually saw an arm sticking out from the branches on her back and found Sharafat still unconscious. The watchman sent for help and everyone was full of praise for Malan Kale. This is just another incident to add to those that make me feel that elephants have the power of reasoning, for I have confirmed this story. I put my questions in a random way to a number of independent sources so that the story should come out naturally. I did not want to guide the answer or encourage the usual embellishments. For once in life I got some authoritative evidence. I had come a long way to learn, so I pressed hard.

How different these old ladies look compared with their wild sisters. They are rusty in appearance rather than smooth and polished like the free elephants, but yet with their extra feeding and care are in far better condition than a zoo animal – perhaps they are less bored and have something like a herd organisation. An elephant must never be bored and it needs its fellows.

How I hate zoos. I've seen animals slowly going mad with lack of exercise and interest. How they must suffer; they are far more intelligent than we imagine. Even safari parks are still zoos since their size must be limited by the lack of land in our overcrowded country. On the other hand I have noticed that small children seem naturally to find an emotional link with animals. There must be some way of helping children to meet and touch animals formerly regarded as 'wild'. Then and then only is there a hope that they will whole-heartedly cherish and protect these animals.

I never tired of watching the wild elephants and never forget how I once saw sixty of them advancing across a plain towards me like an armada. Later in the evening the same party crossed the road led by a big cow. Small ones half crossed, then stopped and waited for a particular friend, who came up and there was much pushing and sparring, with coiled trunk against coiled trunk.

One day we came upon a little party who winded us. Four or five young led by a cow came out of the bushes. Then a big tusker with one tusk and a stump. He moved towards us, so we retreated, following a rule of moving away some sixty yards ahead. At this distance one is beyond the elephant's vision, though its hearing and sense of smell are acute. Peggy and I slipped round the corner, then ran a bit. I gave her a clear lead and brought up the rear, prepared to jettison my sweater if too closely pressed. An elephant will pause and examine such a garment and valuable time is gained. On reaching the next bend we waited and round the tusker came. When he was within sixty yards of us we slipped away in the same manner. We repeated this manoeuvre three times, after which the tusker broke off. He had, in a gentlemanly way conducted us away from the cows and young and we could admire his inimitable, slow swinging stride. We felt rather *de trop* in the face of such dignity and may appear to have been rather overcautious, but the only animals experienced foresters fear are the elephant and the sloth bear.

The elephants had been disturbed by a party of Indian Administrative Service trainees. Having heard of the animals' arrival they had crowded out of the camp and stopped on the other side of a grassy area between them and the herd. The grass was being burnt as part of the routine to encourage tender growth for the deer. The men started to shout and the animals, already upset by the burning, roared angrily and made short rushes to the edge of the fire, upon which the trainees ran away. This advance and withdrawal went on for some time and then the party went back to camp to get their hired bus, the better to see the elephants in the long grass. We had our encounter during this pause. The party returned, some of them crowded as is their wont on the roof of the vehicle, and the shouting continued once more. As the elephants became more angry, the men on the bus roof began to feel threatened and begged the driver to withdraw. Those inside said, 'No,' and that they could see quite clearly, thank you! This harassment of wild life is still all too common – presumably an instinct inherited from primitive man when all animals were a threat. We were lucky to have been so gently moved off by the tusker.

On another walk in the jungle we saw white patches in the shade of the track ahead of us and I dismissed them as the shirt sleeves of some road workers. But I looked again. The dark background was elephant – big elephant. The white was *two* pairs of tusks – big tusks. Using the withdrawal method described above and only running each time we had turned a corner out of sight, we got a series of good views. We had to be careful lest we be seen running, for it would tend to invite a chase by animals much faster than us. And so the two monsters came forward in single file – the two largest elephants and pairs of tusks I have ever seen, one of them a little bigger than the other. I was fascinated by their silent approach and their dipping, swinging gait. Like all great tuskers they moved their heads slightly from side to side as though peering. The massive protrusion of the skull above the base of the trunk prevents them from seeing immediately to their front – hence this movement. On the other hand to look backwards, the whole body follows a zig-zag course, so that the eyes, set well back, can thus look over the shoulders. We enjoyed the thrill and the controlled power. I don't think we were taking risks, though tales of rogues and killings abound. Normally we could hear the animals before we saw them and took care not to move upwind of the herd. By moving downwind of it we could get very close.

The reason for our odd 'stop-go' manoeuvre was that elephants move faster than one first realises. They can run and turn at a horrifying speed though their bulk makes them look slow. On one of our first visits to the Park Peggy and I were playing with mud, water and sticks – always an absorbing thing to do. We were trying to drain the mud road along the edge of the jungle, where I did not want to get the camper stuck when we went fishing the next day. By chance we looked up and there, rounding a corner, was a big elephant, swinging purpose-fully towards us. How black he looked, shining in the rain under the fringe of acacia trees, but his tusks showed white and sharp. We decided to leave at a fast walk. We dared not run as that could have provoked a charge. Taking huge strides, feeling we looked like Groucho Marx, trying not to look hurried, we hoped to get ahead of him out of his vision. Hard as we tried we did not make any ground although he was only strolling after us, and we were beginning to tire. I didn't think the elephant could actually see us very well, but the wind was blowing from us to him so he knew all about us. Just as I was beginning to feel rather anxious we reached a track right-angled away from the jungle and popped down it. When we felt we were at a safe distance we turned and saw him pausing at the junction for some time, testing the air with his trunk held high over his head like a teapot spout. We had time to admire him before, to our relief, he went straight on.

What a fine animal he was. Most elephants look rather baggy, but he was cylindrical in shape. I asked Negi about this and he said that the foresters classify male elephants in two shapes – rotund and barrel. Our elephant was definitely barrel, full of muscle and no bagginess. He said this latter type were powerful fighters and went on to confirm that he himself was more frightened of elephants than of tigers. He also mentioned the existence of very large tuskless males, known as *makhnas*, but did not know if they were natural neuters or not.

Rogue elephants and *musth* tuskers there are, and I give a wide berth to a solitary one, for he could be either. The *musth* tusker is one afflicted with

An Indian bull elephant in its prime. Drawing by the author.

temporary craziness and the condition is indicated by a blackish ooze on its temples. Whilst in *musth* the animal is often most dangerous. This period is not necessarily linked with the sexual urge, though there may be some connection. Mating and *musth* are not always coincident. A rogue elephant is one who has learned his strength and power to terrorise and plunder, and many a hill service bus has been bowled over by one.

One of the tame elephants, Diamond Bud, was killed by a wild tusker in *musth* while grazing outside the camp in the rainy season, perhaps because she would not respond, or because she had the smell of hated men on her. Her bones, soon picked clean, were scattered beyond the camp and more than once in the following winter I saw a herd of wild elephants walking over them and systematically turning them over in a sort of macabre dance. No one could say why they did this, but I think they are deeply conscious of death.

Elephant trainers have told me that those reared from birth in captivity are not so manageable as those captured in a wild state – in reverse of falconry. Can it be that the former have found weaknesses in the character of man and have learned to doubt his omnipotence?

Like men, elephants vary in character, but they have a streak of mischief in their natures. Understandably they dislike anything man-made in their jungles and root up all the milestones on the forest roads. Yellow painted milestones lying about in the road have always been the first indication to us of the arrival of a herd down from the bamboo slopes. Similarly, forest rest houses are damaged if not well guarded. Cattlemen in their grass huts deep in the jungle are raided for their stores of rice and coarse brown sugar. The grass huts are often pushed over and the hearth fire sets all alight. Cattle are sometimes destroyed and villagers fighting back occasionally killed.

The *mahawats* are the elephant drivers of India. They are specialists in the job which they retain with a handed-down, hereditary pride. I say drivers advisedly for to get anything as bulky as an elephant from A to B involves a great deal of muscular effort. To be astride the elephant's neck, the normal riding (driving) position, involves an uncomfortably wide straddle, so it is not surprising that so many of these men are bow-legged and somewhat sunken down on their pelvises. When thus bestraddled there is much of the horseman's knee and leg 'aiding', but the bare foot also prods the base of the elephant's ear with the big toe dominant – a more sensitive guide than any rack and pinion arrangement. Otherwise there is a range of command words, the most common being *ma'lle*, spoken sharply and meaning 'Get on!' I have been told that the words are derived from ancient Sanskrit. I don't know for certain, but I do know that the elephant is an essential part of India's long history and her panoply, so these words could have been handed down from the distant past.

Elephants do delay in carrying out orders as if to assert their own considerable personalities for a moment, but for downright disobedience the *mahawat* administers a sharp blow with the *ankus* (the heavy iron spike and hook) on the two-lobed skull. I look down on this skull covered with short, stubby black hair and wince at the blow, which is hard because the elephant thus chastised draws in its breath sharply in pain. Once a *mahawat* did this and his charge reached upwards and backwards with her trunk as if to snatch him off his perch and dash him to the ground to be knelt on. I felt this was a purely instinctive movement, in fact a feminine *moue* at his roughness. Yet it was a tense second and the *mahawat* touched her uplifted nostrils with his hand in an apologetic gesture, muttering well understood words of affection, for there has to be affection and love between the puny *mahawat* and his massive steed, or the whole relationship would not work. But he must never let the elephant get away with it. His authority must be supreme because he is dealing with a very intelligent animal who will be quick to see and seize upon any weakness in this authority.

In the forestry department there is a quiet little ceremony after nightfall when all the elephants visit a senior inspecting officer in a moving man-to-elephant and elephant-to-man meeting of friendship and mutual respect. The elephants, their hard day's work done, file up to him stripped of all saddlery in what is a visit without restraints, for the *mahawats* do not ride on them but walk behind and there are no sharp orders. In this tranquil evening assembly the forest officer gives each animal a huge cake of concentrated wheat flour. It is as though the elephants are being thanked for their work and they in their turn have been taught to raise their trunks in a salute on a quiet command. I find this coming together, often in the evening twilight, a very lovable affair.

However, a *mahawat* who is too free with his *ankus*, or who fiddles the elephant's rations beyond the accepted norm so that it goes short, and so breaks this bond of friendship, can be killed by his charge, some day, somewhere as quick as lightning. It has not forgotten.

The *mahawat*'s job is hard and, as I mentioned before, he has an assistant to help him. The elephant loves its regular baths and lies languidly in the shallows, trunk clear for breathing while the *mahawat* or his assistant grooms the vast area of wrinkled skin, scrubbing every inch with a brick to remove ticks and scurf, the elephant the while lying with a voluptuous expression on its face. The *mahawat*, or generally the assistant, has to climb high trees with a machete in one hand to cut off green branches. These trees are special, some being better fodder than others and often the search ranges wide. Every year they have to go further and further and take more and more time as the trees are cut back. It requires a surprising area of forest, so difficult to spare, to maintain a relatively small number of these animals. The assistant climbs precariously, chopping off the green branches. To sharp commands of '*Dhat, dhat,*' the elephant lifts these branches onto her back where the man stacks them neatly without the use of ropes and knots. A fully loaded line of elephants returning with this fodder looks like the forest of Dunsinane on the move.

The tame elephant must have this rather coarse fibre and then it needs to change its diet in rotation to elephant grass – a diet of roughage, not too dry, just as the wild elephant does. It must be taken to drink copiously twice a day, when it fills its trunk up with gallons which are poured down into the stomach through its mouth with a loud, lavatorial gurgling.

It is the task of the women, in addition to that which is normal, to bake daily large, soft, wheaten cakes such as the forest officer hands out. The working elephant cannot graze all day long as in the wild and man has found a quick nourishing way of compensating for this. The *mahawat* is well paid in comparison with other camp servants and this pay rather quaintly allows him to draw more rations than the elephant can eat, so he can officially sell the rest. Just so did the British forestry of old fit into the ways of the Indians who would otherwise fiddle the rations anyway. Still, the *mahawat* certainly earns his pay and grows old quickly.

Salim was the nephew of Bashir, the head *mahawat*. Although uneducated Indians are vague about their origins, I think the names of this family of hereditary *mahawats* date back to the forcible conversions to Islam, of the Turko-Afghan invasions, for the men are called Bashir, Hamid or Salim and differ thus from the later Muslim invaders who had names like Nur Khan, Sher Ali and so forth. I believe that the families were in existence and carried on their profession long before either Muslim conquest.

Salim and his widely ramified family were far darker than the other northern Indians round them since they came from the eastern part of the province. He was as near black as could be and the nape of his neck which took the sun like all outdoor workers' was a pure matt black. During the years of our visits to our beloved Corbett Park we watched him grow up from a cheeky small boy with a pet goat to manhood, which comes early in the east. Goodlooking and of an alert intelligence, he was quick to wheedle gifts of fishing hooks and lines, warm pullovers and photographs of the goat out of us. All the servants suffered terribly from cold, though the northern winter was not to us too severe, so we used to bring a reserve of woollies to give them. It was sad to think that Salim's elephant duties allowed no time for real schooling. He was too far away from any school anyway and from infancy had had to look after, amuse and carry about his younger brothers and sisters. In India a little girl of four will mother her little sister of two and carry her straddled on her hip. It is by such things that one's heart is rent and drawn to that ever cheerful, ever hungry country.

I felt that Salim might easily become a slick scrounger, but the stern demands of his elephant calling could mould him. He brought dear Malan Kale round to us to show how he had mastered all the commands and aids, but she obeyed him rather cursorily as though merely indulging the young. She did not recognise him yet as a *mahawat*.

On one of our later visits he approached us thoughtfully. He said that he would lose his job in another branch of the forestry service if he did not subject himself to vasectomy, as he had been told to do. Such was the pressure that Indira Gandhi's unpopular son, Sanjay, exerted on the bewildered masses that led to the widespread reaction in which Indira fell temporarily and dramatically from power. Salim added that he was betrothed, which put him in a fix. I advised him to stall a bit and in the end all turned out well. His marriage went through and he was taken on the *mahawats'* strength. All of them went down from the Park to Ramnagar with all the elephants to attend the wedding and lend lustre to the occasion. So there may be another Salim to cajole and pester visitors.

I knew Hamid, a senior *mahawat*, sweet and gentle in nature and with fine carved features, for the twelve years of my visits to the Park. At forty he looked seventy and once sought our medical help, as so many did. Cold and miserable with pneumonia and dysentery, he was continuing to work. He had to fill his job or others would. No one cared. We gave him a thick pullover, and stuffed him daily with a full course of broad spectrum antibiotics and expectorants, plus an astringent chest rub. Like so many Indians borne up by faith in western nostrums, he improved dramatically. Unlike so many Indians who accepted our efforts with only casual thanks for a recognised service, he gave us three beautiful eggs from his treasured hens, whom the jackals so often carried off. I looked at the little brown eggs, accepted them gratefully, and felt very touched.

But Hamid, the father of ten, had to have a vasectomy. As he had been away for a time I asked him how he was since he looked downcast. A brash clerk intervened to say he had had the operation, sniggered and then looked embarrassed. Hamid was deeply depressed as in an eastern setting it was an assault on his pride and virility. He felt it desperately. What a wretched problem the population explosion is! If the earth is not to be despoiled to extinction, numbers must somehow be controlled, but for the abjectly poor of India, having children when they have nothing else is so obviously their great joy and gives them a sense of identity.

The construction of the Ramganga reservoir in the Park has posed many problems, including the encouragement of intestinal parasites among the axis deer (tiger food), crowded together in the diminished grazing areas on the river bed. The reservoir level drops rapidly in the winter as thousands of new farm settlements downstream demand more and more water and the changes in level present problems for the *mahawats* who never know just how deep the water is near the shore. Incidentally, this constant change of level has prevented the lake from becoming a centre of wildfowl, although it is on the migration line, because a nest built at the reedy water's edge may suddenly be left high and dry and the young exposed to raptors. All in all the reservoir has done nothing except for increasing mankind.

As the lake is close to the elephant lines, it is convenient to water and scrub the animals there when the level is high, but Ram Piari (Beloved of Rama) slipped and fell into deep water. Unable to climb out she swam away strongly and disappeared in the failing light. Her *mahawat* and his family were in despair. The innumerable children wept and would not be comforted. Their elders would not eat. The *mahawat* did not expect to be sacked for negligence, for Narain Negi was a just camp officer. It was simply that Ram Piari was the lynch pin of the family. Her warm, matronly bulk was their bastion.

Many days later she was found at the head of the reservoir where there was still thick undergrowth. There had seemed to be little hope for the elephant, closely shackled as she was with a stout chain. Everyone thought that the chain would certainly have snagged on one of the many trees which the planners had failed to clear from the river valley at the outset of this sorry plan. They had all felt that the old grey cow elephant would have drowned, for the banks were too steep for her to have scrambled up, but somehow she had swum strongly against the current to land near the swift head inflow. What rejoicing – what gifts of sugar balls were given!

Israel, another *mahawat*, was a deplorable specimen. We always tried to doctor him up, but felt it was hopeless to help him, toothless and near voiceless at thirty-five. Israel, tending his elephant at the lakeside, slipped off her back into the deep water and quietly drowned amongst the general splashing. By the time we got back from a walk an hour had elapsed and efforts to save him were hopeless. The Hindus were prominent in trying to bring up the unfortunate Muslim's body; the poor are not proud and forget about caste in time of trouble. They tried so hard, but were poor swimmers and duck divers. I felt sorry I had not been there earlier, though a bit old for the challenge. The women were massed on the bank, calling loudly and incessantly on Allah for help. Israel's sixty-year-old mother was there – she was blind and looked ninety. Her bread-winner was gone. He had not been confirmed by the forestry service in the rank of *mahawat* and there would be no pension. His body surfaced thirty-six hours later – the crocodiles hadn't got it. He was buried according to Muslim rites just outside the camp in a silent, leafy grove.

I would like to think that this great animal, the elephant, will go on into the future, but I doubt it very much as the forests are rapidly dwindling to give place to agriculture. Elephants and farming do not go together. As the forests disappear the elephants are forced to raid succulent crops. Then it is an easy step for the farmers to pressurise or bribe local officials to declare the elephants rogues to be destroyed. Not very long ago a prominent German diplomat in New Delhi shot no fewer than nine tuskers during his tour of duty. All he needed to do was to bribe the local police officer and get him to declare the elephants to be rogues and a danger to the public. May his conscience gore him unbearably when he thinks of so many splendid, innocent beasts slaughtered. The Nazi will out.

The filling of the reservoir in the Park cut the local herd's migration paths from the bamboo slopes to the heavy jungle and grassland. I was told that on reaching the water, the elephants rushed about bellowing in distress and fury. Later, they did find a more precipitous way round, but many did not take it and we no longer saw the large armada advancing, sixty at a time, across the burnt stubble.

Chapter 21

Puddings for Panthers

Put it all down to Tiger Jim, but this is not quite true, as our love for animals and particularly wild ones has always been strong. After all, they are human beings who haven't quite made it and their problems are not so different from ours. A wild tiger particularly attracts us as the most spectacular of all cats. I tell my Indian friends that their jungles will be as insipid as curry without red pepper were they to let the tiger die out, and international interest would dwindle. India in the face of difficulties has done extremely well in a short time to preserve the tiger and has expanded sanctuaries, in the face of political pressure and the need for space to accommodate her exploding population which is increasing at such a frightening rate.

Tiger Jim was well known in Utter Pradesh – a big male in New Delhi Zoo under the Red Fort. He had in comparison with most a large open area in which to pace up and down, but of course for such an active animal a mere nothing. There was a broad ditch full of water between him and the public and when the latter became too irritating he staged a 'ferocious' charge towards them and landed with a splash in the moat making a wonderful opportunity for photographers. In his huge leap when fully extended his forepaws were drawn up under his chin and he zoomed through the air like a projectile. He was in good condition though his coat was not so red as that of a wild tiger. Many photographers claimed that they had taken pictures of wild tigers in order to prove their own virility, but Tiger Jim has a slight cast in one eye and if you look closely at the photos it is always there.

Not so in the work of Brijendra Singh of the Kapurthala family whose pictures of wild tigers and other forest animals were amongst the earliest at the time when interest in wild life in India really started. He took us along with him to try and call up a tiger as Jim Corbett used to, using the same device – a simple one in which, roughly speaking, a leather thong was pulled through the taut skin of a long-shaped Indian drum, producing the rasping moan of a tiger looking for a mate. It was very realistic and carried well. Pulling the thong several times we sent a message through the tree tops of Corbett Park and listened, holding our breath. At last, seemingly from a great distance our call was answered. We were delighted but on further investigation found it was only a fish owl calling from a ravine nearby. Tension fell flat very quickly, but I am sure that with his patient application Brijendra Singh is calling the tiger up at his princely behest.

We were determined to go and see the wild tiger for ourselves rather than in the tourist 'tiger drives' organised in early days by the staff of the Park, though as the tigers' numbers in the reserve increased I began to question the wisdom of going to look for them on foot. I weighed up the risks and believed them to be no more than those of crossing a crowded street in England, but I did take precautions. Peggy and I talked quietly to each other so that a tiger would be perfectly aware of our presence and could cross the road or track before us, or after we had passed, generally stopping to have a good look at us. We have often seen this powerhouse of lithe muscle standing in our path. There is something about his movements that is hard to describe. He is so lissom that suddenly he is there and suddenly he is not. Before he goes we are coolly and, I feel, disdainfully appraised and as he leaves he strolls off slowly and with dignity. There is time to admire his shape and beauty and his remarkable ears, white with black edges. When he does turn away he gives an expressive flick with the tip of his tail as if in contemptuous dismissal of mere man. Although tigers live in fear of him they consciously maintain their dignity. One we met on a long walk looked us over very carefully and as he was rather lean and rangy I thought he was calculating how many juicy collops of meat I would make. Peggy said, 'Doesn't he look friendly,' and I was afraid she might go up and stroke him. I had a funny feeling he would have rolled on his back to have his tummy rubbed like all the visiting cats at our own home. A tiger walking away from you will never look back even if he continues ahead for half a mile. Should he show any such weakness he would no longer be king of the jungle.

As the number of tigers increases so will those of man-eaters and I doubt if I would take such liberties today. The parks are not large enough to hold them and as they move out to the tall sugar cane they can be wounded by angry farmers defending their herds with inefficient weapons. A maimed tiger is a potential man-eater as man is the only quarry slow enough for him to catch easily. At times the only food tigers can find is porcupine, which they seem to think delicious. Unfortunately for them, a porcupine's spines all stick out backwards in its only, but formidable, defence. As it naturally does not want to be a dinner it pivots round and round on its nose, presenting its weapons to the tiger who, always irascible, loses patience and takes a swipe at the prickly ball and gets some of those spines deeply embedded in its forearm. These are not barbed as popularly supposed, but get bitten off short by the desperate tiger who then goes dead lame and a potential man-eater is created.

Some years ago the Conservator of Wild Life, Uttar Pradesh, told me with a laugh that one man-eater was proving a great asset patrolling the borders of a new sanctuary near Nepal and deterring marauding Gurkhas from coming down to shoot deer. I think by now such unofficial wardens are becoming too numerous. The authorities are not so worried as they are beginning to regard the occasional human victims as almost fair game. After all, there are far more people than tigers, and India can surely spare a few.

I did avoid pushing through thick cover as it is very dangerous to disturb a tiger asleep. If when I went fishing I had to force my way through lantana scrub or tall grassland I coughed at frequent intervals to give any tiger warning to move off. Once I saw water starting to pour back into pug (paw) marks in the mud just in front of me. He must have been close and I saw that it was a male for the toes were round, not pointed. On another day I found two tigers sunning themselves on the bank of my favourite pool. They made off, but as I methodically fished down the long stretch of water I had shivers down my spine for I felt them watching me.

A tiger which is harassed may lose its head and attack. This happened during one of our visits to the Park when a scattered gang of road workers, on seeing one, started to shout at it from all quarters. The tiger, feeling it had no line of withdrawal, broke out attacking the nearest man.

A couple of villagers living on the edge of the Park and knowing that a tiger had killed a deer thought they would be clever and retrieve a haunch of venison – meat is always scarce. They reasoned that the animal, as is usual after a kill, had gone to slake his thirst and they pushed through a tunnel of grass through which he had carried his meal. The tiger had not left and dashed down the passage, severely mauling them on his way. In such cases a tiger is at once described by the local population as a man-eater to be destroyed. It is fortunate that nowadays the local authority carries out a sort of drumhead court-martial to give such an animal a fair chance. The story was wormed out of the two villagers by Narain Negi and the tiger was exonerated.

Tigers are very active animals and their shoulders are so supple that they thrust their forefeet forward in long strides. When a male is hunting or looking for a mate he will go as much as thirty miles in a night, so Jim didn't have much room, did he! The animal is generally nocturnal but when the days are long he becomes hungry before it is dark and we have seen him in the evening or the early morning. He relies on a short, surprise rush in order to kill for he cannot sustain a chase any more than a lion can and I have seen a yearling axis deer (cheetal) easily outrun its pursuer. A cub has much to learn or it will starve. Predators cannot be bred in captivity with a view to returning them to the wild in significant numbers, as they have not been taught to hunt and just lie around waiting for lunch to be served, eyeing passing deer with mild interest.

A tiger's roar is the most exciting sound I have ever heard. It is so deep that it seems to thud off the ground. One year, visiting Sariska Sanctuary in Rajasthan, we were allowed as a special favour to park our caravan deep in the jungle. It was a noisy night under the full moon that had turned the trees and rocks to silver, for the large number of peafowl who live there kept up a continual chatter – the hens were particularly gossipy. Then a tiger roared three times – the full roar, not a mating call: 'Shut up! – *Shut up!* – SHUT UP!' he commanded. The king had spoken and for the rest of the night there was not a sound.

Now, as I suppose I am growing old, I have no hope of seeing the wild tiger again. Recently I was given Valmik Thapar's book, *Tigers, The Secret Life*. It is the most remarkable study of tigers you could find anywhere. The author and his photographer, Fateh Singh Rathore, have had the love, patience and dedication to produce a masterpiece which can surely have no equal. Flipping through the pages of this lovely book I was smitten with such pangs of nostalgia, which is a really sharp pain in the midriff, that I could not bear to turn the pages over more. It is relegated to the 'coffee table'.

The tiger has some smaller relations in Corbett Park among all the other attractive animals. The Indian jungle cat, somewhat larger than a big domestic one and with longer legs, is very brave and seems to hold man in truculent contempt. I have seen one stand firm in the path of my car at night. Once on a walk we saw a cat some distance away, coming down the track towards us. We froze and it just walked on; closing with us, and passed two feet away, giving us a dirty look. I think cats, even domestic ones, regard human beings as second class cats only. Another day we were following one up along the track. It gave one glance back just to see where we were and then continued on a hundred yards ahead for some distance. Then it stopped, crouched and pounced into the bushes and to our astonishment dragged some animal of its own size in a rapid snatch across the track and into the bushes opposite. It was so quick that we could not guess what the prey was. Almost immediately a doe axis deer dashed after it like an avenging angel. There was a scuffle and much growling from the cat. We waited for a while and then crept up, upon which the doe ran back across the track into cover. There in the grass at the side we saw a dear little fawn, dark chestnut with rows and rows of white spots placed so close together that its outline was completely broken up in camouflage. It was seemingly unharmed, though a bit wet about the neck. We shooed it over in the direction of its mother and moved away quickly to let her join it, which she did and led the fawn into the protection of other does. It is seldom in the jungle that one sees a drama to the finish and, for once, a happy one. Having unwittingly interfered with the course of nature by walking up and frightening off the mother, we had to complete our action by uniting the pair again, though I feel that as a rule one must not intervene, however cruel nature may be. Death in the jungle is swift and soon forgotten in the happy, sunlit glades.

The rain forest leopard or panther is a very big animal and beautifully marked. His spots are in dark and rich rosettes – the locals call him *Gul Bagh* (a flowered beast). He is just that much smaller than the tiger, which enables him to crouch unobserved in short grass or along a branch and be more difficult to find and see in the jungle.

Occasionally a panther will try to take away a tiger's kill and can come to a sticky end. We discovered the corpse of one in the jungle that had had its neck broken. There were large tooth marks on the neck – it had been killed by a tiger.

One day, wandering through the *sal* trees on an elephant, we came suddenly upon two sloth bears clawing grubs out of an old stump. With sharp barking noises they stood their ground. The elephant, Flower Bud, pirouetted abruptly, nearly unseating us. She feared for her tender trunk, for one swipe of the little bear's claws can remove a man's face. This small, rusty black, pigeon-toed bear, so unlike his big, glossy black Himalayan cousin, is congenitally bad tempered and if disturbed just wades in with his long razor-sharp claws.

I store animals' noises in my memory for future reference. The following year in another part of the forest we saw the unmistakable tracks of a sloth bear, looking rather like a deformed, small human foot, the claw marks showing very square since they are not retractile. Soon after we heard that same characteristic bark, somewhat doglike. It was time to disappear quickly and, hurrying Peggy off, I followed up as rearguard. It is probably the most dangerous of all animals in the Park. Its short-sightedness makes it nervous and irritable.

After this I thought it wise to warn an able young ornithologist about the bear, but he had to go out and see the place for himself. He was, as always, determined to miss nothing. He had a shock of untidy red hair and a shaggy red beard. Cautiously approaching the spot I had described, he saw the bear – and the bear saw him; the large, tousled, red apparition with big, saucer-blue eyes peering over a bush was too much for it. Giving a sharp yip of terror it rushed off in its comic, short, bouncing gallop.

The Park holds substantial numbers of wild pig – a second source of food for the tiger. The wild boar although relatively small is immensely powerful and even a tiger hesitates to attack a full grown male. A young boar joined the camp one day entirely on his own initiative. This was most unusual and he had to be protected by a special notice board to stop children teasing him. What can have made the one animal out of so many leave his natural scene to consort with man? Could it be that for once an animal wished to make the first gesture of friendship? Perhaps I am too sentimental, but he seemed to need man's companionship. Possibly this freak action is how evolution develops, with some animal suddenly doing something different. He was named Guddu by the staff and used to collect rations daily from the kitchen. We had to fend him off when we were cooking puris out of doors. He had his eye on those little wheaten puffs, deep fried in hot oil. Guddu liked his bread hot, but that was not enough. He was a skilful pillager and would search visitors' baggage for tit-bits, sometimes giving them terrible frights at night as he wriggled into their tents. Some of the noisy girl students would shriek when faced with a pig worse than death. Through the years he grew into a mighty wild boar with ferocious tusks. He used to go back to the jungle from time to time to mate, but was always turning up at the kitchen door. Alas, this friend from the jungle came to a sad end. He rifled the baggage once too often and devoured a roll of ciné film, of all things, which killed him.

On our long walks we made our acquaintance once more with the big, silver-grey, black-faced langurs we had seen in Pachmari. Their tremendous athletic leaps were always a feat to wonder at. They were so timid that they took flight when we wished but to look at them and convey our feelings of admiration to them. They would plunge down from the trees in front of us with what seemed painfully loud thumps; they must have very strong bones. However, when we saw them from the back of a riding elephant with our friend Mr Upadayahah, the Chief Wild Life Warden, they were not in the least afraid. Like other animals they as usual assumed we were only an elephant.

Mr Upadayayah looked up at them and shook his head from side to side in the peculiar Indian fashion saying sadly, 'Puddings for Panthers!' Should a panther appear all is panic. They slither down from the trees and rush about in confusion on the ground, becoming an easy prey. Had they remained on the more slender branches, they would have been safe.

High up, sunning himself in the last light, I could see the big leader, his white whiskers framing his black face like a halo. It interested me that the langur troups were inherently inefficient, unlike most animals. They seemed to have intelligence, but no stability. They would post a sentry high up in a tree to look out for danger, but he would soon become bored and desert his post to eat the sour *amla* fruit.

I shall miss all the smaller animals in the Indian forests. Many of them are rare and to see some of them is quite an achievement; unravelling a bit of camouflage needs considerable practice. There is one infallible test. If you think you see some little striped cat sitting motionless among the dry leaves and shadows, you can be sure that it is a figment of your imagination. Small animals, and indeed all animals, are never still. They constantly look round, on guard for danger. The only exceptions are young fawns temporarily left by their mothers, and replete pythons. Both rely on their immobility for protection.

I am often puzzled when approaching wild cloven-hoofed animals, including the boar, on foot for they do not seem to be as alert as their dangerous lives would lead me to expect. I am able to get quite close to them and they stand there peering, to dash off at the very last moment in a wild panic – the axis and hog deer showing the undersides of their tails in a white flag of danger and the axis, that most beautiful of all deer, giving its popping call which sounds like the surprised yelp of a girl who has suddenly had her bottom pinched.

There is one animal which attracts real affection and almost forces me to say, 'What a dear little thing!', though I seldom gush. It is the muntjack with its jittery dog-like alarm bark, so often the signal of a tiger's approach. Its bright, chestnut coat shines like satin in the sun. It is all poise for its slender hind legs are flexed to be released in a powerful spring. Its dainty head with small, curved horns on strong pedicles is grace enough, but to complete perfection it has dark pencilled eyebrows, the envy of any Beauty. It is a solitary denison of the deep jungle and goes about clicking its tusks audibly in what must be almost a nervous tic, for it has many enemies. I always remember how a small one once came right up to me in a jungle clearing, infinitely trusting and appealing. We had been watching the little jewelled sunbirds who arrive in spring and this was an unexpected bonus.

Our very last day in the Park on our very last visit had to come and we were walking along a narrow path, quite close to the camp. It was our favourite place to see wild animals as cars could not drive down it to disturb them, since it was cut by a deep water course. It is unusual to see a dangerous snake in the dry season, although the crested serpent eagles seem to make a good living. Suddenly, down on the track behind me to my right there was a heavy rustle in the bushes and I shouted to Peggy who was following, 'Jump!', for I'd seen the thick, golden brown coils of a large cobra winding up ready to strike. The threat of the jungle is always there and I felt that we had been given a reminder that fortune had smiled on us through the years, but that we had perhaps been indulged enough.

Chapter 22

Under the Haldu Tree I

When I served in India I always felt as if I were looking out at a brightly lit street through a plate glass window, cut off from the people, though I made some sallies into that street to incur the lifted eyebrows of my brother officers. I realised that under my haldu tree I would be well placed to contact the Indian people at first hand as I had so long wished, and to be approachable by a visitor from any part of the country, because the caravan was a motoring curiosity to Indians who are all ardent travellers. Their religions encourage them to travel on pilgrimages, be they Hindu or Muslim. I had their languages and we all had the curiosity. I felt there would be visits by people of all stations in life for we stood in the middle of the camp under a tree with no barriers and no privacy. Once we had drawn back our curtains we were open to visits, whatever the time of day and whatever we were doing. I had to be patient and put up with endless interruptions. It would be a strain, but what an opportunity!

When people enquire what strikes me most about Indians, I can only reply that there are many Indians and all are different. I feel rather helpless for in a life span one can only scratch the surface. I know mine would only be a point of view and an over-critical one, due to my inborn prejudices, but I was determined to swallow them on this, my last opportunity.

Looking out from my caravan on its island under my tree, most of my observations have been of the middle classes of northern India on holiday. To stick to generalities: the foundation of their lives is religion and religious observances which provide a colourful and sometimes threatening background to all their activities. I would say further that few of them take any exercise whatever during their stay in the Park or in their ordinary lives. One hardly ever sees anyone going for a good walk or a jog. There are enlightened ones here and there, but this astonishing lethargy, combined with heavy smoking is, I believe, largely responsible for the very high incidence of heart trouble. So many of my friends, some of them quite young, seem to have either a bad heart or diabetes. Food cooked in clarified butter is, as I have said earlier, perhaps another cause of ill health. Many better class Indians are switching to European-style food, but this I feel is no solution as meat, eggs and vegetables are so often of poor quality owing to the lack of organic fertilisers. I personally find such a meal cooked in India almost uneatable.

Can it be that the Indo-European, sometimes called Aryan – the former invader from the uplands of Central Asia – has gradually found India's cruel and enervating heat too much? Since the end of the eighteenth century and the establishment of British rule the massive inflow of lean, tough northern invaders and fresh blood has stopped. No longer do the lean kine lick up the fat. My more well-to-do friends tell me that they themselves are lazy and this is true.

When I looked out of my caravan window I often saw an unathletic family from the leisured classes piling into an Ambassador car to go to the restaurant, a full hundred yards away. This was, of course, in part to show they owned or could afford to hire a vehicle so as to arrive in pomp – face is all important. When they did walk from their rooms they drifted slowly, many with arms folded, which gave them a backward tilt of the body. The fat women bulged out of their tight bodices and showed a big fold of brown skin and in their flat sandals they looked particularly ungainly in saris, like pouter pigeons. How dark they were, for they came from the eastern part of Uttar Pradesh. Their features were coarse too, unlike those of other Indians of the north who have a high average of good looks. So many of the men coming to see animals wore dark business suits while the elegant sari is the worst form of dress in which to go riding on elephants. It is a garment that makes the wearer constantly tweak and fidget. A slim, small-boned Indian woman in a gorgeous sari for the right occasion can, however, be arrestingly beautiful and I think it is probably the most graceful costume a woman can wear if she is the right shape. Europeans, please don't try! You will make bulky bundles of yourselves, for your bones are too big.

The well-to-do used generally to get up and saunter about in the early morning in dressing gown and pyjamas and were accustomed to sit down to breakfast in this crumpled garb and with tousled hair. The men would wander about later in the day with little packets of spice seeds which they flicked dextrously into their mouths.

Much time is spent sitting and chatting, mainly about money, generally petty cash. The educated Indian will talk 'Kitcheri' almost without realising it. The sitters joggle their legs continuously, showing tension. You seldom see an Indian reading a book, but they are fond of cards and pull out a pack very readily, as we found when staying with the Puris. For me their most disconcerting characteristic is an apparent lack of mental concentration. If you try to answer a sensible question as well as you can you will find the listener does not listen for more than a fleeting second but breaks in and makes some other remark or observation while you are answering. Later, the same question will be asked, showing that he has not listened to a word you have said. Have I been unfair to those I like so much? I can criticise myself too for they must be thinking what an odd fellow I am, with strange failings.

One day I saw an Ambassador car arrive out in the sunlight: this is a by-gone Morris Oxford made under licence in India. A four-seater, this one carried only six passengers and a driver, for its occupants were sturdy Sikhs. Often a family of up to ten lightly-boned Indians will cram into the gallant little car. These Sikhs wearing bright turbans, pale pink, pale blue, peach coloured and even sprigged muslin, with their beards neatly rolled round a sort of chin cord, tumbled out of their car, laughing in a high-pitched titter which did not accord with their manly appearance. It made me want to laugh too – it was such a risible sound. Servants unloaded the roof rack, piled high with *bistras*, the famous all-containing bedding rolls of Indian travellers. I knew they would soon be round my caravan and they were, questioning me first as to its cost, then my origin, the nature of the engine and anything else that occurred to them. I knew too that we would have a merry evening with them if I invited them to a drink, but I knew I would have to keep firm hold on the bottle for the Sikh has a strong head. Patiala Sikhs measure their whiskey with two fingers, but between the first and little ones – a Patiala Peg. However, they eschew tobacco as forbidden by their religion, for a fighting party when the Sikhs were trying to establish themselves was once surprised sitting round the companionable *hookah* for a smoke.

They have a rollicking humour and are undeservedly the butt of many other Indians. They can clown, but they are certainly not buffoons. However, to say to a Sikh in Punjabi, 'O brother, it has gone twelve noon!' if he drives danger-ously or makes some other error, is to imply that with all that hair and turban his brains must be boiling by mid-day. This sally is usually taken good-na-turedly and again with the high chuckle.

The Sikh shows great devotion to his symbolic appearance. It takes him a long time to comb his hair, wind his turban and arrange his beard – a daily discipline. It was a similar discipline that deceived the Persian spies watching the Spartans before Thermopylae. As one who has commanded Sikhs, it was always well known among us that to bring out this soldier's full qualities it was essential to keep him busy, work him and play games with him to exhaustion if you wanted to maintain discipline. On these terms the Sikh was a big, formidable fighting man, one of the best in the Indian army or indeed any other army. Brilliance has its heights and depths and he can soon become discontented and indulge in intrigue, which is a sort of intricate mental exercise in India. This fatal tendency has always been likely to set the Sikhs at loggerheads with a central government.

Yet another party of middle class Indians then arrived at speed to stop at the last moment with the usual squeal of brakes and clouds of dust. They brought the usual servants. The master will not unload his car or do a hand's turn – it would be *infra dig*. He will not even fetch a glass of water for himself, but will shout for it to be brought to him. There is much shouting. An Indian will yell at a fellow, be he only a yard or two away. Those who come from densely gregarious communities have little consciousness of noise and privacy means nothing.

A few hours later there was a peremptory knocking on the caravan door. We opened to see a diminutive girl with big bows in her hair. She cocked her head appealingly and asked, 'Can I see your *carawan*?' I readily agreed though I was busy cooking a curry and it was obvious I was occupied. The child was the advance guard for her whole family who arrived from behind a hut and mounted the vehicle. The springs groaned, as I did more silently. I said, '*Ram, Ram,*' a correct greeting to a Hindu in the army, avoiding the more common '*Namaste*' with hands pressed together which seems to me prayer-like and prissy.

The party appeared to be lower middle-class petty shopkeepers known as *Banias*, far better off than most of India's under-privileged millions. There were two women with their nearly black hair parted in the middle and pulled back tightly in a bun, who wore the red *tikka* on their foreheads (the mark of a married woman). Four or five young men squeezed aboard too. As is usual, particularly in the UP, unlike many parts of India, there was no common style of headdress. One man had a pink, fluffy wool balaclava, its peak pulled down casually over one ear. There were pale blue and buff berets pulled down over both ears, for to Indians the Park was cold. Another had a woollen scarf wrapped round his head, the fringe flopping untidily and an ultimate horror was, as is very common, a World War I type of skull-fitting flying helmet with a jackal fur lining and flapping flaps. Incongruously, the men all wore dark city suits. One of them escaped and twisted my driving mirror to admire his Ronald Colman moustache. This always drives me to a fury as it gets loose when I most need it.

By this time I was tumbling over numerous children. There were some late teenagers, daughters or sisters in tight, bell-bottomed jeans, floppy hats and ponchos in a desperate, but dated attempt to emulate the weird hippy costumes mistakenly taken as the norm of Britain's youth by young Indians who were on the whole much nicer than they look. Their names when introduced were either Darly (Dolly) or Bunty and as usual the youths were called Bubbles or Bunny.

'You are from *Landan*?' they queried. England is never mentioned and London seems to take the place of the whole of our isles.

'How much your *wehicle* cost?' they demanded, still more of them piling aboard.

Then the most important question, 'Have you a toilet?' They viewed our emergency porta-potti with awe.

'Where is your driver?' – that perennial question. I explained that on so long a journey one could not have a driver. It would mean a much bigger caravan with separate quarters. But attention had flitted and I was interrupted.

'Is that a fire extinguisher? Where do you sleep?' I explained how the beds worked, but I could see they weren't listening.

They put superficial questions concerning the engine, the radio and the cassette player – always asking the price. The same questions were repeated several times and I explained again, knowing that nothing was sinking in.

I did not send them all packing though I tend to blow my top easily. Such parties look so terribly abashed if I do and I feel a bit of a cad. I knew that they came from close-packed, noisy dwellings in crowded streets, reverberating with the sound of car horns, the cries of street vendors and the rattles of the performing monkey and dancing bear men. They were simply unaware of crowding, noise and the need for privacy. It all seemed an offence in Corbett Park's deep rain forests and I heaved a small sigh of relief when the visit ended, though still reminding myself that I'd come to study and must be patient.

The party departed, chattering like starlings, and I heard the remark, 'No driver!' and there was much shaking of heads. Clearly I must be of low caste and of no account, for do not all men of consequence have drivers? To drive is to do something manual and demeaning.

This party, like others, had included the inevitable teen-age boy in charge of the younger children. He carried the little ones about, looked after and amused them the whole day through. Anything they wanted, he did, knowing well that if he did not, they would shop him to their parents with angry squeals. He looked shabby and half-starved, worn to a shred. I was fairly certain that he was a bond servant, handed over by his parents to repay a debt or virtually to sell him into slavery as is so common in India, though no one will admit it.

The following day a party of petty tradespeople arrived for a picnic. Indians are ardent picnickers. They did not look at the superb view of rank upon rank of hills, dreaming up to the mountains. No, the family were head down over their meal pots done up in dishcloths. The men sat lissomly, tailor fashion and in comfort, though they were corpulent. Dextrously they began to raise the food to their mouths with their right hands. Normally women of that class eat after their men, but old traditions are slowly breaking down. However, they were eating in a separate group with their backs decorously to the men – not so very emancipated.

With the exception of the better educated, Indian women as a general rule walk a few paces behind their men. I've noticed that when master holds forth with many a stiff-armed gesture, but with flexible wrists and hands, his wife wags her head from side to side in dutiful agreement. It is unusual for her kind to disagree openly.

After what appeared to be a large meal, the men lay on their backs on the concrete platform where they had picnicked. Their distended stomachs rose spherically and for all to see in the camp's midst and they lay and snored unselfconsciously – an occasional belch rolled across the valley. In the east one must exaggerate one's belch as a time-honoured compliment to the cook, listening anxiously for it at the kitchen door.

A brief nap and they stuffed themselves into a small car and left without so much as a glance at the wealth of beauty around. What did they get out of their trip, I wondered? I do so hope they enjoyed it. I couldn't help liking them. It was a workmanlike picnic followed by a quick rest. I had a feeling almost of affection for this uninhibited party who knew what they wanted and did it.

Chapter 23

Under the Haldu Tree II

For our long stays in Corbett Park we were kept supplied with fresh food sent up some thirty miles over bumpy roads. The supplies were arranged by Shiv Kunwar Singh, the proprietor of the dilapidated restaurant. It was a great kindness and not his responsibility. He was a fat, dapper little man and I would see him walking a hundred yards down the road every morning. He claimed to be a great walker and called this his exercise. He was unlikely to get any thinner as he loved rich curry which he made richer still by lacing it with very refined ghi out of a medicine bottle.

There were no means of communication between the Park and the outside world, except by dilatory post, but he was never caught out when, as was usual, unexpected guests arrived in large numbers demanding food, although his cold storage arrangements were constantly bedevilled by electricity failures. Power came from distant Kalaghar, below the reservoir dam, with which the only method of communication was by runner when the ill-guarded pylons were fused by elephants who infuriatedly attacked the humming wires and electrocuted themselves.

Shiv Kunwar Singh is a proud man, very highly educated and with a good writing hand. He is shorter than most of the Gharwali people, though fair, being half Burmese. He could have had a good appointment with Burma Shell, but he forewent this in order to look after his ageing father. He is justly proud of his father who served in the Burma Police and was given the prized distinction of Rai Bahadur and awarded the Indian Police Medal. A great slayer of the fiendishly cruel Burmese dacoits, with whom I too have dealt, he also spied out the land to report on Japanese incursions into Thailand just before they invaded Burma. Shiv's grandfather was equally distinguished in the Burma Frontier Force. An uncle, chosen out of his clan to go to Sandhurst by Sir Harcourt Butler, the then Governor of the UP, was commissioned into the Indian army. Tall and fair as an Englishman, he was killed in the Shwele Bridge battle in Burma. I often saw his son, Brij Mohan, who was almost embarrassingly pleased to meet me, a member of the old Raj. Traditional loyalty has in him become almost a mania. He told me that as he was only an infant when his father was killed, he had no memory of him, nor had he a single token to show

184

proudly to his friends. He asked me if I could possibly get him a photograph of Sandhurst, as indeed I have. I feel it is all rather sad – just another loyal Indian thrown into war's cauldron without so much as a bubble.

Perhaps Shiv saw in me, the old has-been, some vestige of the Raj that has gone and that is why he was so kind to me, though getting up our supplies was an added burden. When I got irritable about the noise in his restaurant at night and was later somewhat contrite, he would say to me, 'I regard you as one of the elders of the family.' The elders are always indulged in the east.

Thus supplied so that we could do our own cooking and avoid the fly-blown horrors of the restaurant, we stayed in the Park until the heat drove us away. I always insisted on adding ten per cent to Shiv's charges for I knew only too well that the jungle road was appallingly rough and by staying put I saved wear and tear on my camper, the only practical means of living close to India's jungles for long periods. Other travellers, not possessing roots in a respected past, who tried to muscle in on my supply lines were haughtily refused by Shiv who said, drawing himself to his small full height, 'I am *not* a shopkeeper!' But shopkeeper indeed he had been, for he had made his little pile with a Coca-Cola stall in the rough and tumble of Ramnagar. In the camp he was always surrounded by a bevy of pretty boy assistants who disrespectfully called him 'Coca'. His sophisticated and charming wife remained far away in their village looking after their land.

The day seemed to be much as usual – we cooked an omelette, baked chapatties for breakfast and then took the 'sick parade'. The British in India always looked after their sick servants and any others who might drop in and the staff in the camp automatically looked to us for help, but I did not want to be patronising and asked permission to give it. This was rather grudgingly given, as the staff said that they had medical supplies of their own. These came up in bulk at rare and random intervals and would be lavishly distributed without any instructions as to their use by one of the sillier reception clerks. There had been none for months. There must be an element of faith in our doctoring, for it was remarkable how those really sick or those with advanced ulcers recovered dramatically.

After 'sick parade' we emerged from our camper and met a party whom we were expecting – a publisher and his friends, in connection with the sales of my first book. He was a regular visitor to the Park and had brought an interesting party with him. Cultured himself, his friends were lively and modern in their outlook. Among them were a caterer, a building contractor, a government official and a tea planter – all old companions who had been at school or college together. They were all upper middle class as is usual in such professions in India. Characteristically they were somewhat loud voiced and had an air of self-assurance, but in no way were they objectionable to the quieter European visitors. They were most friendly and their wives were sophisticated and forthcoming. There was none of the subservience of the women of the next stage down in the social scale, nor were there any signs of the usual distressing lack of concentration. They were indeed most pleasantly vivacious. The publisher's wife had a sparkling vitality. Not a beauty by western standards, although all the wives were good looking, she struck me as being a distinct type which has run through the complex Indian statuary. Her eyes were almond-shaped and long-lashed, her lips full and voluptuous. Her nose was long and curved down – I will not use the term 'hooked' for this suggests abruptness. It was, however, the main feature of the face, for her chin was not strong or heavy as is so often the case in western women, especially the vitamin-reared younger generation. I was greatly struck with her as many an old man would be, but an arrow from Cupid's bow always strikes us dotards only a glancing blow; the wound soon heals. All I can say is that she was the epitome of classical Indian sculpture which I had previously thought to be purely stylized. But no, here it was come to life – gay, attractive and charming.

We were asked to supper, but after a little pleasant conversation were whisked away to a bonfire party. A large bus-load of girl polytechnic students had arrived and organised a singsong. When we joined them they were singing and dancing in the light of a bonfire, jiving sinuously. Many had fair skin and white teeth were flashing, while their hair loosened down their backs was strong and black. The party then began singing couplets and soon on the opposite side of the fire others took up the singing. Positions were taken across the flickering, smoky flames and a couplet was sung which had to be quickly matched by the opposing side. Many were drawn from the traditional proverbs in which Indian folklore is so rich. They made quick improvisations to save being stumped and these were loudly acclaimed. I was struck by the gaiety that sprang from this quick-thinking game and realised that in England we have nothing like it now. What a good way to enjoy an evening with friends: entertainment with no artificial props. Only hand clapping kept the rhythm of the songs and dances, until one of the girls produced an old plastic bucket and used it as a *tabla* (hand drum). I was left with the feeling that India can be vivacious, quick-witted and infinitely friendly.

We went back to a wonderful Indian supper. There were, as is usual, many dishes and all too soon our plates were piled high with spiced foods of exquisite flavours, cooled with curds and a spinach-like dish of tender mustard shoots. The cooking was superb and much preparation and art had gone into it. Indian food at its best need not be too peppery, but is delicately flavoured with many blended spices, freshly ground for the meal. I seek no longer for ambrosia for here it is. After the meal, as is the custom, we took our leave. For a little while we had been part of India.

Next day there was a discreet cough outside the caravan. I knew that asthmatic cough – it was Chahu's. We have known this stunted little sweeper (cleaner) for years now. It became routine for him to have a teaspoonful of cough mixture from time to time. It did him little good, for he was always sweeping up clouds of dust and he got no better, but perhaps it did help him for he knew someone acknowledged his existence and liked him, since in his life he was ignored and looked through. To me he was a little landmark sitting on his hunkers outside the lower-priced hutments where he cleaned. That day he brought his niece, a small girl of about eleven. She had a badly swollen foot, cut in many places when she had taken a moment off from looking after her numerous little brothers and sisters and in playing had injured herself – probably on a broken bottle, for all refuse from the camp was thrown over the wall down a bank, as though it were a steamer that could leave its rubbish behind. New quarters were always being built, but never anything so dull as an incinerator.

She did not know her age so we had to guess at it to estimate the antibiotic dosage. It was silly to ask her. They never do know their ages and she had had no birthdays with presents to mark the passage of time. Old Chahu himself had no idea of his own age. Next day she came for another dressing, bringing with her tiny brothers and sisters – she couldn't leave them behind. She had the good looks which are so common in India and had put on her best clothes. Her dignity and poise were remarkable and she made conversation like a hostess in her own drawing-room. She was much better and her little escort peeped sideways into the strange and wonderful vehicle. Small girls carried their sisters or brothers on their hips, and those carried were little smaller than their small nurses. Where did the strength come from? From the fact that life was an accepted burden. How tiny these children were: pretty little under-nourished dolls. I looked at the little cortège with sadness as it moved off. Chahu had said that our coming each year gave him confidence through the cold winter, so bitter for him and for us so mild. I knew already that we would never be able to come again, for storm clouds were gathering across our homeward path.

Chahu and the other sweepers were full of shrewd observations. They were cynical about those in the camp who were better off and passed them by with unseeing eyes. Sometimes they remarked that the day would come when wrongs would be put right and there would be an uprising against all the graft which left them hungry. But I knew that they were too far down the bread line, bereft of vitality. You cannot revolt at some distant town, so far from your meal of kitchen left-overs. Where would you eat? How would you pay for a meal on £10.50 a month for yourself and your family? In India to make pronouncements is to wield a wand and remove the problem. Indira Gandhi's former election slogan, '*Hathau Gharibi!*' was as if to say, 'Begone dull poverty!' and no more. However, I asked Chahu whether he had in fact received any land in pursuance of recent legislation. He said, 'Yes,' he had a little land and some pigs and for once he looked me straight in the eyes, for his little 'briar patch' had given him pride. Normally his eyes were downcast.

Faquira, the doyen of the sweepers, had a thin, nagging, scolding voice, but many of his remarks were mordantly humorous as he pulled the others' legs.

His son is an epileptic and he once approached me to see if I could help him, but there was nothing I could do except sympathise. Rajan, who used to bring our water and raise clouds of dust round the caravan, giving our area special attention, was an extrovert, who being younger, still saw romance beyond his dust clouds. He improvised ballads at camp fireside parties and some, to our embarrassment, in our praise. It was always a great sorrow to him that he was unable to produce offspring – the one joy in the life of the poor. He once brought his pretty little wife to meet Peggy and see the caravan. She was dressed in her best and peeped out shyly from her sari, but as the years went by she became more and more neurotic at their failure to have children and her husband was always being sent for at a moment's notice to cope with a crisis in their distant home.

Rajan's singing, which we all tolerated, seeing in it a self-expression ringing out from a truly grey background, eventually got him into dire trouble. The camp was invaded by two bus-loads of giggling, chattering schoolgirls. There was no interest in animals and the teachers made no effort to instil it. One girl did look over the camp wall and remark rather inaccurately that she could see a 'loin'. All they wanted was to sing western pop songs round a bonfire. That was their object in coming – to sing, and sing all night to the discomfiture of other campers. Rajan, who had been told to tend the bonfire, just could not resist it and soon with one finger in his ear, he was singing a ballad in the typical, high, cracked Indian way. He revolved round the fire and the girls revolved too. The Principal who had made no effort to organise this swarm of maenads or to control them, suddenly went into action. She reported Rajan, the low caste sweeper, to the Wildlife Warden, a Brahmin. He, as is usual in India, lived in terror of his superiors and, fearing a scandal, took the easy road. He sacked Rajan out of hand for dancing at the same party as the teacher's high class, 'good' girls. We tried to intercede for him but to no avail. I had no leg to stand on in the face of India's prejudices and all I could do was to give him some money to tide him over.

For a year Rajan faced near starvation, but when the warden left for another appointment, I am glad to say that Narain Negi immediately reinstated him. But he was by then thin and listless. We set to, to build him up, but he had taken to smoking *bhang* as so many do to drown suffering and he had lost his sparkle.

On dear, another blissful day spoiled! Two bus-loads of schoolboys pulled up. The occupants soon spread like a plague over the camp lawns where we were sitting under the big banyan tree, idly watching birds gorge themselves on its figs. What brilliant colours they had: orioles, barbets and scarlet minivets. The dark-suited masters, having released their charges, went to the restaurant for tea. We were surrounded, overrun and had to put our best face on it. Being a now rapidly maturing grandfather, I have gained a great liking for children, so I decided to make the most of the situation. I started talking to the boys. They were by no means the riff-raff of the usual bus parties, for they were smartly turned out in blue-grey blazers, and as they were Sikhs their top knots were contained in a twist of stockinet of the same colour. They were Indian Air Force cadets, wisely caught young. We were subjected to a barrage of questions, many of them very much to the point for they had enquiring minds and I was conscious of a ring of bright brown, intelligent eyes. Having found out all about us and the route along which we had come, they asked if they could photograph us. Up went a battery of old-fashioned Brownie box cameras. Later I noticed that many had no film in them, for these are expensive for small boys, but to take photographs made them into mature excursionists.

The boys suddenly burst into ill-suppressed laughter at a figure standing on the verandah – a tourist: a redoubtable erstwhile officer of the Sappers and Miners. This retired British officer was wearing those wide-legged, rather long khaki shorts as we all had in the past when regulations said they had to be half-way down the knee-cap. I must admit he did look rather out of place. One of the elder boys called his fellows to order, saying sternly, 'Don't laugh. He is also human!'

Not everyone we met was so broad minded. There was a more sophisticated couple of Indians: he an international businessman and she in trim trousers and pullover. She was an attractive woman and her strong white teeth shone against her golden complexion. I put out my groundbait to get a lively discussion going, for I love nothing more than a good argument. I suggested that western tourists were exploited in a barefaced manner, referring to the board outside the reception office on which entirely different and far more expensive terms were blandly shown for foreigners *vis à vis* Indians. There was no finesse here. She replied by saying that tourists *should* be exploited. A Swedish friend of hers had gushingly assured her that it was enough for him just to be in India and to see a sacred cow starving in a bazaar. I saw that I was up against the absolute stone wall one so often encounters in dealing with an 'educated' Indian woman. I brought up my battering ram and said there was far too much poverty in India, partly caused by the population explosion and that the masses would not be patient for ever. What was her solution as a well-to-do Indian? My stone wall replied firmly, 'Kill them all!' and I think she really meant it. She and her class who practise birth control are terrified of being swallowed at the ballot box.

Russians were frequent visitors to Corbett Park. Pavel was the most prominent as he was very big and solid and wore American-type T-shirts and that atrocious American, long-peaked sports cap in which he looked like a shoveller duck. Because of this he was the only one who stood out of the anonymous flood. Perhaps I was too much on my guard, but I thought a couple of very cold eyes gazed out over his bland smile. He was an agricultural attaché at the embassy and, unrestricted, he had travelled all over India in his four years there, so that he had an extensive knowledge of the country and its resources. I felt a twinge of jealousy. He had probably seen more of India, my India, than I had, since I had to pay my own way. He was the only Russian to make any advance to us and asked to come with us on one of our well-known walks – a prophet is not without honour! A little puzzled, we agreed to take him. Though elderly, I wanted to put up a good show and set a smart pace and after the first hour, for all his muscularity, Pavel was showing distress. 'Up the old Sirkar,' I muttered to myself, puffing a bit. I told him all I knew about tiger pug marks and pointed out where tigers had sprayed the bushes like house cats to leave an acrid stench demarcating their areas.

So much of the Indian jungle is now covered in impenetrable *lantana* scrub – an interloper, though ideal protection for wild life. It is, however, strangling India's forests. Pavel paused in his stride and spoke musingly. 'If a man were to hide there, he would be difficult to find,' and then, comforting himself, 'But dogs would soon get him out.' From this Freudian slip he obviously regarded the jungle from a different point of view from mine.

Other Russians were probably more characteristic for those times. They used to visit in a large mini-bus from agricultural projects where they were working. They kept absolutely aloof with their overweight women. The camp staff told me they cooked for themselves and lived mainly on potatoes, but when they did have a meal at the restaurant, they would draw all the dishes round themselves and eat head down, glancing neither to right nor left and passing nothing. The staff were very shocked at such bad manners.

These parties did, however, fraternise occasionally with the lesser camp staff and presented many of them with enamelled, red owl buttonhole badges. The staff were very pleased with them, but I, game as ever, said the Russians were making owls out of them. They looked crestfallen and surreptitiously removed the badges. The owl may be a symbol of wisdom in the west, but in the east it is a term of abuse and a symbol of foolishness.

It was always interesting after camp chores were over to see who had arrived at Dhikala. Politicians, film stars and producers trying to sandwich an animal film between their great (and remunerative) epics, ornithologists, zoologists and ordinary tourists interested in wild life came. One day I spoke to a young man tinkering forlornly with a run-down Ambassador. I could offer no suggestions as to how to get it started since it was suffering from in-growing general rust. The young man was bare-headed and dressed in a loose white shirt and cotton trousers. He had a two-day growth of beard. I learned later that this pleasant and unassuming individual was none other than Rajiv Gandhi. Though he was Indira Gandhi's eldest son the general opinion was that he was just a nice nonentity then living in the shadow of his younger brother, Sanjay. The camp staff liked him because he never threw his weight about. I merely remembered him as Indira Gandhi was then well on the way to founding a dynasty with Sanjay as her successor.

One well-known British ornithologist and zoologist invited by the Government of India to advise upon the Park, paid it a short visit. He had a high brow and was bearded like the pard – almost a latter-day Shakespeare. Wishing to bask at the great man's feet, I asked permission to listen to his discourse to the assembled staff. He was most knowledgeable about birds and used all the 'in' expressions – predators had now become raptors and the habitat the biotope. After a while he said with some exasperation that he had the greatest difficulty in identifying those l.b.b.s. We asked him what he meant and he said impatiently, 'Little brown birds!' – *our* frustrated expression for we too have had that difficulty. After this remark his stature declined in our eyes.

He went on to tell the Wild Life Warden that the best way of counting cloven-hoofed animals was to divide the area up on a grid system and collect and sort out all the dung in each section and then weigh the piles. This had been most successful in Africa and, if it were done regularly, it would be possible to work out the numbers and distribution of fauna. There was a shocked silence and the high caste Brahmin warden hastily passed on to other matters. The idea that he and his staff should do such an untouchable job was preposterous and anyway Africa was *not* India. This only goes to show that every nation looks through spectacles of a different colour. What makes sense to one is gibberish or effrontery to another.

Chapter 24

The Last Journey Out

October 1978

Without the mortar of the British Empire the world was coming apart by 1978. Afghanistan, infiltrated by Russia, had had a second revolution. The Bear had turned on Prince Daud and struck him down, putting the ambitious puppet, Tariqi in his place. Pakistan was riven by political instability; Turkey was on the verge of bankruptcy and I had always felt it to be inherently the most dangerous country for a traveller. Tito was getting older and I thought the cobbled empire of Iran was certain to dissolve – its people are so volatile. Although the Shah was still in some sort of control in spite of riots and burnings, I knew it was an even chance that we would meet trouble, real trouble, but Peggy and I just had to go. In the high trees of my garden the collared doves were closing in with their lamenting call. All we had to travel in by then was a stock motor caravan rather like a gaily coloured Mandarin duck, but we were helpless against the little insistent voices: to India we must go, clearly for the last time.

When I told my publishers, John Murray, that I was going out yet again they said they were glad as they were considering another edition of *The Road to India* in spite of the gathering clouds. This confirmed my resolve because the book had been written for young travellers, so many of whom on my previous journeys had said, 'Having your book was as if you sat with us in the cab,' – reward enough for a humble writer. I could not let them down for I knew that the routes I had described so minutely had changed under the pounding of the great transporters on their way to Teheran and beyond, in what was then almost a Klondike rush by road, of export and import. Difficult parts of the journey had been by-passed and new stopping places had been constructed, notably for the TIR lorries. I had to face the fact that my book needed bringing up to date, though when I wrote it eastern routes had changed so little over so many years. I hated the thought, as the modifications needed great accuracy and it would have been so easy to have left it all as it was, especially as I had a terrible fear that these journeys would soon come to an end. It was hard to give of my best as it seemed destined to be futile and in the end it was. My careful amendments were all typed out at a friend's house in Islamabad and sent back to London. Murray's were delighted with them, but by the time they were ready to reprint, the road to India had been closed and few people were buying the book. The edition was abandoned, though a thin trickle of royalties continued for years to come.

With all these uncertainties we set out once more for India in October 1978. In Iran we motored through burnt-out towns where tanks stood menacingly at cross-roads. We slipped silently through before we were noticed and found an excellent by-pass from Qazvin to Rasht on the Caspian to avoid turgid and tormented Teheran. Our high, slab-sided vehicle seemed to tuck its tail well in as we slunk through town after town strung out, eastern fashion, along the road. Occasionally we saw mobs forming in the short side streets and some of them on seeing us set up a war-whoop, but I went faster than I would have advised and left them behind.

It was refreshing to leave the highly populated and productive seaboard and climb up and up through the Shah's forests towards Meshed, spread generously over a stony waste. Our onward journey was uneventful considering this type of travel, and our worst problem was a violent dust storm as we crossed the bad old Bojnourd Passes before the Meshed plateau. The eroded, unstable semi-desert was being hurried across the road by a gale. We fumbled along with headlights on at noon, and as each ten-yard field of view unfolded reluctantly before us through the brown dust we occasionally saw the huge bulk of a transporter blown over flat on its side. Knowing the road so well by then, I had loaded everything at floor level and my low-slung water tank was full, so that at each sideway slap of the gale our little Endeavour righted itself like a teetotum. Dust storms are always followed by rain in this drear part of the world and soon the dust was turned into liquid mud, clots of which were slopped onto our windscreen. By then we were oozing forward at little more than foot pace.

Somehow we crossed the three slimy passes and scrabbled into the yard of the tolerable and newly built 'Inn' just beyond Bojnourd. We tucked in close to the front façade, for it was time to seek security. The term 'Inn' in Iran meant in those days a travellers' hotel and the innkeeper there was a tall and personable man who welcomed us warmly. Hearing on the radio that the petrol refineries were going on strike we thought we had better fill up while we could as we had met political shortages before. So we climbed wearily into our high cab to go and fill up at a nearby station, but no – we were told that the storm had knocked out 'they electrics' and the pumps were not working. We returned to the Inn, assured that the pumps would work next day, to find it less welcoming as it too was plunged in darkness. We negotiated for a meal feeling that as so often our expectations would be thwarted, especially as the cook, temperamental like all his kind, was, judging by the sounds, starting to throw the meat choppers about blindly in the dark. We restored calm by bringing our red candles, each as thick as a barrel and being kept for Christmas, into the gloom. The cook was given

one and he lowered the cleaver with a purr. One was sent on a patrol to bring
beer and the third set a little pool of rosy light on our table with its unexpectedly white cloth. Fate that decrees that man shall suffer unnecessarily had
relented and we were served with a very good meal whose basis was rice from
Rasht province, the best rice in the world. And there was plenty of cold beer,
usually so elusive on these journeys. Surely the stars were now shining again
and brightly over this adobe Inn.

Mine host said he was training as a runner for the Olympics and I saw in this
totally vulgar political gathering the goal of his aspirations. He said he owed
his training and his career to the Shah and I felt sympathetic as I had been
impressed at the progress the much maligned Shah had achieved all along the
route I had used for ten years. I suppose the innkeeper and his family have been
eliminated by now and the pretty little Inn burnt down.

With a sigh of relief we got our petrol next day and by midday were skirting
the great religious centre of Meshed along the so-called Asian Highway whose
construction has never lived up to its grandiose name. Below us on the left
sprawled this great centre of the Shia sect, but the dust storm had caught up
with us and we could see neither the golden dome of the Imam Reza mosque
nor the blue dome of Gauhar Shad. The dust storm swept over us from the right
across the city's rubbish tips – a very foul smelling dust storm indeed. On the
left the glory of Islam: on the right corruption. Just a day in the life of a long
distance traveller.

I had been extremely anxious all the time about Afghanistan ahead. My
anxiety lay in the fact that I knew the Afghans are far tougher than the Iranis
and might well set upon travellers. I need not have worried. Passing through the
well known places – Herat, Kandahar, Ghazni and Kabul, we found an atmosphere of euphoria (for only too short a time). As is all too common, the man in
the street had been promised much by communism, but had not yet realised that
it cannot deliver. As usual, speaking Pushtu caused balm to be poured out
before us. Peggy's three words of the language went down splendidly with an
entirely new horror, a stout lady commissar on the border who followed her
about affectionately, though she was herself the muscle woman posted there to
strip suspect female travellers.

We left Herat by the Russian concrete road to Kandahar. I was pricking fast,
eager to get to my beloved Peshawar, full of memories of better times. It was
always at this point that I felt that the completion of this tricky journey was
within my grasp. The rhythmic clonking of the wheels from slab to slab of
concrete and the high hum of the engine were soothing and started me thinking,
for there was only an occasional affectionately ornamented, antique truck, its
tall wooden structure piled high and with passengers on the roof, boiling along
towards us to distract me. This road, which had caused me so much thought
through the years and about whose purpose I had so often warned my Afghan
friends, had recently been improved and the old concrete slabs were stacked out

in the desert looking like a lot of rejected marmite sandwiches, though for some years previously there had been little effort to repair them. Because of the repairs, were I still Military Attaché in Kabul I would have stuck my neck out this early November day of 1978 and staked my professional reputation to say that the Bear was coming – coming soon and in force. If ever there was a tank road, then this was it.

Some years before I had asked a prominent Afghan if he did not fear the Russians who were by then in Kabul in some numbers. He replied, 'We put them in a compound where we can keep an eye on them,' and winked oh so knowingly, adding, 'But we make a very good thing out of them!'

It was clear to me by the early seventies that the Russians were engineering the seizure of Afghanistan. First they flooded in technicians; I saw them myself in a large encampment next to the Guards' Division in Kabul near the Kabul Gorge route to Jelalabad. Then they ate the heart out of the Afghan apple, creating a fermentation and a ripe breeding ground for planting puppets. By 1978 there were Russian soldiery near the airport and three puppets were down, with Babrak Kamal to go – he went soon after.

We slipped quietly through Kabul, past the flat dusty barracks, where again there were Russian soldiers, and down the road that disappeared into a fold off the plain. Two days later we crossed the Pakistan border one more time at Tor Kham, but it was a very different homecoming from former journeys. The officials from the Frontier Province, all old friends, had gone and been replaced by dour Punjabis. representatives of the austere new regime that had overthrown Bhutto. They refused to understand my Pushtu, once the key to welcome, and I failed for the moment to realise the change. We hung about for hours while taciturn clerks dealt with a huge pile of passports at a snail's pace.

I began to realise that this might be the last of so many passages down the Khyber. Would I ever return through the great pass? I felt the Russians had committed themselves so far that they could not turn back. In order to keep a puppet leader in Kabul and give things an appearance of respectability they would have to go on increasing their hold on the country. I felt it would end up in a great weight of armour and air power, for Afghanistan is as large in area as France and there would be roads to keep open. I could not see the Afghan tribesmen submitting tamely. The Pathans, the most militant of the several races, regard guerilla warfare and blood feuds as a way of life. I knew them so well in the past as both friends and enemies and I felt I could see this far. However, these tribesmen have a weakness which paradoxically is also their strength. One tribe will never combine with another. Their jealousies are extreme so that it is a way of life to raid and squabble with their neighbours. While this would prevent them from combining they would not often be a large target for the Russians to attack and destroy in force. Their relentless hatred would switch to the Russian invader who would never know when the next

Old Pathan holding a rifle – drawing by author.

uprising would occur. I could see years and years of trouble ahead for every-body – the Pathan blood feud would never let go.

Looking at these notes I see I was not very far from the mark. Overall leaders have not emerged. When shock tactics have been used casualties have been too heavy to bear. In a fly-blown country with little medical aid minor wounds soon turn septic. In such tactics neighbouring tribes often fail to turn up, or arrive late, not all that sorry at their allies' discomfiture in the field.

At last, saddened and depressed, we entered Peshawar's lovely cantonments under tall avenues of pepul trees for the last time. The Gymkhana Club looked a bit more down at heel on this final visit. Two other motor caravans were parked under my favourite tree, full of raffish youngsters – under *my* tree! I felt a surge of rage because I had been granted this privilege for several years, owing to old friendships and associations and because I had once been a member of the club. I had kept this special favour a secret, so how had these travellers found the club which lies away from the main route? The high sense of Muslim hospital-ity would not have turned them away, but why, oh why, did they have to be so scruffy? The men had long, greasy locks or a sort of afro-fuzz and beards, not manly, but thin, long and wispy. The girls were wearing revealing jeans or tights and skimpy tops to offend Muslim prudery. I told myself that I was the anachronism and that I was being unreasonable. But I hated them making such a poor showing within a few yards of the little shrine where the light no longer burned. It was a sacrilege, not so much to the club as it now stood, but to my memories of it in its elegant, gay past. I made an effort to be friendly, but could strike no spark for they must have sensed my hostility. They were anxiously studying maps and I could have saved them a lot of trouble since I knew every twist and turn of the journey and the habitual obstructions of the borders ahead.

Still more sad and depressed we set off for India. The journey was decep-tively simple – even the old border pass was no longer needed. As we travelled my thoughts swung back to our journeys through Afghanistan, even to the time when the initial disruptions by the Russians had made our progress probably unsafe. I remembered the seventy miles or so of descent to Kandahar from Ghazni on our way home. The little villages through which we passed in the spring used to be bright with pink and white fruit blossom and the winter wheat was beginning to show green on stony ground, against the drab, near desert brown of the hills. Flocks of sheep and goats were being driven to a distant water hole. Why should this self-sufficient, pastoral life be destroyed to serve a monolith? There would be children, lacking toys, who found sport in throwing stones at my precious caravan – the little girls were the worst! Many of those children would soon lie dead amongst the rubble of their homes, indiscrimi-nately killed. I would gladly have given them my caravan as an Aunt Sally.

Chapter 25

The Last Journey Home I

Winter, 1978 – Spring, 1979

Another purpose of my journey out in 1978 had been to attend a special parade in November at the Rajputana Rifles Regimental Centre in Delhi, together with a small party of other British officers from the old Indian army. The occasion was the re-erection of the war memorial brought in to the centre from Nasirabad which we had seen during our first journey in India. This pure white, marble cupola, supported by pillars on a three-stepped plinth, contains panels and side tablets with the names of British and Indians of the regiment who gave their lives in World War I; the names of those killed in World War II and in India's newer wars are on marble slabs on its flanks.

The service was conducted by a Christian chaplain, a Hindu *pandit* and a Muslim *maulvi*, which I felt must have been unique in its coming together of different religions. The parade included the elaborate, inherited funeral drill and an Attestation Ceremony of the latest draft of recruits as they marched as fully-fledged soldiers into the future. I have never seen drill so smartly executed. Companies marched past the Delhi commander, General Rai, at the fast rifle pace. Each platoon moved as one piece, a many-armed, many-legged machine. The ceremony was flanked by soldiers in dark green, their heads bowed over their weapons in the final movement of the funeral drill. Sitting watching, I became so absorbed in the moving parade that subconsciously I was aware of the flankers only as walls enclosing it, but with a start I came out of my reverie and saw that they were men, tall soldiers motionless for a long while and not stone.

Was all this smartness an end in itself and merely a wonderful and moving spectacle? Granted that we all like outward show, the pomp and panoply, I think not. I felt that the young men were dedicated to die without question for a cause: that of India herself. I felt so proud of them; they were smarter than the Guards. I never knew an Indian soldier who did not throw his heart into the movements as if they were a ritual.

From Delhi we went to spend our usual winter in Corbett Park. It was the happiest stay of all in spite of its confinement due to the reservoir which by then

The three great religions honouring their dead.

At the memorial dedication.

had curtailed the wonderful forest walks. However, on foot we were able to
watch closely some magnificent tuskers, mother elephants with calves and
tigers too. There was an unusual amount of bickering and roaring as each tiger
staked out its new hunting beat in these confines so regrettably narrowed by the
reservoir.

Our friends the Harijans, with all their wounds, stomach aches and anxieties,
were more endearing than ever. The staff too were so friendly and laughed with
genuine delight at my feeble jokes, for in the east an oft-repeated joke gains in
richness from anticipation. My daily enquiry for news from the bird and animal
kingdom was treated as the height of wit and laughing replies were improvised.
But it was all marred by the over-ruling anxiety as to how we were to extricate
ourselves. As the winter advanced and the Shah fell, Iran was in the turmoil of
revolution and the situation in Afghanistan looked more and more menacing
with reports of tribal uprisings and the cutting off of all main routes. We could
not stay in India for longer than six months since the caravan would be as liable
as ever to the penal indemnity of two and a half times its value as graspingly
assessed by the Indian customs. A six months' extension might be grudgingly
granted, but it was by no means certain. In any case, I felt this would solve
nothing as our world was coming apart. I deliberated over our position and
spent much time corresponding from the Park to discover if we could get out by
sea, through Bombay, Calcutta or Karachi, but began to realise that conditions
were so chaotic and charges so penal, that no way out was offered in this
direction. A prolonged strike in India's harbours had left a huge backlog of
shipping still uncleared. I begged Peggy to fly home and leave me to get
through as best I could, but all the time I knew that, growing old, I would get in
a terrible muddle over documents and currency changing, for she had in all our
journeys played such a great part as both navigator and purser. She would not
leave me.

Anxiety tended to build up, particularly as it was fanned to a baleful flame by
the usual hysterical reporting of young correspondents, still wet behind the ears
from the safe welfare state, but now confronted suddenly by the death and
bloodshed of the cruel outside world. Looking back, I feel that the long inaction
necessary until the weather would let us travel, made me over-apprehensive. I
am self-sufficient in quick action, but no master of the waiting game.

Then at last, contrary to the warnings of friends and officials, but with my
knowledge of the countries now in turmoil, I saw a small window through
which we could leap to cut right through the confusion of Islam's vast, rough
intervening miles: Islam torn by harsh extremes and revulsions from the past.
Revulsions against what? In the past fifteen years during which I had motored
through Iran, I had seen much progress. The Shah claimed he was preparing his
country for the time when the oil would give out and the way he had turned his
deserts into sugar beet and cotton fields was remarkable. Perhaps, as he later
said, three or four more years would have sufficed to allow the new well-being

from industrial developments and the irrigation and planting of the country's wide deserts to filter down to those far-flung villages still remaining so poor. He seemed to have started well, but I feel that his government and those holding prominent positions did not possess the character to assimilate the tremendous amount of wealth created under American influence, and his secret police, the *Saveh*, with their cruel methods had finally turned the people against him. With his deteriorating health and corrupt relatives and ministers the collapse of his regime came all too easily and he went without a struggle, leaving his army leaderless and askance. I wonder too if his conscripts got enough pay, or did any pay at all filter down to them. On our journey out from England a soldier sentry on the border had begged me for money as he was hungry.

The quarrels between Iran and Afghanistan had by then shut their mutual borders and the border between Afghanistan and Pakistan was closed as well. The window to dash through was Iran itself, which seemed at the time to be the most troublesome of all. The only route was the sixteen hundred miles through southern Iran, beginning at Mirjawa over eleven hundred miles north-west of Lahore, missing out Afghanistan altogether. As I have said, we had done this journey some ten years before and knew the wide desert valleys flanked by big snowy mountains and knew too the approach road from Lahore through Multan and Quetta. It had been rough going then and the Pakistan stretch had been nearly unmotorable. I remembered trucks getting up such a wheel patter on the deeply gouged-out road as to bounce sideways on. I remembered that Land Rover spring, a specially heavy-weight one that had snapped. How then was I to dash through the window in a flimsy stock camper designed for an adventurous trip from London to Brighton. There would be no hope on this journey of getting repairs done in Teheran as I had done before.

After getting some assurances from the newly constituted Iranian Embassy in Delhi that our tour documents were sufficient and because of information signalled to me by a friend in Reuter's in Teheran, I felt we had a sporting chance, if we didn't hang about. So we left in the old spirit of commending ourselves to our Maker and setting out into the unknown on the 28th March in the Year of Our Lord 1979. I thought of such fortifying expressions as, 'Keeping our powder dry,' and 'Trusting in the Lord,' but my thoughts were ironical, though to be honest I was by then really rather enjoying the adventure.

The Mannings of the High Commission staff had put us up in Delhi at their large flat from where we provisioned our 'ship'. Unusually, they had a big yard in which we could park. We had met these two young people when they had contacted us in Corbett Park and told us how they had liked and used my first book and left them with great regret, having been refreshed by their youth: he a man with a future, having specialised in the Polish language and Poland; she, well-educated, slim and full of grace and chic. They gave us a huge fruit cake to eat on the journey and a bottle of champagne with which to celebrate *if* we got through. We felt that they were genuinely anxious for us.

The camper with its big upper double bunk and slab-sided silhouette was no dasher to freedom, so I decided to follow my old practice of motoring all the daylight hours, even if it involved fourteen hours' non-stop driving, being fed at the wheel. I had done it in the past to make full use of rare good weather in the mountains and to put as many miles as possible behind me. Now I would use it to cut down the number of night stops, for these I thought would be the most dangerous times. I argued that my enemy in Iran would be bodies of armed urban guerillas of no fewer than three different persuasions: just crazy youths seeing themselves as romantic heroes of revolution, who had already tasted blood and found it exciting. Perhaps at night I could hide the caravan, or seek the protection of a controlled area. But surely authority was suspect, now that loot and mayhem were the order of the day. How would I hide a large white vehicle with a red bonnet?

We passed through Lahore quickly because we did not want to get mixed up in riots that might attend President Bhutto's imminent execution and pressed on for Multan. I noted sourly that the road was not banked or ditched and would be all too prone to flood damage. The constant bang of potholes grew more intense, so that at times my 'dash' was reduced to fifteen miles an hour. That day we did not even get to Khanewal, our objective where we had planned to stay with a friend, but spent a short night by the side of the road in the tenuous protection of a nearby military farm. We pushed on next day and, at a filling station, the attendant admitted that the road had been badly cut up by exceptional winter rains. I felt much downcast, as for an oriental to say the road was bad he really meant *bad*.

Multan had grown in size and I thought back a hundred years to the birth of my dear mother while her father was serving there. We stopped the night at a petrol station further on and were courteously treated and much welcomed by a Pathan who was delighted that I spoke Pushtu. Next day we pressed on again across the Sukkur Barrage over the Indus and were greatly tempted to stop and rest, as the vast expanse of water cooled a strong wind in an arid countryside that was becoming hotter and hotter. I had not yet got my long-distance motoring wind, wherein one becomes at one with the machine, all aches and pains sublimated, the only sentient part two ultra-vigilant eyes to command feet and hands to instant action on controls.

We carried on, bonnet down, to Jacobabad, the hottest place in the subcontinent and already almost unbearable at the end of March, as it was now becoming close and thundery. In British days this place was where a bad regiment was sent as a punishment, the idea being, I suppose, to sweat the mickey out of it. We had been told that the road would improve after this town, but it became horrific. Looking back in my mirror the body of the car was a blurred, shimmying shadow. We ran on into a violent sub-tropical thunderstorm, but I decided to keep going, for rain on this flat road would be devastating. We came upon bridge after bridge which had been washed away in the winter and now there was more rain. The bridges were detoured by wide sweeps across the desert to avoid the water courses which they had spanned. Heavily laden local trucks had dug their wheels in deep. To avoid bogging down which would have meant days or weeks without rescue as road patrols are unknown in this area, I had to drive on top of the ruts. To have toppled into these deep cuts would have meant disaster and yet I had to keep along their general line or get lost out in the featureless desert. On about the tenth detour, we came upon a line of trucks bogged down. In desperation I swung wide of them, taking to the open desert and its soft surface. Getting down into bottom gear we churned on, sometimes sideways, spinning the steering wheel this way and that, and the splendid Vauxhall Victor engine got us through where the vastly more powerful, but heavily laden trucks of the professionals with their high clearance had failed. We bumped back up the track to the road to the cheers of the stranded truck drivers. All that we could at first see of the junction was a little notch on the skyline. The notch was the broken bridge, so I had to make for it and climb up on the low bund which was the road, leading in the direction I was to go. It is as such moments that one feels enormous exhilaration. This was what long distance, rough eastern motoring was all about. It was sheer adventure.

We then continued along a deeply rutted road which was in places a series of rain-water holes. It was motoring by eye; each yard had to be gauged and to judge wrongly would be to damage the vehicle. I had always to keep it up on top, one side or the other of the deep, watery holes, for if I took the wrong side then I would hit the bank and slide into them. It was all split-second judgement.

Having driven non-stop for over fifteen hours, we staggered into Sibi – we had achieved 160 miles! We looked for accommodation. It is announced by all tourist organisations in the sub-continent that a traveller can be put up at the various rest houses, but this is not the case. Permission had to be granted by an often absent authority. There was a railway bungalow. The authority had not enough authority. He was quite surly and uneasy and said his master was away. I asked him if this was an example of the well-known Muslim hospitality and his companions looked embarrassed. I only wanted the use of a protected area and a WC since we only used the Porta Potti (that symbol of rally caravanning) in dire emergency.

I was not prepared to argue and decided to visit a unit mess of the Pakistan army. I had intended to avoid this as there is always so much reminiscing and hospitality on such occasions. All I wanted was a safe harbour and sleep. The Pakistan officers were very welcoming, but their commander said there was a real feeling of uneasiness in Baluchistan owing to the infiltration of Russian agents. They fixed us up at a Canal Engineers' rest house. We had arrived on the evening of a big party and it was good of them to have taken so much trouble, particularly as the heavens opened and a vicious thunderstorm broke over the town as we drove up. The guests began to appear so we were able to

slip away and go to sleep in our comfortable caravan, having driven down
sopping wet streets where military patrols were spraying the surface to steal a
march on the mosquitoes. To stay on top of this pest you can never let up.

How snug it was at night, secure in the pouring rain, but then as the rain
stopped hordes of mosquitoes that must have escaped the spray invaded us and,
had they been unanimous, they could have dragged us out of bed. Owing to the
storm it was terribly hot and Sibi is the hottest place in Pakistan after
Jacobabad. We called these terrible mosquitoes Bomber Harris and his lot.
Their high whine as they dived made sleep impossible and, yes, of course, I had
a very upset stomach for the first time in years. It was probably the result of
Delhi's unwonted, rich hotel restaurant fare and the continual pounding of the
road. On such a run one's bottom and legs feel the strain. My stock caravan did
not have the shock-absorbing seats of its predecessors and one's lower end
became so numb that it was difficult even to spend a penny. I limped for months
afterwards. I had driven absolutely non-stop the whole of the previous day,
except for a pee and to fill up with petrol: not a moment wasted – hot tea was
passed to me in a mug, only an egg-cup full at a time or the bumpy road would
have splashed scalding liquid all over my face. We travelled with two large
thermoses full which were kept forward with us. It was during that day that we
realised the serious fault in the cab. The side windows had no louvres to scoop
in the wind and the heater/cooler could not fan enough air through. We were
motoring forever westward with the sun on the windscreen from midday to
sunset. I am surprised that we were not kebabed.

After leaving Sibi we wound up the famous Bolan Pass and I felt the usual
pangs of nostalgia that always twist the heart of an old Frontier soldier. These
grim, polished mountains and shaly hills with clumps of dwarf palms have a
strange appeal, beyond that of lush and verdant scenery. We had intended to
call in at Quetta, the Aldershot of the east and the home of the Staff College
where I had once studied. We rather weakly hoped to get more information
about the road and a political situation which could combust at any moment and
block our 'window', but we decided to push on. I felt that delay might be ill-
advised, but we only got as far as Nushki along an almost unmotorable road
between Quetta and the border. I was not in good shape and antibiotics were not
working.

At Nushki we put up once more at a petrol station. The attendant was very
pleasant and mellowed still further at a gift of those attractively packaged
Benson and Hedges. The station owner, on a flashy motor bike (a yammering
Yamaha – Japan's revenge on the west), was an unpleasantly cocky young man,
fully indoctrinated into Marxism, as were so many Muslims along this route.
Nothing would turn him from his cant – as was usual at that time the Russians
were one jump ahead. The commander at Sibi had been right. But when I said
that he, the proprietor of a pump and a beautiful motor cycle, would probably
be scuppered as a capitalist and the station given to, perhaps, the attendant he

looked thoughtful, even though he went on saying that the Russians were kind, good people, who would free Baluchistan from the oppression of the central government. This province has for long been restless under the rule of Pakistan and there is no doubt that the Punjabi tends to grab the biggest slice of any government handout. Moreover the Baluchis are always a problem because they spread over the borders of Pakistan, Afghanistan and Iran, and for this reason could be got at by Russian propaganda which infiltrated where there was weakness, always taking the initiative. There was plenty of scope for propaganda, for the Baluchis are a discontented people, living mostly on poor land.

That night Bomber Harris caught us up and sleep was fitful. Mosquito-proof netting on the windows shuts in the heat too much and makes everything airless. Our constant aim had always been to avoid the mosquito season and our normal route was free of them at this time of year. However, the discomfort and the poor distance covered had the effect of working up adrenalin for further effort. We made an early start: tea was well before dawn on the summons of our now legless Little Ben alarm clock. We loved it because it always wanted to join in. If we didn't wake up, it would hurl itself to the floor. After a quick breakfast there was a slow start to warm up the engine at the magic hour of sunrise and soon we were pressing on smoothly. There was no trace of the misfiring which had dogged us for a while. Giving the car an occasional fill of super petrol when available to freshen up the normal sludge and a thorough clean of the petrol lines, was paying off. We had the power, we had the road.

The weather, however, was worsening and, remembering how the desert through which we were passing could turn into a sea of yellow, rushing water, I urged the vehicle on while there was still a trace of road. I felt as though I were physically lashing the car, changing down quickly to bottom and then up through the gears, clawing along the bank to avoid falling into a hole, then striding forward for a smooth, gravelly stretch. We came on some trucks stopped and dolefully contemplating a sea of mud and water and deeply rutted road. There was a little French caravan with two youngsters also halted in dismay. We plunged past them into the mud and bounced and side-slipped from bank to bank, encouraging them to follow with a nonchalant pip-pip on my polite horn, which they did. But they gradually fell back and we lost them in the premature gloom of yet another gathering thunderstorm with forked lightning flicking across the 'road'. We certainly were unlucky, for following freak heavy winter rains in a desert which receives but little moisture, we were now getting more and more unwonted spring rain. The flood dazzlingly reflected the low sun through a hole in the black bank of cloud, so that we seemed to be motoring through a lake. In the poor light I could just see the road's mud bank showing clear at intervals like a dotted line to guide me through this sheet of water.

Then we came across a dry stretch which had its own peculiar problem. The wind had blown fat fingers of red sand across the road and these, too high for our negligible clearance, sought to grab us. I was by then buoyed up by the zest of this adventure. Approaching one tongue of sand in second gear I was held but, slamming down into first, I was surprised how this gear in this car could screw me forward. Of course I had not the clearance to get over, but I decided to risk my car's vulnerable underside as the sand was obviously recently wind-blown and would contain no damaging rocks. And so over finger after finger we charged with no sound of a hard crunch, which would have spelt finish to our journey. What a gamble it was! My driver's handbook said when so and so goes wrong, consult a dealer. What would it avail me should I shout, 'Dealer, help me!' in that black, thunderous desert?

In accordance with the unwritten law of the rough road, we were always ready to stop for another vehicle in distress. We had through the years received wonderful, unselfish help from the professionals who in many cases could do a first class welding job by the roadside. Payment offered had always been refused. All I could do in return was to see if those in trouble had water. A stranded truck, gorgeously decorated on every inch of its surface, the pride of the Pakistani owner-driver, appeared in the gloom. We were signalled down by two youths and I asked them if they had water. Yes, they had, but had been left in charge by the owner to guard the vehicle and its cargo while he went to the nearest town for spares: probably Quetta, a couple of days' journey back, where he could scrabble through a bank of rusting parts at the Kabadi (second-hand) Bazaar. They said they had not had any food for three days and I believed them, they spoke so dolefully. So we gave them a large slice each of the Mannings' wonderful cake and some sweets and biscuits – all we could find quickly that was acceptable on religious grounds.

At last we came to a scrape gravel road. These are honest roads as they absorb moisture and do not get muddy. The surface is corrugated, as the scraper or dozer blade judders as it goes forward, making ripples. These corrugations become deeper with wind and time and can rattle a car to bits. But I knew this type of road well in my early long distance motoring. I had travelled along such surfaces for thousands of miles. One just has to be patient and find the speed which best suits the car. With two wheels on the sandy edge, I could cut down vibration.

Fifteen to twenty-five miles an hour seemed to be the answer and we motored into the night to arrive at Taftan, the Pakistan border hamlet. It was as though Pakistan had sought to tear the car apart before our real trial of restless, dangerous Iran had begun. We had done only 315 miles in another fifteen hours, but I felt happy as it was a man-sized job.

We stopped at the Scouts' Officers' Mess at the border, and were given pro-tection and a WC; as the officers were away there was no exhausting reminiscing. We slept well as Bomber Harris had not made the distance. Next morning we met the officers and there was then much talk about the past and cups of tea. They were full of friendship for a member of the old Sirkar, and questioned me closely about other officers. I concealed my fuming desire to press on and succeeded in being very affable. The medical officer changed my antibiotic, dismissing my English one as mere gripe-water, and we set off for the border which bade fair to be tricky. But one of the officers, a pink-skinned, slit-eyed Hazara, recruited traditionally from the Afghan highlands into the North West Frontier forces by treaty with Britain and our successor, went down to the border and introduced me to the customs officers who were in consequence the soul of despatch and speed for easterners.

With our hearts in our boots we approached the Iranian frontier and there to encourage us we saw a German tourist bus which had just broken its back.

Chapter 26

The Last Journey Home II

Spring 1979

Would we ever be allowed to continue? My military rank shown on my passport might deter officials once more as had happened at Lahore on our first entry into India and they could be suspicious of me. I felt I just could not physically turn back, but I need not have worried. The newly appointed police, unsure of themselves, were glad to be cursory with our documents – formerly passports would vanish for what seemed like a year and a day to be sleepily examined by officials absent more often than not. This time, in order to speed things up, we showed them where to fill in their ledgers, having seen it done through the years. Moreover, two of my friends just introduced to me on the Pakistan side were there, working some mysterious fiddle. Their manner was secretive and from the few whispered words I could hear I gathered that contraband of some value was being slipped over the border: there was much suppressed giggling. One said, 'Who signs the permit?' and the customs officer sketched out an imaginary Arabic squiggle and said that would do as a signature. Thereupon everybody again giggled shrilly. But they helped me by introducing me as an old friend to the border officials and in no time we were over, though an indignant Swede who had arrived before us complete with shaggy beard was continually ignored and complained that he had been held up for hours. There is no 'After you, Sir,' in these situations. I knew the atmosphere could get soured all too easily. At customs posts there is much unpacking of cases, and nails lie around to puncture tyres, so I skirted the area as best I could and set off bonnet down through the 'Empire' whose poetry and carpets have always enthralled me.

We had been cheerfully warned that the road ahead would be only fair for a hundred miles or so. We found long stretches of it foul: again there was flooding and we were back on the old game of looping out into the desert to avoid a quagmire. There were fair stretches, but the danger lay in speeding up only to come too swiftly upon the next length of deeply holed road. I had to be ready to brake and, indeed, on switchback sections the vehicle would leap into the air. Jamming on the brakes prevented a series of giant hops. It is remarkable how a dab can damp it all down, but it was difficult to press down on them when I was being bumped upwards off the seat.

We were on the look out for the British road construction firm of Marples Ridgeway whose excellent work had been halted by the troubles. There they were in isolated camps with no armed guard and wide open to roving gangs of Iranian yahoos. One of their dumps had been overrun and looted, but by a piece of superb diplomacy they had arranged protection with the local Baluchi tribes, through whose country the road construction ran. The firm was grubstaking the tribesmen in return for this protection. These Iranian Baluchis were somewhat uneasy, having demonstrated for the Shah whom they held in some regard. I understand that during his reign he had resettled some of them from their almost totally desert lands and had directed more to the Black Gold area, where wages were high. The men of the tribe had now taken to the hills in fear of retribution and were waiting to see which way the cat would jump, while guaranteeing protection for the two remaining British camps for the time at least. As far as I could see, at that time the cat they were watching was likely to tear itself apart in an effort to jump in several directions at once.

We stopped outside the main camp, but the sorely tried gatemen, armed only with staves, rightly would not let us in. They explained that they would call the engineer in charge down some distance to the gate by walkie-talkie to look us over. Being somewhat diffident and not wishing to be a nuisance, for I am never good at asking favours, I pressed on down the road. We soon came upon these British engineers who were preparing a rocky bluff overlooking the road line for dynamiting for, as they said when we pulled up, they weren't going to let the roving bands get hold of the explosives. It must have been most frustrating for these men who had put so much hard work into their brain child, the road, to have it all stopped suddenly. I think they rather welcomed new faces and a crazy elderly couple on the long run was a bit out of the ordinary. So they pressed us to stop for the night at their second camp further west up the road. We were decidedly glad because our plastic roof ventilator had snapped its fastenings, owing to the vibration, and we were left with a gaping hole. Fortunately, we had discovered the fracture before all had blown away and the lid, so to speak, of the ventilator was still hanging on by a sliver. Why do caravan makers have these vulnerable roof ventilators exposed to branches or other damage? It is the one place in a moving home in which one must not have a wide hole. Previous caravans of my own construction or planning had a strong window of toughened glass high up on the kitchen wall in conjunction with a 'hit and miss' ventilator low down, to encourage air circulation. One can overdo all this brittle plastic.

I knew a metal clamp and bolts could be made to get us home, secure from the wet, and the camp would have a workshop. Oh, and yes, I *had* picked up a nail at the customs post and had a slow puncture. How I disliked those tubeless tyres. They were almost unknown in the east at the time and when I sent one forty miles on a bus to be repaired in India it was returned with the caustic comment, 'What good is it without the inner tube?'

We were given a very warm welcome in the engineers' and mechanical technicians' mess. What a steady, sensible lot they were and there was none of that sniping and bickering of a frustrated, isolated body of men. I as an old soldier was very struck by this self-discipline. The technicians were overhauling the big construction plant which had been starved of maintenance in the thrust and drive of putting in this new stretch of road before everything collapsed in Iran. The road had been designed as a continuation of the Asian Highway, so much heralded and at last coming into being, but now again checked here. The Pakistanis had not done much on their side of the border either.

I felt that I gained good marks for I presented my reserve liquor ration to the bar, thinking wrongly that booze would be scarce. It was a strange ration: a two litre plastic orange squash container full or nearly full of Slivovica, that excellent lifter of hearts, Yugoslav plum brandy, on which I have done a high mileage. The container showed a label assuring all that it was indeed orange squash, but we had only put in a dollop of it to enhance the illusion of a big, squashy soft drink. The heart of the thing was good plum brandy, but I did not want any one to catch me drinking base alcohol. Perish the thought!

This plum brandy had sustained us through our winter long trips to India and back. When we were even poorer than now we established the custom of stopping off at Maribor on our outward journeys at a well-placed supermarket on our route. There, in addition to stocking up with food, we bought this inexpensive brandy to sustain us against the evil humours of the road, any kind of murrain or damp emanations from the marshes. When we boldly ordered five cases of a dozen litre bottles each of this tonic, the assistant proffered us but one bottle, whereupon I summoned the manager, a very nice fellow and an ex-RAF wartime pilot who still remembered a word or two of English. I quickly explained my problem. 'No problem,' he replied. Five cases were swiftly loaded on our deck and the bill came painlessly through the till together with Peggy's food purchases. We discreetly withdrew to a nearby car park and with true military precision ripped off the stoppers and decanted the five dozen bottles into light plastic containers marked orange squash. Then we stacked the heavy, empty bottles neatly in their cartons by the dust bin and drove off. And so this swift act of precision must have enriched Yugoslav folklore. Now squalling babies are told that a great ogre stalks the land and every year almost to the day passes through Maribor, refreshes himself with five dozen Slivovica and drives away sober. Yes, I did cross borders with gunwales asquelch with booze, when I should not have, but India has nothing drinkable and if I was to record the wonder of her lands, I felt I should be suitably sustained. So many of her sons have tried the plum distillation in the deep jungle and have voted it famous – what a silly expression! Should they say on the Indian border, 'Have you any liquor aboard?' I answered, 'Of course,' and offered the Sikh a welcome half bottle – just a matter between gentlemen.

To return to the bar of Marples Ridgeway mess: when they learned that the day was our fortieth wedding anniversary they generously opened a bottle of champagne. One of their members, Mark, was the representative of a catering firm who provided exceptional meals. A good board is of the greatest importance when a camp is isolated and dull. Alan Pearce, the administrative officer, had long experience of Pakistan and was ideally qualified to handle a difficult situation with tact *vis à vis* the tribesmen. His heart, like mine, was in the subcontinent.

My roof ventilator was to be put right, but the Pakistani metal worker was so distraught that he could not concentrate. He wept silently for Bhutto, just hanged in a monstrous cat and mouse affair. Did he really sorrow for the man? No, what the mechanic mourned for was an ideal, a release from humdrum existence, since Bhutto if anything claimed to be the common man's champion of the People's Party. He wept for the snuffing out of a ray of hope, some freedom from his oil and spanners' poverty.

He tried to lay a heavy iron ladder against my flimsy aluminium caravan sides to gain the roof. I gently dissuaded him from so roughly scouring my paint and pointed out that the ventilator lid could, if placed diagonally, be pulled down from inside the caravan to be pierced for bolts and a cross bar without destroying the vehicle. When I saw him later and said an affectionate goodbye he was still in tears. Coming from a comfortable land one is so often astounded at the wild depths of feeling and suffering of people who live in a rougher world. It was for this reason that I had driven the caravan and myself almost to extinction. I knew of the emotionalism and wanted to be clear of one troubled country as soon as I could. I did not think that Pakistan would combust as a whole, but I was taking no chances.

What a curse it is that so often during an interesting experience one cannot savour it to the full, or give of one's self. I still felt terrible and was not responding to antibiotics. But the Pakistani staff gathered round me, attracted by the fact that I could speak their language and could tell them stories of my life's experiences in their own tongue. They were delighted to find that I often knew their very villages. It was one of those gentle interludes where brother meets brother.

We were persuaded to stay another day: an easy enough decision as we were in good, friendly company. I felt proud of these Britons, a fine bunch of hard workers, and after I got back to England I tried to repay their hospitality by getting in touch with the Foreign Office through some influential friends, with a plea that the appropriate authorities should take whatever steps were possible for these road-builders' safety.

After this interlude, with my energy restored and armed with new antibiotics by the camp's doctor, we set out for as long a run as possible over as many miles as we could by daylight across the vast deserts of the tortured empire. We bumped and pattered through an abrupt mountain gap, known as the Afghan or Naderi Gate. Then, at last, a fast good road and we sat down on it and motored and motored. All was desert along broad valleys, flanked by snow-clad mountain ranges. Surely few men had set foot on them and why should they? The poor people of such a land could not muster enough calories for the effort and I thought comfortingly that perhaps the beautiful ounce hunted up there unmolested, swiping at snowflakes with his curled, pussy paws. But we could see little of the scenery. Bad weather was in the air and a strong cross wind snatched jerkily at the camper. A dust haze veiled all the magnificence, which on this run outmatches the Afghan upland scenery, for it is all on a much greater scale. Changing direction, we pressed westward, hot in our glass-enclosed cab and it was as if we were indeed pressing, for a strong head wind forced me at times to change down in order to get along at all. As is the wont of these desert winds, it changed quickly and soon I had its strength pressing on my broad rear aspect and we were careering along like a square rigger. But for being bound to the road, there was something akin to sailing. I knew the danger signs of quickly overheating the engine in these conditions and I kept my eye anxiously on the temperature needle, for I am always wary now of brewing up my engine again. I brought the needle back again to normal by turning on the heater which, though it increased our discomfort, seemed to ease the engine as the heat was pumped off into the cab. A further slight change of direction improved matters.

How I hated this slab-sided, high prowed puddleduck of a camper. I felt I was not going to make as good a run as I had hoped in our flight through inflamed Iran, but as the direction of the wind changed we seemed to be putting the miles behind us. It was a monotonous drive as the road was smooth and the view was blotted out by the dust. We negotiated Kerman and Yezd which had both grown hugely since we had last seen them. Everything seemed surprisingly normal, except that most of the signposts had been smashed. Forced by this to stop and ask directions we were smilingly and courteously set on our way. In Kerman a lorry driver even leapt into his vehicle and guided us round the town.

As it grew dark and I grew weary I felt satisfaction at having clocked 570 miles in a vehicle which was relatively slow: a distance I had never done before on this type of road. It gave me the feeling that I was not ageing much. Dog tired by then we started looking for a night stop. On such occasions if you want to do a good mileage having motored on to near dark the choice of harbour must be quick and decisive while you can still see. We were looking for somewhere where we could hide our conspicuous home for the night and there was not much time. With some relief we saw a great, mellow brick fortification on our right flank with an easy lead-off from the road. Though ruined it was something more than the usual *rabat*, or defended daily staging post for the camel *quafila*, and its size would conceal us from any angle from passers-by on the main road.

The fort of age-old brick set in herring-bone patterns was clearly once a defended post of importance. I inspected it, feeling a sense of inexplicable awe. A representation of a horned devil was crudely painted on one recessed wall and beside it there was the thin, sinister figure of one of those whirling dervishes from Konya in Turkey, in a tall pointed hat. The effect was slightly macabre. Though the style of drawing was a conventional western picture of the devil there was also Arabic script too worn and burnt to read written below. Was it the rendezvous of black magic ceremonies? I later discovered that there was once devil worship in this area. There are more sects in Islam than one realises.

'At last peace,' I told myself, when behind a big, wooden door I heard a goat bleat – the devil's familiar? We were not alone. Soon a shepherd emerged from the fort and greeted us. To ensure a good night's rest I gave him a packet of cigarettes and he asked me if there were any more where it came from. I thought, 'Oh dear, another scrounger who will pester us all night,' as the Turks do in some places. Would he even call up companions to raid us as had nearly happened at Dogubayazit on the Turkish border with Iran on our way out? But talking quietly with him I felt he was merely overwrought by our unexpected visit. He begged us to enter the keep but, thinking about goats' fleas and smell, I declined. I asked him about the fort and he said it bore the name of Shah Abbas and described how that great emperor had manned the walls with his bowmen. I am always sensitive to the site of past battles and this explained my reaction to it. He at last got the idea that we were tired and wished to sleep and we cemented the friendship by giving his small motherless son some sweets. We turned in only to be roused by an offering of goats' yoghourt. He explained that on our coming he had missed the bus on which he usually sold this product. I insisted on making up his loss and we went at last to sleep to be refreshed for another marathon drive.

Driving non-stop all day, often against head winds still, we did 508 miles more including taking a by-pass round the edge of Isfahan. How I would have liked to see the beautiful mosques and the Royal Square once more, but Isfahan had been more troubled than any city save Teheran and I felt the smooth, long, anonymous by-pass was our best course. So we slipped quietly round, almost unobserved.

Soon we coasted equally quietly through Saveh and took a new road westwards to avoid troubled Teheran. Then we were wafting towards Takestan, our time-honoured stopping place at the junction of three roads. We were by then travelling on the road up from Hamadan, the second road went off to Qazvin and Teheran, and the third was the road to Bazargan and the Turkish border whither we were bound.

We reached Takestan, but there was nowhere to stay that night as the motel was shut – in happier times we always used to tip the night watchman who let us park and sleep in the garden. Instead of the night watchman we were approached by a number of rather unpleasant looking spivs, who leered horribly and asked if we had any alcohol. I hauled myself up and said in a shocked voice, '*What* would the good mullahs say?'

The collection of softies collapsed in heaps, shrieking with shrill laughter. They would not have let us alone, so we had to move on, dead beat as I was.

On our journey out we had noticed a modern looking motel called the Wild Horse near Abhar, some twenty miles ahead on our homeward way. I was so tired that I felt almost disembodied. When I reluctantly had to stop at a fuel pump and my rhythm was broken, I would tumble wearily out of my seat belt and literally pour out of the cab on to rubbery legs which were ready to buckle. However, I struggled as far as the Wild Horse and pulled round behind as it was obviously deserted. I shunted and tucked the caravan close in to the building so that we could not be seen from the road.

I felt I had made a good choice as the motel was well out of the little town, but a small boy had seen us. Small boys always appear from nowhere in my passage through deserts. The dragon's teeth Myrmidons were mere amateurs compared with these boys. The child said he was in charge and seemed to take our effort at hiding as quite plausible. We corrupted him with a packet of cigarettes. In Iran and more so in Turkey even three year olds smoke. I don't suppose they smoke much younger than this – they would tend to burn their fingers, though otherwise there seem to be no lower limits. We felt we could settle down quickly for the night after a stiff peg or two of the Slivovica we still had left to bring the sparkle back to rheumy eyes.

Alas, the quick deployment for the night in the deft drill that Peggy had worked out on our many journeys was threatened. Two youths hove in sight. They said we were not safe. One told us he owned a dairy farm up a back road and we would be secure there with him. He seemed pleasant enough, but I did not like the other who declared we were in great danger from the revolutionary militia, so I said boldly that if we were molested I would reply to any attack with bursts of machine gun fire. This vainglorious remark impressed them visibly, though I had nothing more sinister than a packet of toothpicks in the car. At best, I knew that we as tourists would provide the interest these bored youngsters craved. There would be many introductions to relatives and I would have to talk endlessly in a language in which my tongue was harsh with rust. No, the effort would be just too much. My aim was to get home, not to cement international friendships any more. I would stay the night where I was. I felt reassured later when the small boy was joined by his father who said he was the official watchman and it was quite safe to stay where I was. He opened up a tolerable WC, too. However, I again became thoughtful when he said the owners who had been running a thriving business were no more, and drew his fingers across his throat explicitly. I insisted on paying him the usual parking fee and the small boy was sent off to buy us *nan* (Iranian bread) and yoghourt, being told not to talk about us.

We made good progress next day and reached Tabriz, the capital of Azerbaijan, by the middle of the morning. We had never done this stretch so quickly before. This city has been so much fought over by the Russians and the British that its inhabitants looked at travellers sourly even in quieter times. Once in the past, having missed our turning, we had got into side streets and were much harassed and bullied by aggressive schoolboys, always the worst in the east. Would it not be better to get round the town by a by-pass road which we had heard about, or by the heavy lorry route to the right which we had never used and which would be terribly rough? I felt however that we knew the road straight through the middle of Tabriz well enough by now, though it was tortuous and extremely crowded, so we decided to use it as there would be no need for us to stop to get directions which would be dangerous. Keeping up as steady a pace as was prudent, we slipped quietly through the tricky town and on along our usual route.

In a surprisingly short time we reached the high ground above Marand, the next town on the way. I thought, 'One last substantial town to get through,' and we could feel reasonably secure in the belief that there were no dangers to avoid. I smiled because the steep hill up from it on the Tabriz side had come as a shock on so many outward journeys. Taking the right-angle bend in the town's main avenue had always presented me with a test, so steep was the hill thus revealed – no run up, just straight up after the corner. The car would be gravid with unobtainable liquor for our six months' stay and other stores – packets of Earl Grey mixture piled high. I hated revving it in bottom gear up to a high shriek. Something must go, I used to think, and no spares for hundreds of miles. It was on such occasions that overwrought, I turned on the navigator to accuse her of putting the hill there on purpose, at which with great insubordination the other rank told me that I was a curmudgeon.

Down, down, we waddled on our homeward way and I looked happily at the gaily coloured fruit stalls, the green, white-veined long melons called *karbuza* (donkey's nose), so delicious that the newcomer overeats with disastrous results. They do not carry dysentery or typhoid generally, but being so cheap, one eats too much. Past the shop which makes coloured baskets. How pretty it all was and how relaxed I felt after all the tensions. What had we been worrying about?

Then a sharp turn to the left and my heart sank into my boots. There all over the road were armed men with short automatics. A thin trickle of blood was running into the gutter. It had hardly begun to blacken. Something nasty had happened in the middle of the mob. I did not wait to see, for the outer edge of the crowd had left a narrow way clear and I slipped silently through. My navigator clutched my arm and said sharply that some of the men were running towards a small truck and pointing up the road towards us. I confirmed this with a brief glance back through my mirror, whilst also keeping a sharp look-out for the old women who always dash across at the last moment like black wet hens.

It had been a case of double surprise: mine and theirs. But I now changed gear hastily up and up, and had made some speed before the enemy had realised that there was a fat duck for the plucking.

I had won some five hundred yards when I saw that the truck was on the road and making fair speed after us. As I had already cleared the line of car work-shops, the last hovels in any eastern town, I felt that if only I could gain a thousand yards their fire would be abortive: the road was too bumpy for steady aim. By then I was doing seventy – my maximum – and how the camper buzzed. I was thankful that the engine was well tuned and run in and that we had used up our heavy stores. What of the truck onto which some seven or eight militiamen had piled? Probably a powerful Chevrolet – all horse power and guzzle. Was it flogged out? Had it been maintained? Was the petrol tank empty? Our salvation lay in these possibilities.

Now down the long road behind I could see our pursuers – a mere dot. In these uplands the visibility is so clear. Yes, they were a mile behind on the lonely road. So far so good, and then the road took a sharp turn to the north. I grew worried as my high Luton bunk overhead was becoming noisy in the wind. I could hear the turbulence above me. Oh hell, I was now motoring slap into the wind and I was slowly alarmingly, so much so that I had to change down to third to push against the strong gusts. Yet I could still hold forty miles an hour. My heart froze! I thought the little truck was slowly closing on us. A minute later I looked again. Yes, it was definitely closer. I was leaning hard against my seat-belt as if to push us on. Then we turned into a series of bends up through shaly hills. Acting and thinking fast, I cut across each left-hand bend (Nigel Mansell stuff); sometimes I had a clear view ahead, at others I gambled. By so doing I could be gaining a few yards. I edged my right-hand wheels so as to leave the tarmacadam and run on the thick, dusty border for brief spells, and yes, as I thought, they set up a plume of dust to blind my pursuers. I was no longer troubled by head wind as the road was sheltered by the hills and as I wound up the tight bends, sometimes I was favoured by it, at others not. I felt hope because Bedfords and Vauxhalls are well geared for hills. I tried to snap my gears in as quickly as possible, so as not to waste a second. I felt we now had a chance. My tank was full and if I could throw my pursuers off in the hills, they might give up. We thundered out of the defile and along a long straight road, and I kept glancing back at the point where the road left the hills. I felt as if I were drawing it out of the huddle of hillocks, like a spider spinning a thread out of its bowels, and still there was no fly on the road, as on and on I vibrated and everything shimmied in the caravan.

We were nearly a mile clear when again I saw a black fly. Our pursuers were still after us. Then, untroubled by a head wind, I kept my distance for what seemed an age. The friendly old Bazorg (Big) Restaurant which I have de-scribed in *The Road to India* was out in the desert on our left. A fleeting glance showed that it was closed as well as the gasoline station beside it. No help there and in any case on whose side would they be? I began to sweat. The black dot was definitely getting bigger, for I was being buffeted by that head wind again. It was setting up a dull roar on the bluff Luton above. Slowly the enemy closed till they were no more than three hundred yards, then two, behind us. I twisted the camper onto the soft edge, sending up plume after plume of dust again, which shut us off in spells. But there they were. Some were waving: then clonk, clonk – a loud noise on our rear. I thought we were hit. The back door had a round hole of bright light in it and the floor cover seemed to be furrowed a bit. I told Peggy to lie across the front seats for the scant protection she would get from their backs. I really was frightened now for her sake and my mouth was dry. I had feared this situation all along and now here it was. Then, after the restaurant, the road went into a deep cut and soon we were winding up and up, changing gear, cutting corners and squealing my big balloon Michelin tyres. On and on I tore, not knowing if the enemy were there, for there was no stretch long enough to see back more than a hundred yards. A near miss by a huge truck piled high with packing cases and well over on our side! I basely hoped our pursuers would run into it for my dust must have hung thick in the airless twisting gorge. Oh, how I prayed!

From now on there was more steep climbing and I kept creating more plumes of dust to cover us. On one longer stretch – no black fly. I felt I must hammer on, though apparently our pursuers had either lost interest or run out of petrol. I hurtled up the main street of Maku, the last village and eight kilometres short of the border, with my loud horn pressed hard down. I was determined to plunge into the border clutter, but still felt not too happy about our reception there.

We prized two slugs out of the vehicle when we got home. I sold the camper but the holes did not detract from its value – far from it. I had wanted to repair the holes, but was dissuaded by my agents – the vehicle had a story and I got a very good price for my ill-treated puddleduck with its battle record.

We plunged on and managed to reach the border with Turkey at Bazargan well before closing time. Parking the camper outside the customs post I saw an armed militiaman with a green cap and gaucho moustache. Would he too try and hold us up? Taking the offensive I ordered him to guard the vehicle. He glanced quickly at the important looking golden buck on the door – my family crest, not unlike the Persian lion – and leapt to obey the command, glad to have something to do. I did not want hippies or professional smugglers to stick heroin on the car skirt with a dab of Bostick, go over the border more quickly on foot than I could with the car to clear, and then remove the dope on the far side. This was a deadly practice about which we travellers had been warned by our embassies. No amount of denial of any knowledge of the dope would save one from a long prison sentence, if it were found: a certain death sentence in a Turkish gaol, for we were old.

I was expecting the usual contumelious crossing on the Iranian side, the filling in of forms and the long delay in getting passports stamped. To my surprise I found that as at Mirjawa the customs officials were very young and ready to shuffle us through with the minimum of delay. They didn't want to write up tedious details in large, dusty ledgers. When I asked where the bank was in order to change money, they pointed out a cheerful individual with his feet up on a small table. Yes, he was the bank, but he had no money. We were not greatly dismayed as we knew we could change money outside the office – indeed, we were scarcely out when we were almost overwhelmed by black market money-changers who offered us very good rates for once. Iran had not yet changed all that much.

Having looked ahead I collected a fair load of petrol in plastic jerry cans at the border, dangerous though they are, but the only ones available in India, as I had heard that fuel was scarce in Turkey. I felt this was going to be a problem as I could not carry enough to cross that country since I had to think of the vehicle's suspension, for there were very rough stretches of road ahead.

We got through the Turkish border with the minimum of delay since there were no tourists and few lorry drivers, and decided to stay the night in the large park provided for travellers and the big container lorries. We were elated at our escape, but it was getting late and we were tired after our long drive, not to mention our narrow squeak and the crossing of double borders. We were soon approached by a small boy who said it was dangerous to park where we were. Like all Turkish small boys he begged for cigarettes, money and cast-off clothing. I sent him packing. All our spare clothing had gone to our Indian sweeper friends in Corbett Park, rather more than we could spare. It grew dark, very dark and I realised that the overhead sodium light standards had been systematically smashed. I began to think of the boy's warning and moved in from the far edge of the park where I had gone to be away from the noise of traffic and the barking of pi-dogs. Earlier, I had seen two armed soldiers with white American-type steel helmets leave the fortified post overlooking us and had watched them start on their patrol. I felt that they would keep off thieves or interference. A little later Peggy heard footsteps, so I got out of bed and waited, listening with torch in hand, by the window which I had left open because of the petrol fumes from our extra load. After more shuffling an arm reached through the open window. I let out a daunting bellow of wrath with a view to unnerving our raider and shone the torch on him and there were the two armed soldiers I had seen on patrol. There can be no doubt they contemplated theft, as the arm was thrust far into the caravan and was feeling round. I continued to bellow in assumed wrath as I felt I had no other weapon. This unnerved them and they backed away, making deprecating gestures. I made all this noise – I am proud of my bellow, it is a very big one – in the hope of bringing down the guard commander, possibly a vain hope as he might be a party to the attempted theft, but it seemed to work.

I then decided to make for a cluster of large container lorries and drove the camper right into the midst of them. These great elephants seemed glad to have a tender calf to mother. In my scanty and atrocious German, together with a lot of gestures, I got the drivers to understand what had happened. They and their co-drivers were all Bulgarians. They agreed that the place was very dangerous, but said we could assume that we were 'in Bulgaria now', and could sleep soundly. They were a friendly and happy lot, as is usual amongst these knights of the road of any persuasion, and they returned my gift of cigarettes with cups of hot coffee. They arranged for a foot patrol all night round their vehicles and ourselves and switched on their very bright cab lights from time to time.

We and the Bulgarians were up early and at the border gates by six o'clock, but had to wait for a sleepy official with the inevitable transistor clamped to his ear to unlock them and check us out two hours later. Oh, for the round-the-clock European borders! I found it excruciating after so much forward drive and thrust on the journey to be needlessly delayed. It tended too to throw the day's run out of gear.

Our drive towards the distant Greek border over the shoulder of Mount Ararat was spectacular and was enlivened by shepherd boys of all ages demanding cigarettes or matches by signs. One small boy, seeing I was not going to give him anything, stooped to pick up a large stone to smash my windscreen, but I saw him and braked hard, sounding my doomcracker horn, and he took to his heels. We were bothered by other young highwaymen and had our door dented in the rear, but by using the triple wind horn suddenly, I gave them pause and so saved my windscreen again. There now arose a menace never encountered on earlier trips. The shepherds, realising that Europeans slowed up decorously when sheep were on the road (their own drivers are more ruthless) had hit upon a new idea. They purposely drove their flocks across in front of us and when we duly slowed down, closed in on us with heavy staves to smash the windscreen. Startling them with the loud horn and pushing forward so that they had to jump for it, we got through unscathed. Eastern Turkey is a wild, cruel land of bare mountains and there is but little law and order, though through the years we never came to real harm, having been careful where we camped and vigilant of stone throwers. Who was the silly mug who offered the shepherds some cigarettes in the first place? They now regard them as a right.

At Horasan we pulled up at the traffic control police post where we had always been given helpful friendship and even on one occasion an escort, to ask anxiously about petrol. The police smiled broadly and said, 'Benzin [petrol] no prob – lem!' This expression had become international since our outward journey. They went on, 'Diesel – yok!' – no diesel.

Soon we were to see miles and miles of tractors and buses queuing up for it and for once we had the bulge on those bullying Turkish bus drivers. We sped on, topping up our tank from our reserves to lighten our overall load. But it was an unwise thing to do as when we got to central Turkey we found petrol was very nearly *yok*. I should have topped up as and where I could have got a litre or so. I still kept my tank full, but had to shop around expensively in the black market. At Sivas, miles from anywhere, I asked a Turk about petrol as I had fetched up at a pump which closed down three cars ahead in the queue. He was a taxi driver who guided us some way to a pump on the old road through the town we had used in times past. It was very good of him as he did not need any himself. Turks are not all brigands. Turkey, splendid in so many ways, was in the outback just a poor, hard country, which blunts sensibilities.

At last we crossed the Greek border at Ipsala and cried *'Ruant Coeli!'* – 'Let the skies fall!' behind us. We were safe. We stopped for the night in the lovely plane groves of Asprovalta and celebrated our freedom with the champagne the Mannings had given us. The journey about which we had worried so much had turned out to be no dash through fire and sword until the very end. Others, however, did strike disaster shortly after the 'window' slammed shut behind us.

> Sorrowful grew the eagle's spirit and heart
> When he beheld the season of youth depart
> Far, far away: when he perceived his turn
> Was nigh to end, the sun's last radiance burn
> The roof-edge of his life. He knew at last
> He must capitulate, and forget the past,
> And take another road, to another land.

> *Khanlari (Contemporary), trans. A.J. Arberry.*

But I can never capitulate. When the collared dove calls again although I fear its voice is too soft to be heard above the cries of terror and clangour of armour, I shall run on creaking legs to leap into my caravan and set forth towards my beloved jungle again.

The End

Tamam Shud